B

Arthur Eperon is one of
travel writers in Europe
worked as a journalist in various cap
He has concentrated on travel writing for the past twenty-five
years and contributed to many publications including *The Times*,
Daily Telegraph, *New York Times*, *Woman's Own*, *Popular Motoring*
and the *TV Times*. He has also appeared on radio and television
and for five years was closely involved in Thames Television's
programme *Wish You Were Here*. He has been wine writer to the
RAC publications and a number of magazines.

He has an intimate and extensive knowledge of France and its
food and wine as a result of innumerable visits there over the last
forty years. In 1974 he won the *Prix des Provinces de France*, the
annual French award for travel writing. In 1991 the French
Government awarded him the Médaille de Mérite (Tourisme).
His *Travellers' France* topped the paperback bestseller list for
eleven weeks.

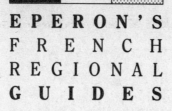

EPERON'S FRENCH REGIONAL GUIDES

BURGUNDY

ARTHUR EPERON

PAN BOOKS
LONDON, SYDNEY AND AUCKLAND

First published 1992 by
PAN BOOKS LIMITED
a division of Pan Macmillan Publishers Limited
Cavaye Place London SW10 9PG
and Basingstoke
1 3 5 7 9 8 6 4 2
© Arthur Eperon 1992
Illustrations © Mary Fraser 1992
Maps © Ken Smith 1992

The right of Arthur Eperon to be identified as author of this
work has been asserted by him in accordance with the Copyright,
Designs and Patents Act 1988.

ISBN 0 330 32223 0

Designed by Peter Ward
Photoset by Parker Typesetting Service, Leicester
Printed in England by Clays Limited, St Ives plc

C O N T E N T S

1 *Départements of France*

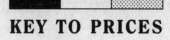

KEY TO PRICES

ROOMS		MEALS	
	A = under 100F		A = under 75F
	B = 100–150F		B = 75–100F
	C = 150–250F		C = 100–130F
	D = 250–350F		D = 130–165F
	E = 350–450F		E = 165–220F
	F = 450–550F		F = 220–300F
	G = over 550F		G = over 300F

Room prices per night for double room without breakfast.
Meal prices include tax and service.

INTRODUCTION

Burgundy gives me a feeling of contentment and well-being. The full-bodied red wine helps, of course; so do the big satisfying farmhouse-style meals. But it is the solid timelessness of Burgundy which is so pleasant – the feeling that no one is going to hurry you, jostle you, nag you from their car telephone or rush you through a meal, a bottle or a decision. The Burgundians say that they learn patience from waiting for their red wines to mature in cask – anything from sixteen months to two years.

Outside Beaune or Dijon, nowhere seems crowded. The nearest I have been to feeling hurried was when I was privileged to be one of ten official tasters at Vosne-Romanée's annual wine festival five years ago. They gave us ninety-five gorgeous wines to taste before Sunday lunch – not even Bacchus himself could have done that. It was just typical Burgundian enthusiasm. They enjoy life. They enjoy celebrations, carnivals and festivals and, however historic the origins of these may be, wine and food play a big part in them, for wine and food are very much part of Burgundy's heritage.

Burgundians are the biggest trenchermen in France. Only the Alsatians would dispute that. The Renaissance chronicler Paladin said that 'the Burgundians dress most modestly, yet their bellies are lined with velvet because of their great food'. Despite the magnificent dress and sumptuous palaces of the old Dukes of Burgundy which you can see in Dijon, the motto of the people was: 'Better a good meal than fine clothes.'

Mind you, I know a vegetarian who drinks little wine but who still loves Burgundy. The Dukes left behind them a fine artistic heritage and, in Dijon, a city as rich in beautiful buildings and lovable old houses as any in France. Burgundy has restful waterways, peaceful towns and villages and fine old abbeys, churches and châteaux.

Burgundy has a centre in Dijon but no logical frontiers. History, not geography, shaped it, and its countryside is bewilderingly varied. At one time the Dukes of Burgundy ruled more land than the kings of France, and were more powerful. The French grabbed the Duchy in 1477 when the last Duke died leaving only a nineteen-year-old daughter, and after the Revolution the new government abolished the name of Burgundy in their division of France into ninety *départements*. De Gaulle brought back the name in 1964 when he grouped *départements* into *régions* for economic planning. So Burgundy now consists of the *départements* of Côte-d'Or, Saône-et-Loire, Yonne and Nièvre. But throughout its history the wine was called Burgundy, of course, and most people still used the word for the region, regardless of what the politicians said. Even now the Beaujolais wine area is not in Burgundy, it is in Rhône. But the wine is Burgundy and the Beaujolais wine and land are in this book.

Burgundy is not a region covered in vines. There are 15,150 acres of vineyards compared with 2,471,000 acres of forest. The forests are largest in the plateaux of the north – in the Senonais bordering Champagne and the Île-de-France, the Morvan, west of Dijon, where they also breed cattle (the old red-coloured local cattle have mostly given way to the white Charolais), and in the Charollais itself in Saône-et-Loire, west of Mâcon. There originated the great Charolais beef cattle of which there are now about three million in the Charollais itself and which have spread to many parts of Europe.

The one natural border is in the west, where the river Loire south from Briare and then its tributary, the Allier, divide Burgundy from the Loire region. The wine town of Pouilly-sur-Loire is on the Burgundy side of the river, although it produces a 'Loire' wine, similar to its rival Sancerre which is just inside Loire.

There are about 1200 kilometres of navigable waterways in Burgundy. The four main rivers – the Loire, Saône, Yonne and Seille – their many tributaries, and the great canal circuit of Burgundy are superb for cruising holidays. Commercial traffic is diminishing and there are delightful villages and hamlets on the banks or within a few minutes' cycle ride. In the west, the gentle river Yonne flows south past the photogenic city of Auxerre (which is usually pronounced Ausserre) to join one of the prettiest inland waterways of France, the Canal du Nivernais, which flows through the rugged countryside of the Parc Régional du Morvan, past red- and brown-roofed villages and pleasant châteaux. It may not go anywhere important but it certainly tells you a great deal about Burgundy. At Decize it joins the Canal Latéral à la Loire and that joins two more canals – Canal de Roanne and the important Canal du Centre – to Chalon-sur-Saône.

The river Yonne meets the Canal de Bourgogne, which passes many interesting places on its way south-east through Dijon to join the Saône river. St Florentin is a good northern base, and between there and Montbard two superb Renaissance châteaux stand close to the towpath – the beautiful Château de Tanlay and the magnificently furnished Ancy-le-Franc. The twelfth-century Fontenay abbey is 6 kilometres away from Montbard. As the canal climbs through many locks to its 3350-metre summit tunnel just after the market town of Pouilly-en-Auxois, it does a lovely looping descent past the hill village of Châteauneuf through the valley of the river Ouche and down to Dijon – a super stretch of country. It would take you about ten days to cruise from St Florentin to Dijon sightseeing; in a fortnight, you could continue to St Jean de Losne where the canal meets the Saône, or just follow Saône to Pontailler. Different boat companies let you leave your boat at one or the other. Several British operators offer boat-hire holidays in Burgundy. Both of the good cruises I have mentioned here can be booked through two very experienced operators – the excellent Vacances-Franco-Brittaniques (VFB, Normandy House, High Street, Cheltenham, Gloucestershire GL50 3HW – 0242 526338) and boat-hire specialists Hoseasons (Sunway House, Lowestoft, Suffolk NR32 3LT – 0502 500555).

Canal du Centre, which joins the Saône at Chalon-sur-Saône to the Loire at Digoin, was once a very important commercial canal, built in 1794 to serve the steel town of Le Creusot where the great Schneider steel works has stood since 1836 (now called Creusot-Loire – *see* page 157). Le Creusot is still an industrial area, but the canal is being switched to pleasure use, with a good new holiday-cruiser base at Montchanin, west of Chalon-sur-Saône.

I have written about touring wine villages in the section on wine (pages 24–57) but the basic wine areas are Chablis, standing isolated north-west of Dijon; Côte de Nuits and Hautes Côtes de Nuits from Dijon south-west almost to Beaune; Côte de Beaune and Hautes Côtes de Beaune around Beaune, and to the west as far as Santenay; Côte Chalonnaise to the west of Chalon-sur-Saône; Mâconnais, the highlands around the town of Mâcon, especially westward around Pouilly and Fuissé, all very close to the borders of Rhône; and Beaujolais in the hills just over the border in the Rhône *département* but not, of course, in the Rhône valley, which still produces a Burgundy wine.

Côte de Nuits and Côte de Beaune form the Côte d'Or – indeed a golden hillside. Beaune (*see* pages 65–72) is not only the wine capital but also a wonderful town with superb old buildings and stretches of the old ramparts. Inevitably, it is very crowded with visitors in June, July and August and the time to see and feel its real character is in April, May, lateish September and October. We were there recently in early November – the weather was still pleasant, the restaurants, bars and shops were all operating but not crowded, and you could park even in place Carnot, around the corner from the Hôtel Dieu.

Midsummer can be very hot in Burgundy, winters cold, so

May or September and October are the best times to go. For the wine villages the *vendange*, the grape harvest, is the most wonderful time to be there, but you need help from the growers, the oenological stations which test the amount of sugar in the grape and the Almighty to guess when that will be: it could be early September; it could run into October. I once waited for three weeks, with everyone telling me that it would be 'any time now', then I had to leave twenty-four hours before it began. In 1976 it started on 30 August in Côte de Beaune! But my bet is around 23 September – my wedding anniversary. Anyway at this time the villages will be in action – even if they have finished picking and are drinking to celebrate a good vintage or drown their sorrows for a bad one. And there are always the little local wine festivals, *paulées*, after the picking is finished. Then the villages are great fun.

During much of the year many villages are dead during the day – truly dead. You could believe quite honestly that they had been suddenly abandoned. In Beaujolais, many of the wine villages are hidden on tiny local roads which are little more than tracks in places. There I have failed to raise more than the bark of a dog for two or three hours. Everyone is busy in the vineyards. Looking after vines is a full-time job every month of the year – mostly for the whole family. There are still old vine-growers' houses around, with cave entrances and wine-making equipment on the first floor and outside steps to the living rooms – sometimes with an open-arcaded gallery along the front. Other bigger houses are built around a courtyard, with the caves along one side.

Unlike Bordeaux, holdings are small, nearly all family-owned and very little outside labour is used except during the picking, when not only is the entire family kept busy but other pickers are hired – mostly French and foreign students. They truly earn their pay. Picking machines have not been introduced at the rate they have in Bordeaux as it is not very economic for small growers to buy one, though the cost of paying, feeding and lodging pickers keeps rising. Margaret Loxton has painted some superb pictures of well-fed, strong-armed Burgundian men and women picking the grapes – Burgundy would lose something if they were replaced by a machine. The vines might not be too pleased, either, and it is the life's work of Burgundians to keep the vines happy and healthy.

Burgundy's feeling of near-isolation has been shaken in the last few years, particularly in and around Dijon. This is the meeting place of four motorways – A6, A38, A31, A36 – giving fast routes to Paris, Lyon, Marseille, Nancy, Metz, Lille, Mulhouse, Strasbourg, Germany and Geneva. Even more significant is the fast TGV train from Paris, with links to Marseille, Berne and Lausanne. The train from Paris takes 1 hour 35 minutes, and the last time I caught it around 6 p.m. it was carrying many young businessmen. It seems they commute most days but stay in Paris if they are working late, which must be quite expensive. In fact, so many Paris businessmen now work in Dijon and return to Paris on the same day, that they can hire working space with phones, computers and copying machines in Dijon station. I would stay overnight – Dijon has so many good restaurants these days with a much friendlier atmosphere than Paris.

Burgundians *love* to put up flags, turn out the village bands and feast, drink and dance. Almost every wine village has its great annual fête and some have several.

One fête well worth joining is St Vincent Tournante on the Saturday and Sunday after 22 January. St Vincent is the patron saint of winegrowers and 22 January is his Saint's Day. Each year he 'changes house': a different wine village is chosen annually and members of the village's St Vincent Society blend a wine to be drunk at the fête.

On the chosen day, members of the Society from the whole area assemble at the chosen village around 8 a.m. and carry their statues of the saint in procession around the village, through the vineyards and back to the church for Mass. Then the caves are opened, the feasting begins and the *folklorique* groups and musicians perform old Burgundian dances and songs. For 20 francs you buy an attractive Burgundy goblet inscribed with the village's coat of arms. And you fill it, free, with the Cuvée St Vincent chosen wine as often as you can empty it. For about 120 francs you buy a Repas Gastronomique, usually of Kir, parsleyed ham, coq au vin, cheese and a cassis dessert. The big dance begins at 9 p.m. and goes on all night. So does the drinking.

That is a true Burgundian feast.

HOW TO GET THERE

FERRIES
(joining convenient roads to Burgundy)

Hoverspeed (Hovercraft and Sea Cat)
Dover–Calais, Boulogne. Folkestone–Boulogne.
A good ferry-rail route is Hoverspeed Dover or Folkestone to Boulogne, trains from Boulogne station to Paris Gare du Nord. TGV Paris Gare de Lyon to Dijon.
(International Hoverport, Marine Parade, Dover, Kent CT17 9TG. Tel. 0304 240241.)

P&O Dover–Boulogne, Calais. Portsmouth–Le Havre.
(Channel View Road, Dover, Kent CT16 3BR. Tel. 0304 203388.)

Sealink Dover–Calais, Boulogne. Portsmouth–Le Havre.
Newhaven–Dieppe.

Sally Line Ramsgate–Dunkirk.

ROADS
Motorways through Paris:
From Calais – A26 to join A1 near Arras.
From Boulogne – join A26 at St Omer.
A1 to Paris. A6 from S of Paris by Auxerre to Beaune.
For Dijon turn on to A38 at Pouilly-en-Auxois, 37km before Beaune. From Beaune, A6 to Chalon-sur-Saône, Tournus, Mâcon. More attractive route Paris–Beaune is by N6 through Fontainebleau, Sens, Auxerre, Avallon, Beaune, but it is narrow for overtaking lorries in places.
Le Havre to Paris by A16 via Rouen.

Route via Reims and Champagne instead of Paris:
A26 from Calais (and Boulogne joining at St Omer) to Reims, A4 to Châlons-sur-Marne, N77 to Troyes, N71 to Dijon.

AIR
Air France (158 New Bond St, London W1Y 0AY. Tel. 071 499 9511) or *British Airways* (West London Air Terminal, Cromwell Road, London SW7 4ED. Tel. 081 897 4000.)

Heathrow to Lyon, then train to Mâcon, Beaune, Dijon, etc.
TAT (book through Air France) Paris Orly to Roanne (just over
S border of Burgundy, SW of Mâcon.)

RAIL

Fast TGV trains run Paris (Gare de Lyon) to Dijon in 1 hour 35
minutes (313km). About fifteen trains per day. Beaune (1 hour
58 minutes) and Chalon-sur-Saône (2 hours 16 minutes) are on a
side-line from Dijon, about three trains per day. Some TGV stop
at Montbard (1 hour 5 minutes).

Another route is Paris–Mâcon in 1 hour 40 minutes. Some stop
at Le Creusot (1 hour 25 minutes). TGV seats must be booked
before boarding.

Ordinary express trains run from Calais/Boulogne to Paris
(Gare du Nord). TGV Paris to the Channel Tunnel outside
Calais being built (1992).

HISTORY

A family argument started the wars between Burgundy and
France. For centuries after, the people of Burgundy thought of
themselves as Burgundians first and Frenchmen by accident.
Some still do, though most now admit that they are French.

In 1369 Duke Philip of Burgundy (Philip the Bold) married
the widowed Margaret of Flanders to get his hands on the rich
province of Flanders, plus Artois, Nevers and Franche Comté.
Then in 1380 his brother Charles V of France died, and Philip
became the leader of a Council of Regency, ruling France for
Charles VI, who was only twelve years old. Soon after Charles
VI came of age, however, he suffered attacks of paranoid
delusions – at one stage he believed he was made of glass. The
Regency Council was recalled and Philip the Bold of Burgundy
virtually ruled France until his death in 1404. The Regency was
then taken by Charles VI's brother, the notorious rake Louis,
Duke of Orléans, whose mistress was Charles VI's wife Isabella.
However his cousin John the Fearless, the new Duke of Burgundy, was determined to be Regent. The cousins hated each
other and in 1407 John of Burgundy had Louis of Orléans

ambushed in a dark alley and bludgeoned to death. This started a near civil war in France as Louis' father-in-law, Bernard of Armagnac, took up the fight. All Frenchmen were divided between Burgundians and Armagnacs in a most extraordinary way. In Paris, the University and the butchers were Burgundians, the clergy were Armagnacs. To make life more complicated, Henry V of England invaded France, claiming back the old English lands, and his crushing victory at Agincourt in 1415 left France in chaos. In 1418 John the Fearless of Burgundy won control of Paris in a coup, with great slaughter of Armagnacs. On 10 September 1419, a meeting was held on a bridge at Montereau, south of Paris, to try to make peace between the Dauphin (Joan of Arc's 'gentil Dauphin' who later became Charles VII of France) and John the Fearless. Charles had one of his knights murder the Burgundy Duke with a hatchet.

The new Duke, John's son Philip the Good, set out to avenge his father's murder. He made an alliance with England, signing a treaty with Henry V and Queen Isabella, Charles VI's wife, declaring that the Dauphin Charles was the illegitimate son of the Queen's adultery. The treaty recognized Henry of England as the true heir to the French throne, arranged Henry's marriage with Charles VI's daughter and made him Regent until Charles VI's death.

The Dauphin Charles himself had doubts about his own legitimacy – not surprising, considering his mother's reputation – and hid in the Loire valley. It took the peasant girl from Lorraine, Joan of Arc, to persuade him that God had told her he was the true heir and that he was to give her an army to drive out his enemies and put him on the throne. It was the Burgundians who finally captured Joan of Arc at Compiègne and sold her to the English.

The Dauphin made peace with Philip the Good by recognizing the virtual independence of the Burgundian Duchy, which stretched through Artois and Picardie to Flanders, nearly all of what is now Belgium, much of Holland and Luxembourg, Burgundy itself and Franche Comté. Philip had palaces in Lille, Ghent, Brussels, Bruges and Hesdin, and although in documents he referred to Dijon as his capital, he in fact ruled from Brussels, for his power and wealth were centred in the

Netherlands. His son, Charles the Rash, extended his empire to the rest of Holland into what is now Germany, Lorraine and Upper Alsace. But he overreached himself: in 1477 he was killed in a battle to hold Lorraine. His heir was his nineteen-year-old daughter, Mary. It was a wonderful opportunity for the cunning Louis XI of France to invoke the *French* Salic Law, which stated that women could not inherit, and to grab all the Burgundian lands his army could occupy. He took the Duchy of Burgundy, Artois, Picardie and Franche Comté. Mary quickly married the German Emperor Maximilian of Habsburg, whom she had intended to marry earlier. The Emperor failed to hold Burgundy against Louis but held Flanders and Mary's non-French lands.

Louis was clever enough to grant Burgundy special privileges, and as the people were not very keen to become part of the Holy Roman Empire – the German Empire – Burgundy reverted to the French crown.

The German Empire did make an effort to take Burgundy in 1513. On 7 December, Dijon was facing disaster. The Emperor had besieged it with an army of 30,000 Germans, Swiss and men of Franche Comté. The Governor of Burgundy, La Trémoille, had only 7000 men defending the city. The Swiss opened fire and made breaches in the walls, but La Trémoille played his trump card: he sent out a group of negotiators to arrange a peace – with a procession of wagons loaded with wine. The Swiss soldiers got drunk, and agreed to lift the siege. In return France was to pay 400,000 Écus and give up the Milanese in Italy. Dijon and Burgundy were saved. But Louis XII of France said that he did not understand the strange treaty and refused to ratify it. He had to fight the German Empire in the Milanese and he lost the territory anyway.

The first Burgundians came from the Baltic Scandinavian island of Bornholm (Burgundarholm). The Romans called them Burgundiones. They crossed into the Middle Rhine around the fifth century as the western Roman Empire was in decline, but in AD436 were utterly defeated by Attila's Huns and their King Günther was killed. The defeat is told in the first story of the thirteenth-century poem of the legend of the Niebelungenlied. The survivors of the tribe settled near Lake Geneva and became allies of the Romans in their fight against the invading German tribes. By AD470 they were strong enough to take Lyon and then took over most of Switzerland and much of what is now Eastern France.

They did not mix with other peoples in the area but were Romanized quickly and by AD500 had produced a version of Roman law for their people. They adopted Arian Christianity – a belief that the Son of God was not Divine – in preference to Catholicism. But the Merovingian kings took them over with the whole of Gaul and they became part of Charlemagne's huge Empire. Burgundy, now much smaller, came under the Franks. The murderous raids by Scandinavian Norsemen in the ninth century drove monks from the western areas to take refuge in Burgundy, and the great Burgundian abbeys became powerful, their schools spread learning and culture through Western Europe. The abbey at Cluny put Burgundy at the head of Christendom. It had 1450 dependent abbeys and monasteries around Europe, with 10,000 monks, and was also one of the greatest artistic centres. The abbey's wealth made Burgundy prosperous.

In 1031 Robert, second son of the French king, was made Duke of Burgundy, starting the three-hundred-year line of Capetian Dukes, named after the Capets, kings of France. They were a colourful lot. The first Robert, contemporary of William the Conqueror, divorced his wife in a great scandal, killed his father-in-law, then walked to Rome to receive absolution from the Pope. Another suddenly gave up the job of Duke and became a monk; most of them fell out with the church and were excommunicated; and two married into the French royal family. Suddenly, in 1361, the young Duke, Philip of Rouvres, died of the plague and the French kings came to power again.

King John of France had been taken prisoner by the Black Prince in the great English victory at Poitiers. With him was his young, fourth son Philip. One of the English knights treated the French king disrespectfully, so Philip hit him. It was the English king, Edward III, who said, 'You are indeed Philip the Bold', and that label stuck. When they had been ransomed and

returned to France John made young Philip Duke of Burgundy – the first of the Valois Dukes. No one would have
believed then that they and Burgundy were going to become
great enemies of France.

The last of the Capetian Dukes, Philip of Rouvres, had just
married Margaret of Flanders when he died. Philip the Bold
married the ugly widow and was rewarded with several rich
provinces.

The Valois Dukes were flamboyant and great self-
publicists. They encouraged their colourful labels – 'the Bold',
'the Fearless', 'the Good'. 'The Rash' is really a rather bad
translation into English – in French he was 'Charles le Tém-
éraire', which adds a certain amount of courage to the reck-
lessness.

They were certainly ostentatious. To afford to marry Margaret, Philip the Bold borrowed a fortune and pawned his
jewels. She was the richest heiress in Europe, but he was still
permanently broke though always magnificently dressed. As
Regent of France, he stole half the Royal income, and when he
founded an order of chivalry, he could not afford to pay for
his own insignia. His heirs had to pawn his gold plate to pay for
the funeral.

Philip the Good had palaces in six towns. The greatest artists
of the time worked for him: painters and sculptors decorated his
palaces, poets and musicians were kept at his Court. The painter
Jan van Eyck was an important courtier, treated like a noble and
entrusted with delicate diplomatic missions.

To celebrate his marriage with Isabella of Portugal, Philip
founded the Order of the Golden Fleece, still one of the most
exclusive in Europe. It was created in honour of 'God, the
Virgin Mary, and St Andrew' (his patron saint), and it was so
exclusive that its motto was 'Autre n'auray' ('Not for Others').
They dressed in scarlet tunics trimmed with squirrel fur and a
similar long cloak. When a member died, his heirs had to send
his necklace medallion and Fleece costume back to the Grand
Master of the Order.

As well as great works of art, Philip collected practical jokes,
such as bridges that collapsed and dropped you in the water if
you stepped on them, or sprays which wet ladies from under-

neath if they trod on the pad. He also collected mistresses – thirty were known publicly.

It was Philip the Good who held the famous Vow of the Pheasant banquet at Lille, with a magnificent pageant and decorations. One 'decoration' was a full-size church with an organ and singers. Another was a full orchestra hidden in a pie! He announced at the banquet that he was going to lead a crusade to take back Constantinople from the Turks, then made all the knights present swear on a live pheasant wearing a necklace of precious stones that they would go with him and perform remarkable feats. He promised to challenge the Great Turk to single combat. What he did do was impose such heavy taxes on his people to pay for his extravagances that the city of Ghent started a revolution in his Flemish provinces. He killed 20,000 people to put it down.

Philip's son Charles the Rash was even more flamboyant in his court life: daily meals were a banqueting ceremony, and he had musicians and poets sing or tell stories of chivalry, romance and heroic deeds for an hour or two each night before he went to bed. He must have been the only Burgundian Duke, almost the only Burgundian, to water his wine. He married an English princess, Margaret of York, to gain an English alliance, but Louis XI of France, a cunning king, bribed both Edward IV of England not to invade France, and Swiss mercenaries to do France's fighting against Charles in Lorraine. The Swiss beat the Burgundians and killed Charles. His stripped body was found in a frozen pond, partly eaten by wolves.

During the Revolution, the destruction of the beautiful and once-powerful old abbeys of Burgundy was zealously wanton. Cluny, greatest of all, was sold to a property asset stripper from Mâcon who pulled it down systematically for building materials. The very name of Burgundy officially disappeared under the Revolutionary division of France into ninety *départements*.

On 14 September 1944, the French army under Général de Lattre de Tassigny, which had landed in Provence from North Africa with the British and Americans, met up with Général Leclerc's Armoured Division which had landed just after D-Day on the Normandy coast near St Lô. They met at a hamlet called Nod-sur-Seine, just south of Châtillon-sur-Seine.

The wartime Resistance was extremely active in Burgundy, especially in Dijon and around Châtillon, as it was southward around Lyon. One of the great leaders was a priest, Canon Félix Kir. He was for many years Mayor of Dijon and Parliamentary Deputy (Member of Parliament) and his work to make Burgundy prosperous again after the war was almost legendary – in fact a book was written entitled *Did Kir Really Exist?*. To help both the wine and blackcurrant growers he served *blanc-cassis* (white wine and blackcurrant liqueur) as the only apéritif on official occasions. The drink was renamed Kir after him. He would not, I am sure, have approved of the modern snob version Kir Royale, using champagne as the wine. I met him once and he told me two things – that Kir should be made with Aligoté dry white wine and that in street-fighting against well-armed troops you should try to avoid going into the streets; you must stay inside buildings even if it means making holes in the walls to get from one to the other!

Another great Burgundian did not believe in street-fighting. Sébastian le Prestre, later Marquis de Vauban, was born in 1633 at St Léger, near Avallon in north Morvan. His family were minor local bigwigs. One of his uncles was on the staff of the Prince of Condé (the Great Condé), Commander of the French army, and Le Prestre joined the army under his command, fighting in the Fronde uprising of nobles against the king. He was captured when Turenne defeated Condé in 1653, switched sides and became Chief Engineer to Turenne. He was to become the greatest military engineer in history. He fortified more than thirty towns and strengthened the fortifications of at least three hundred others. He lined France's northern frontiers with fortresses and fortified the Channel and Atlantic ports against English and Dutch attacks. He directed more than fifty successful sieges. The French claimed that a town defended by his fortifications was impregnable, a town besieged by him was lost. Louis XIV gave him a small fortune for capturing Maastricht and he bought the medieval château of Bazoches in the Morvan (*see* St Léger-Vauban, page 229). This was partly a snub for the Le Prestre family: his father had lost a legal battle over the family inheritance and one of his uncles owned the family château near to Bazoches.

Le Prestre retired, then made a political mistake. He began to worry about the terrible conditions of the ordinary people in a France almost bankrupted by Louis XIV's overspending, by dishonest officials, and by disastrous wars. In the reign of the Sun King, nobody in his position was supposed to even *think* about the common people. Furthermore he wrote a book, *Projet d'Une Dîme Royale* ('Project for a Royal Tithe') suggesting ways of improving the living conditions of the poor, including a 10 per cent tax on all land and trade. Nobles were exempt from taxation in France, and some of the most powerful men in the country were the profiteering revenue farmers – the men who could sell rights to collect taxes in an area. And there were the successful merchants, too. All were furious at this attack on their fortunes. The king backed them. The book was banned, seized and burned. Vauban was in disgrace. He died shortly afterwards.

WRITERS

The strange life of Colette (1873–1954) took her to many places, from a fine but lonely castle in the Corrèze to seedy theatre dressing rooms, but her best-loved novels were set in the big village of St Sauveur-en-Piusaye, south-west of Auxerre, where she was born in 1873 and went to school. Her father was an invalided army captain and her mother was the very Sido of her novel of that name. *La Maison de Claudine* (1922) had some fine descriptions of life in a Burgundy village and, above all, of the Burgundy countryside. The house in rue de l'Hospice is still there, with a plaque marking her birthplace reading *Colette est née ici*, but it is a private house and you cannot visit it.

It is difficult to believe that the mournful Romantic poet Alphonse de Lamartine (1790–1869) (*see* page 87) was a Burgundian, although he was born in Mâcon and lived in the Mâconnais whenever he was not involved in politics in Paris. He was an admirer of Wordsworth, and followed the English poet's example of writing much about the countryside.

His family had several manor houses around Mâcon and he lived from the age of seven at a hamlet west of Mâcon then called Milly and now called Milly-Lamartine. The house is still there and there is a bust of him in front of the town hall. One of his favourite houses was Château Monceau, just off N79, 6 kilometres north-west of Mâcon. He liked to think of himself as a great land and vineyard owner but he was a spendthrift and during his last days in the château he was hounded by creditors. In a little gazebo in the garden at Monceau he wrote *History of the Girondins* (1847) in which he called for a 'revolution of contempt' against the monarchy.

His father gave him the château at St Point, further west. There you can see the study where he wrote, his bedroom and his salon. He is buried in the little church with his English artist wife and other relations.

Lamartine inherited so much property – houses and vine-yards – that it is difficult to understand how he became so poor in the period in which he lived, when money, land and markets were so much more stable than they are today. But his sorties into politics undoubtedly caused this problem. He became a Deputy in 1833 and was a sort of freelance Radical, much opposed to the reign of the 'Citizen King' Louis-Philippe, who had virtually stolen the crown from his young nephew for whom he was supposed to be ruling as a Regent. When Louis-Philippe had to abdicate and fled to England as 'Mr Smith', Lamartine became Foreign Minister, but left-wing uprisings destroyed the Government and Louis Napoleon (later the Emperor Napoleon III) rose to power. Lamartine stood against Napoleon for the Presidency but received only one vote for every 500 in favour of Napoleon. He retired to his Burgundy estate to con-centrate on writing, but never wrote poetry better than his *Méditations* which he had written at Milly and St Point when he was thirty. He was embittered by the way Frenchmen had treated him, but was regarded very highly as a poet until later years when he lost much of his popularity.

His best known poem is still 'Le Lac'. In 1816, when he was twenty-six, he went to the spa resort of Aix-les-Bains to recover from an illness and there he met Julie Charles, wife of a Paris doctor, who was seriously ill with a lung complaint. They fell in love. He returned to meet her the following summer, but she was too ill to make the journey from Paris. She died that September. On a hill overlooking the lake he wrote his beautiful poem.

Gabriel Chevallier was a Lyon journalist, but he used to take holidays in a Beaujolais wine village: Vaux-en-Beaujolais. There he noticed that the local people not only consumed a great deal of their own product in their inn but openly and freely relieved themselves of it in public. He wrote a joyous book about 'Clochemerle', a fictional village in which the Communist mayor decides that in the name of progress Clochemerle must have a *pissotière* – a urinal – and to annoy his rival, the village priest, he places it in the alley which leads to the church. If you have read *Clochemerle* you will know what rumbustious, rollicking, bed-romping, sinful scenes result from this simple attempt to clean up the village. If you have not read it, I do suggest that you hurry to buy a copy. It is superb satire. It has been translated into English – and just about every other language in the world. It has made Vaux-en-Beaujolais the most visited village in Burgundy, and Vaux has truly cashed in. It has opened a tasting cave – in fact, Chevallier opened it. It has changed the name of its Beaujolais-Villages wine to Cave de Clochemerle. It has changed the name of its inn to Auberge de Clochemerle. And, of course, it has built a fine new *pissotière*. Vaux also has a brotherhood called Compagnons du Gosier Sec or Fellowship of the Parched Throat.

FOOD

You will certainly eat well in Burgundy. In fact it is possible to eat *too* well.

Considering I have known Dijon for more than thirty years, I should have known better one November recently than to accept an invitation to a renowned restaurant after spending the day at the Dijon Gastronomic Fair. Here Dijon feeds people from all over France with delicacies they may not have tasted before, from snails and coq au Chambertin to the superb hams of the Morvan, many types and sizes of sausages, dozens of varieties of the unsurpassed Dijon mustard, and all sorts of *cassissines* – sweetmeats laced with blackcurrant liqueur, crème de cassis. People come from far and wide to taste and buy, and you can't get away *without* tasting. I completely lost count of the

number of slices of *jambon persillé* (that delicious ham and parsley in white wine jelly) and ham that I tasted, and of different sausages – *boudin* (black sausage), *andouillette* with different mustards, *bresli* (thinly sliced, cured and air-dried beef), *judru* (large dry pork sausage flavoured with *Marc de Bourgogne*, the wine spirit). I was fed with *gougère*, the cheese choux-pastry rings and *escargots à la bourguignonne* (snails in garlic and parsley butter), and, of course, *pain d'épices*, the spiced honey gingerbread in which Dijon specializes and which Ghengis Khan gave to his warriors as part of their rations. If Burgundy is supposed to be light on cheeses, I cannot explain where all the varieties I tasted came from.

That night I went to the Toison d'Or, a restaurant in a lovely fifteenth-century mansion which is open to the public but is also headquarters of the Compagnie Bourguignonne des Oenophiles – the illustrious brotherhood of wine-lovers. I had real old dishes of Burgundy – *oeufs en meurette* as a starter, which is eggs poached with onions in a sauce of young red wine. Then I had one of the most famous dishes of Dijon – *râble de lièvre à la Piron*, named after the Dijonnais satirist and bon vivant of Louis XIV's reign. It is a saddle of hare marinaded in the wine spirit *Marc de Bourgogne*, cooked in its marinade and the juice made into a lovely creamy, peppery sauce. I followed with a spicy, flavoursome St Florentin cheese and a dessert rich in crème de cassis.

However, I did not feel that I had over-eaten that day, and that is the joy of Burgundian dishes. Modern chefs talk about the great gastronome Curnonsky and of simple cooking of natural ingredients, then offer us complicated concoctions of unnatural mixtures. Burgundian cooking belongs to the soil, even at its most refined. It is farmhouse cooking raised to greatness – and its lusty, thick sauces are not achieved by simply throwing in flour.

Not just Burgundy but the whole of France is proud of Charolais beef, produced by those rotund, pretty white cattle which have long since strayed way past Charolles to England, South America, Australia and many more countries. Charolais beef can be very good in the hands of the right chef, but the main reason for producing it is that the cattle are extremely fleshy and therefore more profitable. I prefer Scotch beef – but I hope the Burgundians don't read this! I *do* believe that beef grilled over vine cuttings tastes very special.

The most famous dish of Burgundy is *boeuf à la Bourguignonne* (boeuf bourguignonne to foreigners outside Burgundy). Even in Dijon, I have been served cheap beef with a cheap wine sauce poured over it. The real thing is made of best beef marinaded, then simmered slowly, in good Burgundy wine. To taste it properly cooked, go to the Porte Guillaume restaurant of the Nord Hôtel in Dijon (*see* page 85).

Coq au vin is claimed by both Burgundy and the Auvergne, eaten all over France and sneered at these days by snooty Parisian readers of Gault-Millau guide (which itself sneered at Dijon's Porte Guillaume restaurant as 'one of the ultimate bastions of coq au vin and persillé, essentially for use by tourists'). There *is* a snob version – coq au Chambertin. But that is more in the name than the wine, for even if Chambertin is used, it should be a fresh, young wine. Everyone has their own views on coq au vin. Some use a young bird, some say that it should be old and have chased a lot of hens in its life! But in Burgundy it must be flambé with half a glass of *marc* and cooked in the wine with thyme. Don't be fobbed off with a chicken just covered in red wine sauce. And the wine, of course, must be Burgundy.

Chicken dishes abound, among them *poulet au Mersault* (cooked in Mersault wine) and *poulet Gaston-Gérard* (chicken in a sauce of Gruyère cheese, white wine and mustard) named for the Mayor of Dijon (1878–1969) who started the Gastronomic Fair.

Poulets de Bresse are free-range chickens of the white Bresse breed, with a minimum of 10 square metres of ground for every bird, fattened on maize and buckwheat. They are the only chickens with an AOC – an Appellation d'Origine Contrôlée label – and are produced under the strictest regulations only in the Bresse area of 400 square kilometres.

I always regarded *Poulets de Bresse* as belonging to Bourg-en-Bresse in Ain, but the other big centre is Louhans which is in Saône-et-Loire in Burgundy. They are plainly cooked in cream to bring out their special flavour.

Pork is produced in most parts of Burgundy and the pigs are kept the old-fashioned way in a sty or on a hillside. Most of the pigs are made into sausages and other forms of charcuterie. You can buy lovely *tourte* (pork pâté baked in pastry). Air-dried *saucissons rosette du Morvan* are a fine cold snack with wine, though most fresh or smoked sausages are served hot.

When I was young, *Saupiquet* was a gourmet meal but now it is regarded as a poor man's dish on a cheap menu. That is because it is made with cheap cuts of bacon, not good Morvan ham. It is sliced ham in a creamy, slightly sharp sauce, made with cream, wine and wine vinegar.

In spring do try the peasant's snack – *petit-salé aux pissenlits* – which is salt pork with young dandelion leaves. You don't have to eat it outside: I don't believe the legend about taking dandelions indoors even if the French do call them 'wet the bed'.

The Morvan forests are still rich in game of outstanding quality – *sanglier* (wild pig), *marassin* (young wild pig), venison, hare, pigeon and pheasant. *Lapin rôti* is rabbit covered in mustard and baked. *Lapin à la moutarde* is with a cream mustard sauce.

Freshwater fish are still eaten with delight, especially as the old peasant dish of *Pôchouse* (sometimes called *Pochou* or *Pau-*

chouse), which is a freshwater fish stew. If you want to start an argument, ask what goes in it. Eel, white wine, onion and garlic are essential. Some insist on just carp and pike, some go for tench, and fishermen of the Doubs river insist on perch, while others insist on *burbot* (freshwater lotte). At Verdun-sur-le-Doubs they created in 1949 a Confrérie des Chevaliers de la Pôchouse – a brotherhood of Knights of the Pôchouse. Freshwater fish is also served with a *meurette* red wine sauce.

Let's face it – the snail was eaten by starving peasants and war victims and how it became a gourmet delight I shall never understand. The snail of Burgundy, *escargot de Bourgogne*, is, it seems, different from most of those eaten in France – bigger, fatter, juicier. It would be, being Burgundian! But it is dying out, for it was found mostly in the vineyards and has been killed by agricultural fertilizers and weedkillers. Their protective hedgerows are going, too. So 95 per cent of snails consumed in France are imported, and some are imported frozen and ready prepared – *badly* prepared. The Romans ate them but they were poor man's food until late last century when gourmets took them over, as they have taken over so many peasant dishes. The *escargots de Bourgogne* you are offered in Dijon may well have been imported live from Germany, Eastern Europe, Greece, Turkey or south-east Asia. You can only hope that they were fattened and prepared in Burgundy, with a very garlicky butter.

Still a vineyard-worker and peasant dish is the Burgundian version of *potée*, a soup-stew – 'bacon and vegetables, neither salt nor spices'. Cabbage is nearly always included.

Another old dish which still exists in the Saône valley and Bresse is *Gaudes*, a maize-flour porridge with cream, served hot or thick, cold and sliced.

The north of Burgundy grows far more grain than can be eaten locally, despite the popularity of various types of bread, and of tarts and pastry-covered pâtés.

Pain d'épices de Dijon, made of honey and flour, was a recipe brought back by the Crusaders from the Turks. A touch of anis is added in Dijon. You will find all sorts of cakes and sweetmeats in the bigger towns. Burgundy and Franche Comté still argue about who invented the feather-light deep-fried balls of batter called *pets-de-nonne*, probably for pride in its name (nun's fart).

Dijon definitely claims *nonnettes*, its special gingerbread cakes, which are made in different shapes according to the seasons.

Gougère, the cheese pastry served with wine or as a cheese course, is generous cubes of *Gruyère de Comté* or some similar cheese in choux pastry. Gâteaux and desserts are often rich in blackcurrants, or sauce made from cassis liqueur made from blackcurrants. *Poire Belle Dijonnaise* is a delicious sweet of poached pear with a raspberry sauce, cassis, cream and roasted almonds.

CHEESES

Once in a lifetime we should all try, if only for interest, *fromage fort*, the favourite cheese-spread of the vineyards and farmers of Burgundy. Unfortunately it is not often offered in the shops. You are more likely to find it in a small market town than a big city. It is old, hard or over-ripe cheese, grated and mixed with leek water, butter and usually *marc* spirit and kept in a closed pot, occasionally stirred, for several months. It can literally blow its top. It is eaten with onion, spread on bread or toast. I cannot promise that you will like it.

There are many local cheeses, not often found outside their area, and Gruyère-type cheeses are imported from the next region – Franche Comté – produced there in the mountains. You will find many local goat cheeses in Burgundy.

The best Burgundy cheese I have tasted is *Citeaux*, made by Trappist monks at their abbey, 14 kilometres east of Nuits-St-Georges, which was where I bought it. I am told that the great lady Maître-Fromager of Dijon (Mme Simone Porcheret, 18 rue Bannelier) has a few each week. It is rich but easy on the palate. *St Florentin* from the Yonne is a commercially-made soft cheese, cows' milk, brine-washed, which makes its presence known on the nose and the palate. A red-brown small disc, with a spicy taste, it is lovely with a glass or two of Côte de Beaune red. *Soumaintrain* is the original farmhouse version of *St Florentin*. Usually wrapped in vine or chestnut leaves now but Colette describes it as 'wrapped in beetroot leaves'.

Époisses, washed with *marc*, has an even stronger smell and flavour. It is often kept in ashes over winter or used to make *fromage fort*. A very special version is *Ami de Chambertin* – *époisses* washed in Chambertin wine.

Montrachet is a delicious, creamy, goats' milk cheese, soft and mild, made in a cylinder about 10 centimetres high, matured for a week and wrapped in vine leaves. It is best from the end of spring to autumn, when made with fresh milk. Other times it is made with frozen milk.

Other cheeses worth seeking are:

Bleu de Bresse – from just over the border in the Lyonnais but goes well with Mâcon or Beaujolais wines. Produced since 1950 to rival the soft blue Gorgonzola of Italy. It doesn't, but it is softer and creamier.

Cendre d'Aisy (Montbard) – soft cows' milk cheese cured in *marc*. Very strong flavour.

Charollais (Charolles) – goats' or cows' milk or a mixture. Hard, nutty.

Chevroton de Mâcon – small discs of goats' cheese often stored until dark brown and brittle to be used for *fromage fort*. They then develop a disgusting smell. Eaten very fresh and creamy, they are fine. Often eaten with sugar. Also called *Mâconnais* or, when brown and nasty, *boutons de culottes*.

Claquebitou (Beaune) – fresh, soft goats' milk cheese flavoured with garlic and herbs. Sold mostly direct from farms. Look for notices on farm gates.

Dornecy (Nièvre) – goats' cheese from local farms and dairies (just west of Vézelay).

Lormes (Nièvre) – strong, cone-shaped goats' cheese.

Mâconnais – *see* Chevroton de Mâcon.

Pierre-qui-Vire (Côte d'Or) – made by monks in monastery in St Léger-Vauban. Strong, smelly; very nice.

Roucy (Dijon) – square-boxed, flavoursome commercial cheese. Cows' milk.

Vézelay (Morvan) – farm produced goats' cheese, in cone; soft and gentle.

WINE

No one knows how wine came to Burgundy.

Pliny and Plutarch told a story that the Gauls invaded Italy because they thirsted for its wine and when thrown back across the Alps they took vines and the secrets of making wine with them. A Roman romance, it seems. The popular modern belief is that the vine came to Burgundy from the Greek colony of Massilia (Marseille) around 600 BC and that after importing wine from the Aegean in amphora for some time the Gauls were persuaded to bring back cuttings. Now there is a suggestion that they themselves, in their wanderings, brought back the vine and developed it.

I do not know. I am just very grateful indeed that wine did come to Burgundy, whoever brought it, and that the Gauls invented the wooden barrel to replace the amphora.

I am also grateful to the monks to whom we owe the beginnings and rise of many of the great vineyards of Burgundy. When parcels of land were given to their monasteries by kings and nobles trying to buy their way to Paradise, the monks found that wine was a great cash crop, and they needed cash to build and extend their great monasteries. The monks of the Monastery of Cluny created and extended the vineyards of the Mâconnais in the tenth and eleventh centuries, and the strict Cistercians of Pontigny built up Chablis in the twelfth century. The Cistercians became renowned as wine producers, showing that poor soil, fit for little else, could produce superb wine. The hard work of the vineyards was done by hired labour, for the Cistercians had such a strict daily programme of services and prayer from 2 a.m. that they had little time to do much cultivation themselves. The Cistercians established a branch of their order at Clos de Vougeot (*see* page 31). I wonder what these austere men would have thought of the Bacchanalian feasting and drinking of the Chevaliers du Tastevin who now use it as their headquarters?

The harsh order of Cistercian nuns founded the Abbey of Notre Dame du Tart and bought a vineyard at Morey which they owned until the Revolution and which still produces superb wine. It is called Clos de Tart (*see* page 30) – an unfortunate name for a nunnery wine when marketed in Britain.

A far earlier claim is made for Aloxe-Corton. Emperor Charlemagne gave Aloxe (pronounced Alosse) to the monks of Saulieu in AD775 when he rebuilt their abbey which had been destroyed by raiding Saracens. Charlemagne drunk so much Aloxe that when he was old his white beard was stained red. It is said that his wife nagged him so much that to appease her he ordered part of the vineyard to be planted with white grapes so that he could drink a non-staining white wine!

Beaune wines were claimed to be the finest reds in France by the beginning of the thirteenth century, and when the Popes moved their court from Rome to Avignon in 1309, the wines of Burgundy became renowned at the Papal Court, despite the rival claims of Rhône wines. In fact, Petrarch accused the Cardinals of delaying their return to Rome for love of Burgundy wines.

When the Revolution came, the monasteries were disbanded, the nobles who did not lose their heads lost their lands, and the big vineyards were broken up and sold to farmers and vineyard workers. Unlike Bordeaux, where the nobles later got back their lands, Burgundy vineyards are still divided among many small growers and often they own parcels of land, sometimes miles apart. The French inheritance laws, whereby all the children inherit instead of just the eldest son, has helped to keep properties small.

Last century, Burgundy, like all French vineyards, was struck by two disastrous diseases. A powdery mildew (*oidium*) cut yields right back until the remedy of dusting vines with sulphur was discovered. Then there was the terrible vine louse (*phylloxera*) in 1875 which killed the vines. It came from the United States and ironically was only cured by grafting on vine stock also imported from the US, which was immune to the pest. There is still only a quarter of the acreage of Burgundy under vines as there was in 1875.

The growing, production and naming of wines are very strictly controlled under AOC (Appellation d'Origine Contrôlée) laws, including maximum yields for each acre, so that abundant harvests do not bring increasingly abundant quantities of wine. The grape varieties are very strictly controlled. Quite simply, red wines must be made of Pinot Noir grapes or of Gamay. White wines must be of Chardonnay or of Aligoté.

Pinot Noir is used for all the great red wines of Côte de Nuits (just south of Dijon to just north of Beaune), for Côte de Beaune (down to Santenay) and Côte Chalonnaise (further south and including Mercurey). Two-thirds of the red grapes of Mâconnais are Pinot Noir, the other third are Gamay. Pinot Noir, incidentally, produces a white juice – the colour of the wine comes from the skins, which is why the juice can be used for making champagne.

Gamay, the grape of Beaujolais, produces a lighter wine, which is drunk younger and brings quicker cash to producer, *négociant* and even the retailer. In the Côte d'Or, a wine called Bourgogne Passe-Tout-Grains is made of one-third Pinot Noir, two-thirds Gamay.

The best white wines of Chablis, Côte d'Or, Côte Chalonnaise and Mâconnais are made from Chardonnay, the grape which has become so popular in wines of Australia, New Zealand and the US in recent years. It is the main grape of champagne, too. In Chablis it is known locally as Beaunois. Other great

Chardonnay wines are Pouilly-Fuissé, Meursault and Puligny-Montrachet.

Aligoté is the other white grape used in Burgundy. Wines are not sold under village names, simply as Bourgogne Aligoté, except for the village of Bouzeron, outside Chagny, but you can often tell where it comes from when the producer also bottles it and puts his village on the label. Aligoté is drunk young.

Sparkling wines have been made by the champagne method in Burgundy since 1822, but recently a good Crémant de Bourgogne has been produced. Pinot Noir or Pinot Gris (white), Chardonnay and Aligoté grapes are used. Rully was until recently the great centre for Crémant.

The grades of wine are Grand Cru, Premier Cru, Villages AOC (village's name is allowed), and Régional. In the last grade are wines called Bourgogne Hautes Côtes de Beaune, Bourgogne Hautes Côtes de Nuits, Bourgogne Passe-Tout-Grains, Bourgogne Aligoté, Bourgogne Aligoté de Bouzeron, Bourgogne Grand Ordinaire, Bourgogne Rosé and simply Bourgogne. Chablis AOC and Mâcon AOC are regional names, too. Fixin (Côte de Nuits) is allowed its own appellation. Beaujolais has a different system.

Although Pouilly-sur-Loire and its neighbouring wine areas are in Burgundy, the wine is officially a Loire wine (*see* Pouilly-sur-Loire, page 209).

Some of the villages with great individual vineyards have added the vineyard name to their village name. They include Puligny-Montrachet, Gevrey-Chambertin, Aloxe-Corton and Vosne-Romanée.

CÔTE DE DIJON AND CÔTE DE NUITS (CÔTE D'OR)

If you are following a wine route, you would need a great deal of time to stop at all the great wine villages, but in some of them there is little to see. The N74 south from Dijon is regarded as the great wine road of Burgundy, but most of the villages are, in fact, just off it, on the D122, called Route des Grands Crus. Chenôve is virtually part of Dijon these days, although technically a town of 20,000 people. Clos du Roi vineyards were owned by the Dukes of Burgundy, and the Dukes' old wine cellar (Cuverie des Ducs de Bourgogne) has two superb thirteenth-century wine presses capable of pressing the contents of one hundred wine casks in one go. They were built for the widow of a Duke. Chenôve was once a centre for breeding Burgundy snails and also for collecting them to be sent to other parts of France, and it was said that at snail feeding time the noise of their chewing sounded like wind rustling through a wood.

Marsannay, a village of 6000 people, is the only village producing a quantity of wine in the old Côte de Dijon. It produces Rosé, and is allowed to use its name – Bourgogne-Marsannay-Rosé. The Pinot Noir grape is used but the skins removed quickly from the vat. Domaine Clair-Daü and Domaine Bruno Clair both produce a wine with a lovely strawberry flavour and robust enough to stand up to Burgundian dishes. The red has an earthy flavour. For tasting, Régis Bouvier, 52 rue de Mazy (tel. 80.52.21.37) produces a fruity red called Clos du Roi, in a vineyard known since the middle ages and owned by kings of France. Fixin, where the Côte de Nuits begins, is just west of D122. It produces red wine often underestimated because it is not kept long enough. It can be coarse (*sauvage*) when young, and should be kept five to ten years, when it is robust and reliable and goes very nicely with red meats and cheese. Domaine Bruno Clair produces a good red and also a white from Pinot Blanc grapes – heavy unless very young and not so good as Chardonnay whites. (*See* Fixin, page 163.)

Gevrey-Chambertin on D122 has more Grands Crus wines in its commune than any in Burgundy. The sprawling village of Gevrey added the name of its greatest vineyard, Chambertin. The monks of the abbey of Bèze started making wines here and the monks of Cluny controlled the abbey in the middle ages and built the château to store and protect their wines. A local story says that a peasant named Bertin copied the methods of the monks in Bèze and his wine became as good as theirs. His vineyard was called Champ de Bertin (Bertin's field) then Chambertin. Le Chambertin is now a truly full-bodied wine, superb with game and roasts. Clos de Bèze is the only wine as great as Chambertin itself and is allowed the title of 'Chambertin – Clos de Bèze'.

Certain surrounding parcels of land are allowed to add the name Chambertin to their own. Latricières-Chambertin is not so powerful as Chambertin but has a lasting flavour. Charmes-Chambertin is best known, less tannic and almost too easy to swallow. It can be drunk younger than the others. Chapelle-Chambertin, with a small production, is very fruity. Other Grands Crus wines are Griotte-Chambertin, Mazis-Chambertin and Ruchottes-Chambertin. There are twenty-four Premiers Crus Gevrey-Chambertin and some, like Clos St Jacques, are almost equal to Grands Crus wines. The Gevrey vineyards cover 1250 acres and produce 1,900,000 bottles a year.

They proudly tell you in Burgundy that Napoleon loved Chambertin and took a wagon-load of it in his baggage-train wherever he went. What they don't say is that he usually put water in it! Anyway, it must have tasted a little shaken up, especially when he got to Moscow.

More impressive to me is the accolade given by that great Anglo-French bon vivant, Hilaire Belloc, novelist, essayist and poet, who died in 1953. He wrote when he was old that he had dreamed of confessing his sins to St Peter at the Gates of Heaven, though his memory was fading. 'I'm sorry, St Peter,' he said. 'I cannot remember now the name of the French village, nor of the girl, nor even what we ate for dinner. But, my God, the wine was Chambertin!'

The Burgundy poet, Gaston Roupel, a Gevrey man, wrote of the wine, too. 'It blends grace and vigour. It unites firmness with power and finesse . . . an admirable synthesis of unique generosity and complete virtue.'

Not many Gevrey-Chambertin producers are interested in giving tastings to passing travellers or amateurs as they have too many trade callers, but the Goillot-Bernollin family, in a seventeenth-century house at 29 route de Dijon, where they have produced good wine for a hundred years, have kindly received readers of *Eperon's French Wine Tour*. They prefer you to phone (80.34.36.12) but if they are there you can call between 9 a.m.–12 noon or 2 p.m.–5 p.m. (*See also* Gevrey-Chambertin, page 170.)

Gevrey spreads so far south that its slopes stretch to those of Morey-St-Denis and Morey shares the same geological make-up. Before the laws of Appellations Contrôlées were passed, Morey wines were sold as Gevrey or as Chambolle, the commune which borders it to the south. So Morey-St-Denis wine is less known than most, underestimated by many and well worth buying. It has five Grands Crus wines, plus part of the Bonnes Mares which lies mostly in Chambolle.

Clos de Tart, of the old Cistercian convent, and the Premier Cru wine Clos de la Bussière are both produced in a typical medieval abbey close, completely surrounded by walls, to which the old buildings are attached. Clos de Tart is very unusual because it is not broken up into several separate producers, each offering a slightly different wine, but has been owned since 1932 by the Mommessin family of Mâcon and Beaujolais fame who use 100 per cent new oak casks every year, like the greatest Bordeaux producers. The grapes are destalked and undergo long vinification with their skins. This all makes for tannin from the oak when the wine is young and, unfortunately, the French in particular do tend to drink it too young. When kept long enough, it has a superb spicy strength of flavour. You can't drink a good Côte de Nuits Burgundy young.

Another Clos owned by a single proprietor is Clos des Lambrays. Watch this wine. It was only made a Grand Cru in 1981 after a programme of replanting had begun. Former owners had allowed the average age of vines to reach seventy years – which may be all right for a man like me but doesn't produce great Burgundy. There are several good Clos de la Roche wines which take time to develop (try Ropiteau).

Clos St Denis, founded in 1203 as College of St Denis de Vergy, was added to the title of Moray in 1927. It produces a charming wine with finesse. The Premiers Crus wines have a lot of flavour but are not quite so rich as Grands Crus. The ordinary Morey wines really taste of fruit and can be absolutely delicious. One of the most respected producers is Jean Taudenot (tel. 80.34.35.24). If you really intend to buy a few bottles, you can taste free from 8 a.m.–12 noon, 1.30 p.m.–7 p.m. The family have been *vignerons* for many generations in their lovely old Clos and produce not only Morey-St-Denis but Charmes-Chambertin, Gevrey-Chambertin and Chambolle-Musigny. The main wine route now joins N74 with sorties westward a few kilometres for some vineyards.

Chambolle-Musigny added the name of its best vineyard, Le Musigny, out of sheer pride. Grand-Cru Musigny wine has received all the accolades. And, of course, it is very expensive. There are other good wines, too – elegant, not powerful, but a subtle taste and a gorgeous bouquet. Bernard Amiot produces a straight Chambolle wine with a lovely taste, charming bouquet and a sensible price. The Premiers Crus wines of Les Amoureuses vineyard have more than a charming name.

Clos Vougeot has been famous in Europe since the Hundred Years War. There are 124 acres inside its stone walls. The Cistercian monks who owned them built a fort in 1367 to protect them from roving bands of thirsty French and English soldiers and above all from *les routiers*, the freelance mercenaries who would fight for either side so long as the loot was good.

When Gregory XI became Pope in 1370, the Abbot of Citeaux, Jean de Brussières, sent him thirty barrels of Clos Vougeot wine. The Pope promised to remember this thoughtful act. Four years later he gave de Brussières a cardinal's hat. The monks never sold their best wine: they reserved it for gifts to kings and other important, influential people.

In 1790 in the Revolution, all church property was confiscated and auctioned for the nation. Before he handed over the keys, the monk in charge of the cellars, Dom Goblet, is said to have smuggled out enough of the last vintage to satisfy him for life – but I am sure that St Peter forgave him at the Golden Gates. The Clos was bought as a single vineyard, but in 1889 it was broken up. There are now just under eighty owners. This means that even Clos Vougeot wines can vary considerably and picking one, even if you have the money, is not easy. There is a snob value, too, in owning a parcel of the vineyard.

The fine old building is well preserved. Vineyard owners have to keep up the old walls and the rest is the headquarters of a prestigious brotherhood started in 1934 to boost sales of Burgundy during a slump. The Confrérie des Chevaliers du Tastevin originated when wine merchants and growers met at Nuits-St-Georges. In 1944 they bought the Renaissance château of Clos Vougeot as a meeting place for their 'chapters'. Dressed in scarlet and gold robes, the officers of the brotherhood initiate new members at gastronomic banquets with superb wines. They hold about twenty chapters a year. The greatest banquet is on the eve of the Hospice de Beaune sales. On the Monday is the Paulée de Meursault. These events are called 'Trois Glorieuses' ('Three Glorious Days') (*see* pages 38–9). The Confrérie also chooses the best wines to carry the Tastevinage label. It has a very Burgundian motto: 'Jamais en Vain, Toujours en Vin' ('Never in Vain, Always in Wine').

The respect in which Clos Vougeot has been held for centuries is summed up in a story told by Stendhal who said that on his way home from campaigning in Italy, a Napoleonic colonel named Bisson paraded his regiment in front of Clos Vougeot and made it present arms in respect to the great wine. (Clos open daily except 25 December–2 January from 9 a.m., evening closing time seasonal, tel. 80.62.82.75. Guided tours of half-hour followed by a quarter-hour audio-visual story of Confrérie.)

The Clos is 270 metres up with a gradual slope to vineyards beside the N74 road. On the whole, higher vines produce better wine. Clos wines are rich. Premiers Crus wines have less body but still have finesse. Vougeot Village wines are, of course, much cheaper and pleasing, but not exciting.

You are not likely to be asked to taste Clos Vougeot wines unless you are better connected than I am, but you can taste some very good Premiers Crus wines at Domaine Bertagna in rue du Vieux Château (tel. 80.62.86.04). Les Petits Vougeot wine has superb fruit and a lovely bouquet, Clos de la Perrière is rich (open 8 a.m.–7 p.m. every day including Sunday).

The village of Flagey-Echéveaux is across the plain between the N74 and A31 motorway. There are two Grands Crus wines – Echéveaux and Grands Echéveaux, and straight Flagey wines sold as Vosne-Romanée.

The village of Vosne-Romanée, just off the N74, 2 kilometres before you reach Nuits-St-Georges, produces some absolutely magnificent Grands Crus wines which are extremely pricey. Burgundians say: 'If Chambertin is King of wines, Romanée is Queen.' Certainly it is delicate in fragrance, subtle in taste and outstandingly seductive.

Most highly praised is Romanée-Conti, a wine which I have never had the luck or money to taste, though I *have* tasted La Tâche, which in some years is regarded as better. For over two centuries the Romanée vineyard was owned by a family called Croonembourg and when it was sold in 1760 there was a great rush of buyers. Louis XV's grabbing mistress, Pompadour, intended to get it but for once was outwitted by the Bourbon Prince of Conti. Now it is owned by a company (Domaine de la Romanée Conti) who own other vineyards of Vosne-Romanée. I have had an excellent Romanée-St-Vivart 1985 (another Grand Cru Vosne-Romanée).

Richebourg runs Conti and La Tâche very close in some years. Serena Sutcliffe has called it 'velvet come to life'. I remember especially the sumptuous 1983 of Domaine Jean Gros, also a Premier Cru Clos des Réas 1985 of the same Domaine – lovely smell and full of flavour. Jean Grivot makes a gorgeous Richebourg, too, and other wines, including a Premier Cru Les Beaumont. (You can taste some of his wines if you phone 80.61.05.95.) Buying is inevitably costly and you will have to keep it a few years, but what a splendid drink it will be!

Nuits-St-Georges is a delightful town and I love staying in it (*see* page 196). It is second to Beaune as a wine trade centre. The wine area stretches for four miles, so there is a great deal of wine produced. The best wines have real depth of flavour. It is another example of wines which are often drunk too young, when they are too tannic – good wines should be kept four to eight years.

Louis XIV was advised to drink glasses of Nuits or Romanée with each meal as a tonic. He probably needed a bottle or two after his activities – the Sun King was so addicted to love-making that when a mistress took a long time preparing her toilette, he would bed her lady-in-waiting to pass the time. Perhaps that is where the title lady-in-waiting came from! Anyway, Louis seems to have had no trouble taking his medicine, and, of course, both wines became fashionable at Court. Wine has been produced from the vineyards since AD1000.

Nuits wines are rich and intoxicating. Do try a mature Les Vaucrais. Les St Georges has strength and finesse and is considered to be the supreme Nuits wine. As in Beaune, the hospice owns vineyards and sells its wines at auction each year, usually on the Sunday before Palm Sunday. There is also a white made from Pinot Noir grapes, nothing like Burgundy Chardonnay nor so good.

Henri Remoriquet produces some of the most respected Saint Georges Premier Cru and an ordinary AOC Les Allots. Both are fruity and age well. (You can taste Monday to Friday at his caves, 25 rue de Charmoise. tel. 80.61.08.17.) His grandparents were vineyard workers who saved up to buy a few parcels of vines in 1892. Now he and his son have also started a vineyard in Hautes Côtes de Nuits in the south hills. The family of Xavier Dufouleur, 17 rue Thurot, have been *vignerons* since the sixteenth century and made excellent wines traditionally, matured in oak casks and reaching their best in ten to twenty years. (Tastings cave open 8.30 a.m.–12 noon, 2 p.m.–6 p.m. No need to phone.)

CÔTE DE BEAUNE (CÔTE D'OR)

The first great vineyard of the Côte de Beaune is Aloxe-Corton, just north-west of N74 on the pretty little D18 which runs up into the hills. The village of Aloxe-Corton itself lies beneath a hill (the Massif du Corton) and its beautiful little manor house Château de Corton is almost hidden by vegetation. To me, it is a true working Burgundian wine village, with vines so close to the houses that you could almost pick grapes from the windows.

Le Corton vineyard itself is a narrow strip just beneath the wood which crowns the hill, but the vineyards around it are also able to use the title Corton before their name as they produce such superb red wines. The Corton area, however, spreads around the hill to the other side, which is in the prettier village of Pernand-Vergelesses, and this, too, has vineyards producing Grands Crus Corton wines, as do some small vineyards in the twin villages of Ladoix-Serrigny. They also take a part in growing grapes for the magnificent white wine Corton Charlemagne – flinty, slow in maturing and a true rival to the best Montrachet. Alas, some Frenchmen still drink it too young, despite warnings! The other good wines are all red. Red Corton is more powerful than other Côtes de Beaune and it starts off very tannic. It really does need time to develop and soften – a good ten years. Considering its price, it would be ridiculous to drink it too young. It is very rich. My own favourites are Corton-

Clos-du-Roi, which takes longest to mature, and the extremely rich Corton-Bressandes.

Premiers Crus wines are not usually as rich, but are ready to drink much sooner and are attractive and satisfying. Outstanding and rich is a Pernand-Vergelesses Île des Vergelesses, which must be mature. Pernand Village wines can be earthy, even harsh, but are good value. Ordinary Aloxe is a good buy, too. Pernand makes a lot of Aligoté white.

Aloxe and Pernand had been producing wine for a long time when Charlemagne, who rebuilt their abbey, gave some of his vineyard to the monks of Saulieu and he, of course, is credited with first making white wine so that his beard would not be stained red (*see* page 25). Voltaire liked the red. It was sent to him by the man who built the Château de Corton. Voltaire kept the Corton for himself; to his guests he served Beaujolais.

The Château is now called Château Corton-André after the André family who bought it in 1927. They have an estate of 174 acres in Burgundy and another in Côtes-de-Rhône. They produce four different Grands Crus, Cortons as well as a Clos Vougeot wine, and other Burgundies. So the old Château cellar is a splendid place to taste wine. It is better to phone first but not necessary (tel. 80.26.44.25).

Savigny lès Beaune, on the little D2 road 6 kilometres northwest of Beaune, is an absolutely delightful village at the entrance to the lovely valley of the tiny river Rhoin. The attractive D18 runs north to Pernand, just missing Aloxe-Corton, and the D2 itself follows a pleasant route to Bouilland. Just beyond, you can turn right along D25 for a charming drive to Nuits-St-Georges. From Savigny are wonderful views over the countryside, marred only by some noise from the A6 motorway passing through the vineyards only a kilometre away.

After Beaune and Pommard, Savigny produces more red wine than anywhere on the Côte de Beaune and its wines mature faster than their neighbours, which pleases the wine trade. The wines have a superbly rich perfume of fruit and flowers and those produced south of the river are mostly seductively light. Domaine Simon Bize makes outstanding wines. A little white is made from Chardonnay grapes or from Pinot Blanc.

Like Beaune, Savigny lives by and for wine. The motto of La

Cousinerie de Bourgogne, the wine producers' brotherhood, is 'All Gentlemen are Cousins', and they meet in the communal cellars, over the door of which is written in Latin, 'There are five reasons for drinking: the arrival of a guest, a thirst, an oncoming thirst, an excellent wine and any other reason you care to think of.'

Savigny lès Beaune is a good centre to stay for visiting the vineyards and the attractive countryside without the hustle of Beaune (*see* page 238).

Chorey lès Beaune, once a quiet village just off N74 north-east of Beaune, finds itself these days within 2 kilometres of the meeting of the A6 and A31 motorways. It produces no Premiers Crus wines, most of its wine is sold as Côte de Beaune-Villages, which is best drunk fairly young to keep its fruitiness. The village has a superb hotel-restaurant Ermitage Corton serving great food and wines (*see* Beaune, page 72).

A good place to taste is Domaine Goud de Beaupuis, Château des Mulots (8 a.m.–8 p.m. daily, tel. 80.22.20.63 if possible. English spoken). A family Domaine since 1787, they use an old stone pressoir and mature wines in oak barrels for twenty-two months in eighteenth-century caves.

Beaune is the heart and metropolis of the Burgundy wine trade. It has such a rich heritage of beautiful historic buildings and streets that to know them truly you would have to live there for a long time. And the wine and the heritage are so closely knit that it is difficult to describe one without the other. So please also read the story of Beaune the town on pages 65–72.

The hospice, of course, is mainly kept going by the famous sale of wines from vineyards presented to it over centuries. (*See* pages 67–70.) But many producers and *négociants* are in historic buildings and you can visit them not only for their wines but to see the surroundings. Patriarche Père et Fils, for instance, have the biggest cellars in Burgundy in what was the convent of the nuns of the Visitations, founded by the grandmother of the Marquise de Sévigné and bought by Jean-Baptiste Patriarche in 1796 when his cellars at Savigny lès Beaune became too small. The nuns' cellars have been joined to other underground pass-ages, including the fourteenth-century cellars of the monks of

Chartreuse. Patriarche are *négociants*, but they also own vineyards and the Château Meursault.

Using the little silver flat Burgundian cup called a *tastevin*, you can taste twenty-one wines the proper way, not gulping down twenty-one glasses! You are given a comment card, which says 'Taste sensibly'. The visit (1 March–15 December, 9.30 a.m.–11.30 a.m., 2 p.m.–5.30 p.m.) takes 40 minutes and costs a fee, which is given to charity. The building itself is beautiful, with elegant seventeenth-century arcades.

J. Calvet, the great international wine company founded in 1818 and exporters to Britain for more than 150 years, have superb cellars in the medieval fortifications of Beaune and you taste wine in a fifteenth-century tower. (Visits daily except Monday 8 a.m.–11 a.m., 2 p.m.–5 p.m. 6 boul. Perpreuil. tel. 80.22.05.32.)

One of the most interesting visits in Burgundy is to the cellars of Bouchard Aîné, 39 rue Ste Marguerite (tel. 80.22.07.67 – 9 a.m.–12 noon, 2 p.m.–4.30 p.m.). You cannot taste unless you are in the wine trade but you will learn a great deal about Burgundy wine, and drink a Kir (one part crème de cassis, alcoholic blackcurrant liqueur, to four parts Aligoté white wine). You can buy a choice of wines. So many people wanted to visit these family-owned cellars that Terry Price, the English PR man, has been forced to ask you to phone. It's worth the trouble.

Cave Exposition de la Reine Pedauque, Porte St Nicolas (tel. 80.22.23.11), is in ancient caves with hundreds of thousands of bottles and barrels, including the greatest Crus of Burgundy and some of the oldest wines. It was set up by the owners of Clos des Langres near Nuits-St-Georges and in Mâcon and Beaujolais. Visits and tastings are welcome in business hours and English is spoken.

It is worth remembering that the appellation Beaune on a wine is different from Côte de Beaune, which is wine from certain small parcels of land on the Beaune 'mountain', and from Côte de Beaune-Villages, which is a blend of two or more red wines from sixteen picked wine villages, such as Savigny lès Beaune, Puligny-Montrachet and Meursault.

Wines simply called Beaune are produced on the slopes around the town, up to about 330 metres. Most are red. The vineyards are cut in half by the D970 and near the Savigny border the A6 motorway cuts right through some vineyards, such as Les Marconnets, which produces some of the best Premiers Crus wines, of which there are more than thirty. They do vary enormously, but some are delicate and can be drunk youngish (4–5 years), others are more robust and need longer. One of the very best is Bouchard's Grèves wine from their tiny vineyard Vigne de l'Enfant Jesus. You will notice that most of the vineyards are owned by *négociants*. Beaune has for centuries been the main centre for the sale and shipping of Burgundy wines and when the big estates owned by the church and aristocrats were taken away and sold in the Revolution, the wholesalers and shippers moved in quickly and bought the vineyards before the peasants could.

Ordinary Villages-Beaune is, I think, underrated in many cases but is usually drunk too young in France. Some wines are fruity when quite young but most of the wine is at its best at five years old and goes very well with richer food which would kill the taste of a fine Côte de Nuits. White wines often have a coarse, rustic flavour, not unpleasant.

I tell the story of the Hospice de la Charité in the section on Beaune. Through centuries rich men and women have left vineyards to the hospice, perhaps in exchange for a little parcel of land in Heaven, and the list of vineyards they own and wines they produce is formidable. The wines are sold, of course, at the huge annual auction held on the third Sunday in November, but you cannot attend unless you can ingratiate yourself with somebody in the trade and persuade him to take you as a personal guest. It is an old-style traditional auction: a taper is lit and when it goes out it is replaced with another until the bidding stops. When the second candle has gone out, the wine is sold. Prices are high because there is prestige in bidding and in having the wine on your trade list when it has been raised and matured. But the prices paid are a relative guide to the general price level that year. Usually the biggest money-spinner is a white. That night a candlelit dinner is held in one of the huge cellars of the town walls. On the Saturday night before the sale is the banquet of the Chevaliers de Tastevin at Clos Vougeot. On Monday the eating and drinking moves to Meursault where three hundred growers take two of their bottles each and demolish them at another banquet. The three events are called the Trois Glorieuses. It is no time to be in Beaune unless you are well connected with the wine business – every hotel bed and restaurant table has been booked long before.

Pommard, the next village, astride D973 and stretching to N74, is the tough-guy of Burgundy – producing a full-bodied sometimes unsubtle and rather tannic mouthful which goes splendidly with old Burgundy dishes like *boeuf à la Bourguignonne*. Unfortunately it has suffered in the past from false labelling, especially outside France, and there is such widescale production that there are great variations in quality. And it is yet another wine which suffers from quick-profit merchants persuading people to drink it too young. It takes time to open out. Some wines from good vineyards made by good wine-makers are wonderful with old-fashioned man-size meals. Like modern cooking, modern Burgundy can be too light for a winter's night. The best Pommard wines are generally reckoned to be Les Grands Epenots and Les Rugiens, and there is a movement to have them promoted from Premiers Crus to Grands Crus. Rugiens is on the higher ground between Pommard and neighbouring Volnay, which makes more subtle wines.

Most of the vines are grown by small *vignerons* with caves beneath their old houses in the village.

Wise words on Pommard have come from Jean-Louis Laplanche, owner of Château de Pommard: 'We only bottle the best cuvées from each harvest under the Château de Pommard label, carefully selected by repeated tasting. This allows for the great vintages as well as the lesser ones to offer a wine of great distinction. One may have more body and warmth, another has more balance and subtle aromas. Therefore do not be swayed by preconceived notions of the "Vintage of the Century" or by little annotated cards. Each bottle is a separate achievement.'

The Château used to have a huge notice outside just after World War II reading 'Free Tasting Every Day'. It was next to a warning notice saying: 'Safe Driving Demands Sobriety'. So many people wanted to taste it that they made a nominal charge to cover something towards the cost of wine tasted. The wines must be kept four to ten years according to the vintage. For instance, when I was last there in 1986, the 1980 wine was soft and ready for drinking and the 1979 and powerful 1981 needed several more years. (Visits Easter to third Sunday in November, 8.30 a.m.–6.30 p.m.)

The Parent family, in place l'Église by the church with an oddly shaped belfry, have owned Pommard vineyards since 1740, supplied wines for Thomas Jefferson when he was US Ambassador to France, and still use the old traditional methods. Their Clos Micault, aged for at least ten years, is the sort of beefy, old-style Pommard which I love. Their Les Epenots wines are fruity and elegant. (To taste you must telephone 80.22.15.08.)

Pommard was named after Pommona, Roman goddess of fruits and gardens. Friends of Pommard included Henri IV, Louis XV and especially Victor Hugo. Today the wine is extra pricey – Americans are blamed.

The wine of Volnay, 2 kilometres along D973, could hardly be more different – a gorgeous perfume, delicate, elegant. It has a definite scent of violets – even I can notice it! The Dukes of Burgundy had one of their most beloved vineyards there and a favourite country house. When Louis XI of France's force of Swiss mercenaries beat and killed the Burgundy Duke Charles the Rash, Louis celebrated by looting the whole 1477 vintage and having it taken to his château of Plessis-lès-Tours. Far too good for him! Volnay is a hamlet of only about five hundred people who mostly live in lovely solid old Burgundian houses standing proudly above the vineyards. Do try the wines of Hubert de Montile's Domaine if possible.

The lovely old hamlet of Monthélie has only two hundred people and until 1937 its wines were sold as either Pommard or Volnay. It is rather similar to Volnay, with a lovely scent, but even lighter and noticeably cheaper. It is a splendid luncheon or summer dinner wine. There is a white wine which you can taste, perhaps, in the village café, and you might be able to taste the best of Monthélie by phoning Robert de Suremain at Château de Monthélie caves and asking for an appointment (tel. 80.21.23.32).

Meursault, a little town between the D973 and N74, (*see* page 185) has a church with a beautiful Gothic stone spire and produces what some people, especially the people of Meursault, believe to be with Puligny and Chassagne Montrachet 'the best white wines in the world'. With its ripe-grape and cinnamon perfume and hint of hazelnuts in its strong, long-lasting flavour, it bewildered me when I first tasted it. I could not decide just how dry it was! But it *is* dry, and some wines are actually flinty, while others are very rich, too. I wish that I could afford to drink it more often – such as every day. Louis XV's Cardinal de Bernis would celebrate Mass with no other wine because, he said, he did not want his Creator to see him pulling a face when he made his communion. Good red wines are produced, too.

Patriarche Père et Fils own the sixteenth-century Château de Meursault, which until recently belonged to le Comte de Moucheron. The cellars, holding half a million bottles and one thousand oak maturing casks, were partly dug by the monks of Citeaux abbey in the thirteenth century. The white wines produced here are gorgeous even by Meursault standards. The great park with ancient trees was partly replanted with Chardonnay grapes in 1975. Visitors may taste wines and walk round the park (every day including Sundays, 9.30 a.m.–11.30 a.m., 2.30 p.m.–5.30 p.m.). It is one of the most rewarding visits in Burgundy.

Back on D973 is Auxey-Duresses, at the entrance to a gorge dominated by Mont Melian. There are many pretty roads around here, and although most vineyards are too high to make great wine, they produce red and white wines which are very good value, having not yet become fashionable. Most red is similar to Monthélie. Alain Gras produces a nice one. White is very pleasant drunk young.

The attractive D973 continues to La Rochepot (*see* page 213). Equally attractive is the little D17 west to St Romain, a hamlet with a ruined castle high on a spur and the highest vineyards on the whole Côte d'Or, producing an excellent fresh apéritif white Chardonnay and a very quaffable rustic red with the flavour of cherries.

Puligny-Montrachet, a charming place, is the next village you reach near to the N74 after Meursault, but take the little D13A vineyard road, then follow it across N6 to Chassagne-Montrachet. From a mere 18 acres Puligny and Chassagne produce sheer nectar – almost certainly the best white wine in the world. Alexandre Dumas, gastronome and wine worshipper as well as world best-selling novelist, said that Puligny should be drunk on bended knee and with head bared, and even an agnostic like me can agree with that. People who do not agree have probably been drinking them too young, especially the greatest Grands Crus wines such as Le Montrachet, Bâtard-Montrachet, Chevalier Montrachet and Criots-Bâtard-Montrachet. 'It is really a vinous crime to drink Le Montrachet at under ten years of age,' says Serena Sutcliffe, and although the other Grands Crus can be drunk earlier, they do need to be kept until the lovely greenish-yellow colour of the young wine turns to gold in the bottle and the full taste of honey and fruit develops. They should be served at 55°F (13°C) cellar temperature – not from a fridge. Most Chassagne can be drunk younger than Puligny. Many wine experts say that Grands Crus Puligny should be drunk without food, for they are too powerful for fish.

All this talk, of course, can be academic to many of us, for they cost enough to warrant the bended knee. But if you cannot taste the Grands Crus wines there are some Premiers Crus wines such as Les Pucelles and Les Folatières which are a delight, and the village wines are excellent and inexpensive.

Chassagne-Montrachet red is underrated, more is produced than white and although the French drink them both two to four years old they do get smoother with age.

Alongside Chassagne-Montrachet on N6 is the village of St Aubin whose old *vignerons*' houses are so interesting that it is an historic monument. If you want to drink wine with a true Burgundy flavour but lighter, fresher and considerably cheaper, this is the place to stop. The reds taste of strawberries and are drunk at around three to four years old; the best whites have a distinct affinity to Puligny-Montrachet. Try La Chatenière white, very aromatic with a lovely flowery taste. Domaine Roux Père makes a beauty. So does Marc Colin whose caves you can visit if you phone first (80.21.30.43). The village of Gamay alongside gave its name to the Gamay grape – the 'Beaujolais grape'.

The last vineyards are at Santenay, west of the little industrial town of Chagny. Santenay is really a string of three hamlets along the banks of the little river Dheune, beneath a mountain. It has a fine thirteenth-century church with beautiful nave and some charming old wood and stone sculptures. It used to be called Santenay-les-Bains 'where wine and water meet' and it still produces a mineral water recommended for gout and rheumatism. It is said to have the highest lithium content in Europe. Its wine has changed a great deal in my time. The old *vignerons* produced dark, earthy, beefy wines from old vines more like those from Côte de Nuits. Now more modern methods have also produced a light and fruitier wine, drunk much younger. You can taste the excellent wines of the Prieuré family, who have made wine here since 1804. Do try their La Maladière in the fifteenth-century caves at Domaine Prieuré-Brunet. This is a good Domaine to visit because there is no need to phone and the family own vineyards producing great and good wines all over the Côte de Beaune, including a superb white Bâtard-Montrachet (tel. 80.20.60.56. Visits 10 a.m.–12 noon, 3 p.m.–7 p.m.).

Santenay, like all good spas, has a small casino. When healing the body at spas it is traditionally essential to destroy your financial status by gambling. On weekends, steelworkers and miners from Le Creusot used to crowd into the Santenay casino. Now with the slump in those industries, tourists are the main gamblers. I suggest that you call first at Domaine Prieuré-Brunet and invest your money with more wisdom and pleasure.

CÔTE CHALONNAISE

The long line of vine-covered hills from Dijon breaks up at Santenay. From there, vines are grown on favourable slopes and the area is called Côte Chalonnaise. But the town of Chalon-sur-Saône is out on the plain and has little to do with wine, so wine people tend to talk of the Région de Mercurey, named after the best known wine of the Côte.

The best wine villages are mostly on tiny winding roads just west of the D981 from Chagny, and are well worth seeking. Bouzeron, the first village, produces very good Aligoté white wine, so good that it is allowed to use the name Aligoté de Bouzeron on the label.

Rully is a charming village dominated by a big hilltop church (*see* page 217) and for long was so little known that its red wines and most of its white were made by the champagne method into sparkling wines just called 'Burgundy'. The few floral and spicy still whites were bargains. My wife Barbara knew.

Then the prices of Chablis and Pouilly-Fuissé, not to mention Meursault and Puligny, shot up so fast that trade buyers came around looking for a substitute. Now 70 per cent of Rully white is still wine, it has reached world markets and the price has gone up as people realized how good it is. Now it is usually priced equally with an AOC Chablis and only just below overpriced Pouilly-Fuissé. The theory is that Rully white wines should be drunk when two or three years old, after which they are supposed to lose fruit and toughen. They are certainly delicious young. But Barbara has cunningly bought bin ends of four- to six-year-old wines and they have all been slightly less fruity but very satisfying, with real finesse – and noticeably cheaper! Armand Monassier of Prieuré gave us some whites and reds recently dating back to 1975 and they were superb.

Red wines are real Burgundy Pinots, quite light in colour and with a raspberry flavour. To taste and buy phone either Domaine du Prieuré (85.87.13.57) or Caves Delorme-Neulien (Domaine de la Renarde – 85.87.10.12). Domaine de la Renarde owns all the 45-acre Varot vineyard and another 100 acres in Mercurey, Givry and Bouzeron. Jean-François Delorme makes a lovely velvety red Rully. In the château is a glass goblet which belonged to a sixteenth-century Lord of the Manor. It holds more than five pints and it is claimed that he could drain it in one draught – a shocking waste of good wine.

You can use little vineyard roads to go from Rully to Mercurey, but they are mostly one-car wide and the roadside grass is allowed to grow window-high to cut for hay, which makes navigation difficult in summer. The easy, much longer way is down D981, then right on D978.

Mercurey production is nearly all red. The whites are heavy and not so attractive as Rully. Reds are heavy, too, sometimes rustic, and go well with old local dishes such as *boeuf à la Bour-*

guignonne. Some wines taste of iron, but it is a pleasant taste. I think that the wines are best five to six years after the vintage and their lowish rating with the French was caused by the same old trouble – people were persuaded to drink them too young.

A lighter, more elegant wine is produced by the Marquis de Jouennes d'Herville, son-in-law of the great Antonin Rodet. It is best after four to five years and is called Château de Chamirey after his seventeenth-century château, which is classed as a national monument. His red and white wines have won many international awards. The whites are aromatic – the best white Mercurey I have tasted. It is well worth visiting Château de Chamirey. Phone if possible (85.45.22.22), they speak English. As a village, Mercurey is rather spoiled by the main Chalon road running through it.

Givry, although only 9 kilometres from Chalon, and on D981, is more interesting and more attractive (*see* Givry, page 171). For centuries it was a very important wine producing town. In the sixth century Gregory of Tours was already praising it as 'the wine of Chalon'. In the middle ages it was rated with Beaune and equally heavily taxed in Paris. It was on the table of many monarchs but the one who matters to Givry is inevitably Henri IV, *le Vert Galant*, who loved wine as much as he loved women. Before you reach the village, notices on the D981 tell you that it was his 'preferred' wine, as do the bottle labels. We must blame the eighteenth-century Burgundy poet and historian Courtépée who wrote that Henri got to like the wine when his favourite mistress Gabrielle d'Estrées was staying in the nearby Château of Germolles, and that he made it his daily tipple back in Paris, exempting it from duty. However, when ten times more wine than Givry could ever produce suddenly appeared for sale duty free, the tax had to be put back. The truth is that Henri not only loved wine but was a diplomat of high order who liked to please his subjects. So, when in a wine area, the local wine was his favourite. Among others Suresnes, Anjou, Arbois, Ay, Jurançon and Pommard have claimed to produce Henri's favourite.

Givry wine kept its popularity until the First World War. Then it fell so low in people's estimation that it still does not have a Premier Cru. But it does produce a very good light red wine with a pleasant smell, a lingering taste and delicate flavour which goes well with old-fashioned sauces. The wines remind me of Loire wines. Caves left over from its heyday are enormous – the biggest belonged to the family of the late Baron Louis Thénard who worked hard to get Givry back on the map. One red, Le Cellier aux Moines, was described aptly by Serena Sutcliffe as 'having the smell of all the herbs of Provence'. The white wine is pale and fruity, like a lightweight Meursault, and it is nearly all drunk locally.

Buxy, 8 kilometres down D981, is an old, busy, pleasant little town which, with the village of Montagny 3 kilometres west, produces the delicious Montagny white wine that we will go far out of our way to buy at local prices. It is greeny gold in colour and tastes like a crisper version of Pouilly-Fuissé from further south in Mâcon. It is said to keep the mouth fresh and the head clear, and it was the drink of the learned monks of Cluny, not of roistering kings. Drink it between two and three years old. It is delicious.

Cave des Vignerons de Buxy is much respected in the trade in France and Britain. We have found it excellent for Montagny and for other ordinary Burgundy wines. Buxy, by the way, is another of the towns with an 'x' in it that the French say you should pronounce 'ss' – Bussy. Not all the locals do. The town's market is on Thursday.

THE MÂCONNAIS

The Mâconnais vineyards stretch for 50 kilometres from Tournus on the river Saône to St Vérand in the south and are about 15 kilometres wide from the river Grosne valley to the valley of the Saône, but to tour them would be a winding, circuitous route. The scenery of the uplands is varied and very beautiful with forests at the summit of hills, arid slopes and damp, rich meadows in the valleys. The vineyards are planted in terraces on the slopes where morning sunlight falls. The rest is heathland where goats produce milk for little chevroton cheeses.

The hero of the Mâconnais was a winegrower from Charnay-lès-Mâcon, a little village now almost on the western edge of the town. Claude Brosse was an ordinary winegrower but a giant of a man, who decided that the wine of Mâcon deserved to be better known. So he loaded two hogsheads of his best wine on to an ox cart and took it to Versailles, hoping to attract the custom of some noblemen. He arrived after thirty-three days and went to Mass in thanks for his safe journey. King Louis XIV was there and was annoyed to see a man still standing when everyone else was kneeling in prayer. He sent one of his staff to tell the man to kneel, only to discover that the Burgundian giant *had* been kneeling. Louis sent for Brosse and asked what had brought him to Paris. Brosse explained and asked the king if he would like to taste the wine. Louis did, and said that it was far better than the Suresnes and Beaugency wine being drunk at Court. So, of course, all the sycophantic courtiers wanted Mâcon to serve at their tables. Brosse took his wine to Versailles every year – and became rich. No doubt he bought-in his neighbours' wines, too!

The great abbey of Cluny was north-west of the town of Mâcon and the Cluny monks planted the first grapes in the area. Now the grapes grown are Chardonnay for white wines, which are the most important, and Gamay, the grape used in Beaujolais for most of the reds, with some Pinot Noir.

Most Mâcon Blanc is made without using oak casks – kept in a vat and bottled young. But in the cellars of the greatest Mâcon wine, Pouilly-Fuissé, you will see barrels and even old traditional wooden vats.

Nowadays an increasing amount of the Gamay red wine-makers are copying Beaujolais and making wines by semi-Macération Carbonique method, which means that they can and should be drunk young. The Gamay grapes, which are black with white juice, are never crushed in making the wine. The fermenting juice at the bottom of the vat induces fermentation within each individual grape, which lasts for four to six days. In the full Macération Carbonique method, the vat is saturated with added carbon dioxide. However, grapes are still pressed by many producers. Macération Carbonique does accentuate the beautiful bouquet of the wine while losing none of its fruitiness.

If you want to see something of the Mâconnais vineyards in a short time, you could start at Mâcon, forgetting the northern stretch from Tournus, and make straight for the Pouilly-Fuissé villages (Pouilly, Fuissé, Solutré, Vergisson and Chaintré) then for Loché and Vinzelles. But you would be missing some superb scenery west of the Saône.

Mâcon is a busy place on the Saône with a river port used for centuries to transport wine. The town adopted the Spanish St Vincent, who became patron of *vignerons*, and it holds the French National Wine Fair in the last two weeks of May, so if your wine bottle has a round golden sticker saying that it has won a Gold, Silver or Bronze medal at Mâcon, there are few higher accolades in its class (*see* Mâcon, page 86).

Pouilly-Fuissé is a gorgeous white wine, made with Chardonnay, rich but with a lovely flavour which makes it more refreshing than Chablis or Puligny-Montrachet. Alas, it is too popular, especially with Americans and Japanese, and the price is too high for some of its old supporters. There is much debate locally about which village produces the best wine. They all taste splendid to me!

Château Fuissé wine, I believe holds the record for prices at auction.

Until a few years ago, you could not trust a Pouilly-Fuissé label outside Burgundy. I came across some in Britain which was obviously Chardonnay from the south-west. Good cheaper substitutes are Pouilly-Vinzelles and Pouilly-Loché, named after nearby villages, but production is small and they are hard to find, though the great Georges Duboeuf offers them (*see* Beaujolais, page 51). The wines are more rustic than the real thing but are luscious.

A Fuissé substitute more easily obtainable is St Véran, from seven different villages, including Chasselas, which also produces the famous dessert grapes, and a village confusingly called St Verand with a 'd'. Although it matures more quickly than Pouilly-Fuissé, it should be two to four years old to enjoy its full nutty flavour.

Forty-three villages make Mâcon-Blanc-Villages, mostly produced by co-operatives. Best known are Lugny, Clessé, Viré (easy to reach because it is 3 kilometres west of the N6, 19 kilometres north of Mâcon) and Chardonnay (8 kilometres south-west of Tournus) where the Chardonnay was probably developed, some say by the monks of Cluny. The wines are fruity, with a flowery perfume, best when two years old, often drunk one year old in France. They sometimes have the musky taste of some Australian Chardonnays. The cave co-operative at Viré makes a good wine, fresh and fruity. It has a mural showing Viré's twinning (*jumellage*) with another village – Montmartre in Paris! You can taste there, in business hours, paying by the glass. I like that idea. I am sometimes too much of a coward to taste without buying a bottle or two! No need to phone, but the number is 85.33.11.64.

Mâcon Rouge and Mâcon Supérieur Rouge (1 per cent more alcohol) are best drunk young (two years) when they are fruity and fresh. They go well with charcuterie or poultry. Like all Gamay wines, they are often drunk cool or cold (not iced) in France. They are not usually as good as Beaujolais but are cheaper. A wine of Gamay mixed with a third or more Pinot Noir is called Bourgogne Passe-Tout-Grains. Mâcon rosé is not much good.

You can taste wine in Mâcon at the Comité Interprofessionel des Vins de Bourgogne et Mâcon, Maison de Tourisme, avenue Maréchal-de-Lattre-de-Tassigny.

BEAUJOLAIS

Nearly all of the Beaujolais is in the *département* of Rhône, in the Lyonnais, not in Burgundy, but the Beaujolais wine *is* Burgundy and the little wine villages of the Beaujolais produce enough grapes to make about 150 million bottles of wine a year!

It is wonderful countryside – a land of hills, packed tightly together with the little valleys between, threaded with streams, with twisting narrow roads made for carts, not cars, and with villages which are mostly just hamlets with a handful of red-roofed houses and a spired church. There is no wine tour of Beaujolais. There are no main roads taking you from one wine village to another. You just try to map-read, and you get lost. So the only plan is not to have one except to decide that you will find by hook or by crook two or three villages you especially want to visit and see what turns up in between. It is no good worrying about time – or tyres. In 1991 I (who should have known better) drove my old automatic Jaguar around the Beaujolais. I shall never forget it. I should have hired a little Peugeot or a 2CV.

Beaujolais must be drunk young. Only a few Crus wines are better for keeping five to six years. Nor is it a wine for a lot of deep thought and pretty words after solemn tasting. I agree with what the great wine producer, *négociant* and writer Alexis Lichine said in his very readable and extremely useful *Guide to the Wines and Vineyards of France* (Papermac, 1982), 'Forget the delicate sniffs and sips, the ruminatory gargles, the suspenseful silences with which we approach the great Burgundies and Bordeaux. The wines of Beaujolais are meant to be swallowed and gulped and unabashedly enjoyed'.

But please allow yourself a sniff long enough to enjoy that lovely fruitiness of the Gamay grape at its best.

All this fuss about Nouveau Beaujolais bewilders me and I am glad that the silly fashion is fading. It all started in Lyon and Paris in the old days when cheap bistros served the wine direct from barrels, kept in the smoky bar, and by November it was going pretty nasty and vinegary. So when the new wine arrived, the bistro owners happily announced, 'Le Nouveau Beaujolais est arrivé!' Even I can remember in the late forties and early fifties when much Beaujolais never reached a bottle. In Lyon the joke was that three rivers flowed into the city, the Saône, the Rhône and the Beaujolais.

The earthy Beaujolais growers would drop their *tastevins* laughing if they could see snob amateurs of Paris and London solemnly going through a tasting ritual, then pronouncing wise words on the merits of the year's Nouveau when the wine has not had time to stop revolving round the bottle after its journey.

Georges Duboeuf, who is variously called the King or the Pope of Beaujolais and who is known personally to every great chef and wine-trader in the world, has improved Nouveau Beaujolais greatly and sends a lot of his carefully chosen wines to be independently tasted and analyzed to make sure which are suitable for drinking young. Despite that, one nasty November night a few years back I arrived at his cave to taste and take away the new wine, but after a smell, a swirl and a swallow had to admit that I didn't want to drink any more because it gave me hiccups and an acidic stomach. He disappeared into the cellar and brought back for me a bottle of Fleurie which was two years old, flowery, soft and delicious. That is another advantage of Beaujolais – it can be drunk at cellar temperature when not accompanying food. In fact that is the current fashion.

Fleurie is one of the nine Crus wines – single villages which may sell under their own names, and all in the north of Beaujolais, where the granite-based soil produces a better, fruitier Gamay wine than any I have tasted even from Touraine.

Nearly half of red wines produced are ordinary AOC Beaujolais. They are light, fruity, very quaffable and should be drunk at one year old or younger. Beaujolais Supérieur can be kept a little longer but is not seen much outside France. Most of the wines that are seen outside France are Beaujolais-Villages, which are more full-bodied and satisfying but still fruity and easy to drink. They are best from one to two years old.

Many bigger wine villages making Villages wines have tasting bars of some sort. Some open only in tourist season, others on Friday, Saturday and Sunday. At most you must pay a nominal amount for a glass or a tasting. A pleasant place to taste a light Villages wine is Château de Corcelles, a fifteenth-century fortress with Renaissance galleries in its courtyard, fine woodcarvings in the chapel and a seventeenth-century Grand Cuvier, 80 metres long, with wine maturing in huge casks. It is at Corcelles-en-Beaujolais, just west of the N6, 8 kilometres north of Belleville (tel. 74.66.00.24 – check opening times). Another is La Cave Beaujolais at Château des Loges, Le Perreon. From St Georges-de-Reneins on N6, north of Villefranche, go west on D20 and D49 to just north of Vaux-en-Beaujolais (Clochemerle). Wine-making equipment is modern, wine is fruity and light except Château les Loges (full-bodied, maturing excellently) and you taste in fine old eighteenth-century caves of the château. (Pay for tastings – 9 a.m.–12 noon, 2.30 p.m.–7 p.m. tel. 74.03.22.83).

Georges Duboeuf, *négociant* par excellence, and man with 'the best nose and palate in Burgundy', is at Romanèche-Thorins, just west of N6, 15 kilometres south of Mâcon. Everyone wants to visit him, so you must make an appointment (phone 83.35.51.13), and visits are for serious buyers. He travels through Beaujolais and Mâcon each year, tastes 8000 wines and brings back 3000 for exhaustive laboratory analysis.

First of the Crus wines you meet coming from Mâcon is St-Amour at St-Amour-Bellevue. The wines are sprightly, fruity and delicate. They take about three years to ripen, as true Amour should. The name came to the village because its owners, the Canons of Mâcon Cathedral, did not allow their holy vows to stand in the way of their *droits de Seigneur*, and fully instructed the local brides on the night before their wedding. Wayward girls must have been very glad of the excuse next night. Wines of Château de St-Amour are outstanding – as are the aptly named Domaine du Paradis, bottled by Georges Duboeuf. Even the local restaurant is called Auberge du Paradis. If you cannot drink the wine with the right companion on St Valentine's Day, don't miss 20 August – St Amour's Day.

The wine of Juliénas, the neighbouring commune named for Julius Caesar, is said to be the epitome of Beaujolais. Deep purple, gloriously fruity at six months to a year, spicy as well at two to four years. Slopes are very steep, making picking difficult and expensive. Its producers' association has a convenient tasting cave, Cellier de la Vieille Église, in a fine old church with coloured frescoes devoted to Bacchus and his worshippers. You can taste Juliénas and St-Amour (every day in June, July, August; shut Tuesdays rest of year, 10 a.m.–12 noon, 2.30 p.m.–6.30 p.m.). Château de Juliénas wines are excellent. Its Domaine de la Seigneurie du Juliénas wine has body, tannin and is gorgeous after a few years in bottle.

Chénas wines are less known and not quite so good as Moulin à Vent. If kept for a few years they have a lovely flowery smell and super fruitiness which stays a long time in the back of the throat. The co-operative in a Louis XIV château is one of the best places to visit in Beaujolais. Its wines are outstanding and you have a chance to compare Chénas with Moulin-à-Vent. (Visits Monday to midday Saturday 8 a.m.–12 noon, 2 p.m.– 6 p.m.; also on Saturday afternoons from 1 April to 30 October – 74.04.11.91. No need to phone. Tastings free.)

On the road from Chénas to Romanèche-Thorins you can see the windmill of Moulin-à-Vent on a hill overlooking the vines – a symbol of Beaujolais. And there is a tasting cave at the bottom of the hill. Deep in colour, smooth and rich, Moulin-à-Vent is best drunk after three or four years. Good vintages improve for ten years. I agree with experts that the wine is often more like a Côte d'Or wine than a Beaujolais, which is why I think it should be served at around 60°F and not 55°F.

Fleurie, west of Romanèche-Thorins, is 'easy to say, easy to drink' and is one of my very favourite luncheon wines. It is charming, very fruity and can easily seduce you into drinking more than you intended. Parisians drink it within eighteen months of the vintage, Burgundians often keep it three years, and any time between two and three years seems right to me. It has real style. Happily there is quite a lot of it. The Cave des Producteurs de Fleurie was made famous by its president for many years, Mlle Marguerite Chabert, 'Queen of the Beaujolais'. One of the best two wines is rightly named after her, 'Cuvée Président Marguerite', a typical elegant, feminine wine. 'Cardinal Bienfaiteur' of this cave is more powerful and needs to be kept longer.

Chiroubles, Cinderella of the Beaujolais Crus, has gone to the ball, by courtesy of Nouvelle Cuisine, and is light, fragrant, tasty, and ready before the others! It was hardly known fifteen years ago, now it is favourite Beaujolais of the young French who, alas, drink so much of it by February after it is made that it is difficult to find by summer, when it would be so refreshing with salads or at picnics.

Morgon wines have a different bouquet and, for me, a different taste from the others. The vineyards are around the villages of Bas-Morgon and Villié-Morgon, with the best wines said to come from the hill between, Mont du Py. They used to be made so that they seemed dead when young, rich, robust and mouth-filling when kept two to four years, and were so popular that the wine trade would say of wines that improved with keeping, 'Ils morgonnent'. Now, wine-makers are aiming at lighter wines. Jean Descombes is the great grower. Domaine Lieven, bottled by Duboeuf at the Domaine, belongs to Princesse de Lieven, who is Mrs Charles Piat (a name you may have noticed on Beaujolais bottles of an unusual shape!). You can taste (small charge) in Caveau de Morgon at Villié-Morgon in the attractive cave of the Louis XVII Château de Foncrenne, in a big, pretty, public park. There is a display of old wine-making tools and a small zoo. Tasting daily 9 a.m.–12 noon, 2 p.m.– 7 p.m. If you phone (74.04.20.99) you can see a seventeen-minute film in English on Morgon wines and taste the wine of the year.

A new Crus was added in 1988 called Régnié. The wine comes from the vineyards around the two steeples of Régnié-Durette, villages SW of Morgon close to D47, The cherry-coloured wine has a slight taste of redcurrants and is often served cold (13°C) with pâtés, terrines or hot starters.

D43, a pretty road south from D47, which joins Belleville to Beaulieu, leads you to Mont Brouilly and the village of Brouilly, home of the most southerly Crus Beaujolais, Brouilly and Côte de Brouilly. Mont Brouilly rises to 500 metres and the vineyards are on all slopes. Vines for Côte wine grow on the south-facing slopes. It is a better wine than Brouilly itself, very rich and grapey. Brouilly produces more wine than any of the other Crus. It is normally light, fruity, simple and very quaffable, but some are luscious and heavier, like Château de la Chaize, a splendid Brouilly produced in a cuvage 110 metres long in the château outside Odenas. Château de la Chaize was built by François de la Chaize, brother of Louis XIV's confessor. It stands in a huge property and in its vaulted caves, the largest in Beaujolais, is an antique pressoir famous in Beaujolais. The château is now a private home, almost enclosed by vineyards.

Odenas is on the fairly wide and modern D43, 16 kilometres north-west of Villefranche-sur-Saône, the end of Beaujolais. You must turn left 5 kilometres after leaving Odenas on the little D49 to reach Vaux-en-Beaujolais – the village of Clochemerle (*see* page 258). There may be a lot of traffic in high season. The Clochemerle story has brought the world to see the village, the church, the auberge (renamed Auberge de Clochemerle). There is a new cave where you can taste the wine renamed Clochemerle and, of course, a new pissoir. They had to erect one, didn't they? And the people of Odenas have been known to say that if you drink Clochemerle wine you will need it, but they are Brouilly snobs in Odenas.

Lyon is only 31 kilometres down N6 from Villefranche. But it is on another planet from the Beaujolais villages.

When travelling Beaujolais, it is easy to remember that the

tractor only arrived in these villages after World War II and was condemned by old *vignerons* who believed that it would ruin the vineyards. Little else seems to have changed.

CHABLIS

Chablis is produced in twenty communes in the northernmost part of Burgundy, around hills of limestone. Chablis itself is an interesting and pleasant town (*see* page 128). The white wines made from Chardonnay are a lovely pale yellow with a greenish tinge, are drier, crisper and fruitier than most other Chardonnay. They are often gorgeous. Alas, there is a lot of variation, and different views on how they should be made. The ordinary AOC Chablis can be drunk after one or two years, but ages well. The fine Premiers and Grands Crus need at least three to five years. It is always stressed that Chablis is perfect with shellfish, which it is, but it goes splendidly too with any delicate fish, with hors d'oeuvres, with smoked salmon, and with white meats such as chicken, turkey, guinea fowl and cold pheasant. When I was honoured by being made a member of the wine fraternity 'Pilliers Chablisiennes' (Pillars of Chablis) in 1991, we ate a seven-course banquet with three glasses of different Chablis at every course except the red meat, with which we drank Vosne-Romanée and Gevrey-Chambertin.

The seven Grands Crus are all on the slopes of the big hill across the little river Serein from Chablis town. They are Blanchot, Bougros, Les Clos, Grenouilles, Preuses, Valmur and Vaudésir.

There are eleven Grands Crus communes. Apart from the Grands and Premiers Crus and ordinary Chablis wines, there is some Petit Chablis, little drunk outside France, and which is really an AOC Chablis from a few villages around Chablis town.

There have been many growers in Chablis since the big estates were broken up in the Revolution, and this can make cooperation difficult.

Spring frost has always been the great enemy here, any time from the end of March to mid-May. Two protective methods used are spraying to give the vines an insulating coat of ice and using oil burners. The water method needs great skill and experience and no wind, and oil burning is expensive in fuel and labour. Oddly weedkillers have lessened the danger as fewer weeds mean less humidity. Whole vintages have been lost to frost and the danger is still there.

Most growers now use stainless steel or lined cement vats for fermenting, but there are many arguments about maturing wine. Some use old oak casks, others new oak and some modern makers use no oak casks but bottle younger wine straight from the vat, producing a young, fresh wine delicious with oysters or most shellfish but no good for chicken or other poultry. I prefer the traditional old Chablis, kept in vat until the spring after the picking and then aged in barrel for a year. Grands Crus and good Premiers Crus made like this improve for several years. It is best if you buy in Chablis to ask when a Grand Cru or Premier Cru should be drunk. My 1985 Premier Cru was not ready until 1990. Nor was a 1983 Grand Cru Preuses.

You can taste at La Chablisienne, the cave-cooperative to which two hundred growers send wine. Formed in 1923, it has done much to see Chablis through bad years of frost. It produces many wines, including the excellent Grenouilles (9 boul. Pasteur, tel. 86.42.11.24. Monday–Saturday 8 a.m.–12 noon, 2 p.m.–6 p.m.). Simonnet-Fèbvre (La Maladière, 9 ave d'Oberwessel, tel. 86.42.11.73. Phone if possible in office hours) are not only growers but excellent *éleveurs*, buying must and bringing up wines. They produce young bottled wines, superb long-keeping Grands Crus Preuses and magnificent rich and delicate Fourchaume, plus an interesting red Irancy (*see below*). Domaine Laroche has won many awards, produces lovely Premiers Crus wines matured in oak and superb Grands Crus Les Clos to be kept ten years. Some wines are kept in the original cellars of the monks who fled here in the ninth century and started it all. There is also a thirteenth-century wine press (10 rue Auxerroise, tel. 86.42.14.30. 9 a.m.–12 noon, 2 p.m.–6.30 p.m.).

Irancy is a red or rosé wine from the Yonne made with Pinot Noir with a little rustic grape called César added. The wine has been known since the twelfth century. In good years it is full-coloured with fruitiness, rustic at first, smoother with age.

Simonnet-Fèbvre carry this wine and also a lighter red from Coulanges-la-Vineuse.

St Bris-le-Vineux, south-west of Chablis, produces a white from Sauvignon grapes – light, dry and quite fruity. A VDQS wine (Vine Délimité de Qualité Supérieure) which is one below an AOC wine, it is a good apéritif, goes with shellfish, light fish and hors d'oeuvres, and is also used for Kir.

Pouilly-sur-Loire, on the Burgundy side of the river Loire, just north of La Charité-sur-Loire (*see* Pouilly and La Charité, pages 209 and 134) produces similar smoky Sauvignon wine (Pouilly-Fumé) to the wine Sancerre produces on the other side of the river. The wine is all called Loire but Pouilly is in Burgundy. Pouilly-Fumé has become so popular recently that prices have risen greatly. A dry white wine called Pouilly-sur-Loire is made from Chasselas grapes. It is fruity, light and quaffable. Drink it very young. Guy Saget makes magnificent Pouilly-Fumé. A co-operative cave making good wines, Caves de Pouilly-sur-Loire, is opposite the Relais Fleurie on the old road through the village, branching off N7. Try their Moulin à Vent (dry, fruity) and Vieilles Vignes (more body) – (tel. 86.39.10.99. Monday–Saturday, 8 a.m.–12 noon, 2 p.m.–6 p.m.).

INFORMATION ON WINES

Comité Interprofessionel des Vins de Bourgogne et Mâcon, Maison de Tourisme, ave Maréchal-de-Lattre-de-Tassigny, Mâcon, Saône-et-Loire.
Comité Interprofessionel de la Côte d'Or et de l'Yonne pour Vins AOC de Bourgogne, rue Henri Dunant, 21200 Beaune.
Union Interprofessionel des Vins de Beaujolais, 210 boul. Vermorel, 69400 Villefranche-sur-Saône, 74.65.45.55.

Old-fashioned wine press

HOTELS AND RESTAURANTS IN WINE VILLAGES
(not mentioned in Gazeteer)

HOTELS

Morey-St-Denis
Auberge Castel de Très Girard, rue Girard (80.34.33.09): pricey Logis with good cooking, swimming pool. ROOMS C–G. MEALS C–G.

St Amour-Bellevue
Auberge du Paradis (85.37.10.26): small inn with fairly good meals. Cheap. Exact prices unavailable. (*See also* Restaurants.)

RESTAURANTS

Vosne-Romanée
Toute Petite Auberge (80.61.02.03): simple auberge, excellent cooking. MEALS B–C. Shut December, January; Thursday.

Auxey-Duresses
La Crémaillère (80.21.22.60): only 8 kilometres south of Beaune, so very popular. Burgundian dishes with superb wine list. MEALS C–F. Shut first fortnight March; Monday evening, Tuesday.

St Amour-Bellevue
Chez Jean-Pierre (85.37.41.26): attractive, only 12 kilometres south-west from Mâcon. MEALS B–F. Shut February; Wednesday evening, Thursday.

Chénas
Daniel Robin, aux Deschamps (85.36.72.67): (*see* page 146). Good meals, delightful restaurant, family's own wine. Terrace views over vineyards. MEALS E–G. Shut mid-February–mid-March; evenings except Saturday, Sunday; all Wednesday.

Auxerre

[MAP 4, page 274]

A very attractive and interesting old town terraced up a hillside. Tree-shaded boulevards made from the old city walls still encircle busy narrow streets running down to an ancient port on the Yonne and at the head of the Nivernais canal, which has been converted into a pleasure-boat harbour. The harbour is a leading centre of inland waterways holidays.

The town looks superb from across the river, with the Gothic spires of its churches rising above old rooftops. On a sunny day, with the cathedral, the spires and the fine arched bridge reflected in the river, and the blue sky as a backcloth, it is one of the loveliest scenes in Burgundy. Renaissance houses, and some earlier, line attractive streets and narrow lanes which lead to little squares, and along the old quays are pleasant riverside walks under the trees.

The Romans built up Auxerre as a garrison town called Autessiodurum on the important road from Lyon to Boulogne.

In the fifth century, a local man, Germanus, became bishop. Now, as St Germain, he is one of the most popular saints in France. Son of rich Gallo-Roman parents, he became a lawyer, practising in Rome until sent back to Auxerre as a military adviser. When converted to Christianity, he gave up sharing his wife's bed, slept on bare planks, wore a hair shirt, and lived on two or three meals of coarse bread a week. He was a brilliant administrator, which would account for his popularity with the French, who admire bureaucrats. He has a church named after him in Paris opposite the east side of the Louvre, called St Germain-l'Auxerrois, to avoid muddle with another Burgundian St Germain-des-Prés, a Paris bishop. A Benedictine abbey

Auxerre Cathedral

called St Germain was founded in Auxerre in the sixth century by Queen Clotilde, wife of Clovis, first Christian king of the Franks. Within a hundred years it had six hundred monks and two thousand students.

The abbey church and the cloisters remain, with a fine fourteenth-century belfry 51 metres high, now standing separate from the church owing to demolitions. The crypt is really two crypts, one built on top of the other, to fool pillaging Norsemen. They include frescoes of the stoning of St Stephen, dating from AD850 and said to be the oldest in France.

The superb Gothic cathedral is dedicated to St Stephen (St Étienne). It was built between the thirteenth and sixteenth centuries on the site of a sanctuary founded about the year AD400 by St Amatre. His building was destroyed by fire in 1023. A Romanesque cathedral was begun immediately, but in 1215 Bishop Guillaume de Seignelay decided its style was too dated and had all the work done again from top to bottom. It was not finished until 1560 – the stonemasons of those days must have known they had a job for life! The result was certainly outstanding – pure Flamboyant style, looking rather lop-sided but with exquisite tracery on the façade and magnificent thirteenth- to fourteenth-century glass. The two rose windows are lovely; the doorways interesting.

Inside, the cathedral is very spacious and cool. It was almost stripped by Huguenots in 1569, who even pulled down the organ pipes, burned the choir stalls, threw the bells down from the tower and left behind little but wreckage. Now the inside is graceful if not beautiful. The old stained glass is a blaze of colour. Although incomplete, it shows 350 scenes from the Bible and Legend. Joan of Arc prayed here when she passed through disguised as a boy in 1429 on her way to Chinon to persuade the Dauphin to give her an army. She returned with 12,000 men on her way to taking the Dauphin to be crowned King Charles VII at Reims.

A window shows her at the head of her troops. Ironically, it was in this cathedral that the Burgundians and English met in 1423 before advancing to beat the French and Scots at Cravant. The Burgundian commander was Claude de Beauvoir, Baron Chestelux, who was able to return Cravant to its owner, the Bishop of Auxerre, for which he was rewarded. He and his descendants in perpetuity were created hereditary lay canons, with the right of attending services in full armour, booted, spurred, wearing their swords over their surplices and carrying their falcons on their wrists.

There are fine views over the town from the cathedral

tower. Auxerre is rich in old churches. St Eusèbe has a fine twelfth-century tower, fifteenth-century spire and sixteenth-century stained glass windows. It belonged to a priory which has now gone.

Lovely houses are spread around the streets of the old town centre, especially sixteenth-century half-timbered ones. Several are in place de l'Hôtel-de-Ville. In the same square is a statue of a poet much loved in France, Marie Noël, who died in 1967 – it is one of several painted statues by a local modern sculptor, François Brochet, which are scattered around the town. Marie Noël's statue is near to my favourite corner of Auxerre – Tour de l'Horloge, the fifteenth-century Tour Gaillarde, once part of the old defence walls. The belfry and clock tower, with a seventeenth-century clock, were added by a Duke of Burgundy. The clock, showing the time on one dial, the movements of the sun and moon on the other, was mentioned by the novelist Rétif (or Restif) de la Bretonne (1734–1806) who served his apprenticeship as a printer in a nearby workshop. He was an extraordinary writer, producing more than 250 novels and sometimes setting them up directly in type – even quicker than using a word processor. Some of his works were licentious but his great talent was for observation, so strong that in his *Les Contemporaines*, which ran to forty-two volumes, he described in some detail 250 trades in which Parisian women were engaged, from Grande Couture to selling herbs! (I feel that Balzac must have read him.) He was the son of a Burgundian farm worker from Sacy, but wrote in Paris where he was a printer, so a constant theme is how the simple countryman is perverted by town life.

It was in place de l'Hôtel-de-Ville that on 17 March 1815 Napoleon, having escaped from Elba and marching towards Paris with a small army, met his old commander Marshal Ney and his troops. After Napoleon's defeat and internment in Elba, Ney, one of his most successful commanders, was loaded with favours by Louis XVIII and given command of a Royal army. When Napoleon landed from Elba, Ney marched with a big force to meet him, swearing that he would 'bring him back to Paris in a cage'. But when they met, Ney embraced Napoleon and joined him, giving him the army he needed. Ney commanded the Centre at Waterloo and after the return of the monarchy, he was shot.

Beside the clock tower is a vaulted passage leading to place Maréchal-Leclerc with a plaque recalling Cadet Roussel (1743–1807), a local man who was the blighted hero of a popular French song.

Musée Leblanc-Duvernoy, rue d'Eglény, has a wonderful collection of Beauvais tapestries and good ceramics.

South of Auxerre is the lovely Yonne valley and to the east are the vineyards of Chablis. It is an excellent place in which to stay, explore and eat and drink well. It is famed especially for cherries.

TOURIST INFORMATION 1–2 quai République
(86.52.06.19).
MARKETS Sunday morning, Tuesday , Friday.
FESTIVALS Jazz in June. St Martin's Fair early
November.

HOTELS

Parc des Maréchaux, 6 ave Foch (86.51.43.77). Very attractive Napoleon III mansion in a park. No restaurant but bar. ROOMS C–D.
Seignelay, 2 rue Pont (86.52.03.48). Old timber-framed coaching inn. Burgundian dishes, tree-shaded courtyard for summer meals. Good value. ROOMS B–D. MEALS A–E. Shut mid-February–mid-March; Monday (October–June).

RESTAURANTS

Jean-Luc Barnabet, 14 quai République (86.51.68.88). Jean-Luc has moved from Petite Auberge de Vaux to seventeenth-century relais de poste superbly placed on river quayside. Regional and inventive cooking. Menus good value. MEALS E–G. Shut mid-December–mid-January; Sunday evening, Monday.
Jardin Gourmand, 56 boul. Vauban (86.51.53.52). Attractive

dining room, terrace. Varied choice, inventive dishes. Set menus good value. MEALS C–F. Shut December; Monday low season.
Petite Auberge, Vaux, 6km SE by D163 (86.53.80.08). Comfortable, on river bank. MEALS D–E. Shut Sunday evening, Monday.

Beaune

[MAP 2, page 271]

Beaune is a superb town, crammed with treasures and magnificent old buildings in narrow cobbled streets and attractive squares. To enjoy it to the full, of course, it does help to love wine and to avoid going there in June, July and August, when there are too many people and far, far too many cars. Beaune is so bound up with wine-making that even its old and most beautiful buildings are used to this day by wine-makers, *éleveurs* and *négociants*, so please read also the section on Beaune under Wine (pages 34–43) or you might miss such splendid places as old monasteries, rampart towers and the ancient caves under the town. You can hardly find a street without fine old stone houses and mansions, and happily much of the central area is for pedestrians only.

Beaune was the capital of the Dukedom of Burgundy up to the fourteenth century, before the Dukes moved to Dijon, which upset Beaune considerably. Diplomatically, the Dukes made Beaune the seat of the Appeal Courts and the High Court for four hundred years more. The High Court, called the Grands Jours, was a council of barons, knights and lawyers. Incidentally, the Dukes did not hesitate to bribe courts, in their own Dukedom and in France, by sending presents of Beaune wine. They bribed kings and church dignitaries, too. A bribe is still called 'pot de vin' in France.

The town walls, fortifications and towers that still exist were built from the fifteenth century onwards. After the death of the last Duke, Charles the Bold, in 1477, Louis XI grabbed the Dukedom of Burgundy but Beaune resisted until forced to surrender after a five-week siege.

The quarrel between Beaune and Dijon reached comic heights in the eighteenth century, stirred up by the Dijonnais satirist Alexis Piron, the man from whom Dijon's saddle of hare dish was named. Dijon had been beaten by Beaune in a shooting contest, so Piron wrote a comic poem of revenge, comparing the people of Beaune with the donkeys used on their land and wrote that he would starve them to death by cutting down all the thistles on the banks. As Piron almost certainly knew, the important wine merchants of Beaune, the Lasnes brothers, had the sign of a donkey as their trade mark. The elders of Beaune pompously banned Piron from their town. Inevitably, he went there, and went to Mass, about which he said, 'Those who came to ogle the women were obliged to pray to God, for these ladies would have frightened even John the Fearless.' Then he went to the theatre, where he was recognized and booed and hissed heartily. One poor man trying to hear the play shouted, 'Be quiet – I can't hear anything,' whereupon Piron shouted, 'That's not through lack of ears.' The audience rushed at him and he was saved only by a friend who rushed him away and hid him in his house all night.

Stendhal claims that all this happened in the pleasant little town of Autun. But how could Dijon and Piron declare war on such a pleasant, harmless little place as that?

The Dukes kept a mansion in Beaune long after moving to Dijon. It is still there, a stone and wood house of the fifteenth to sixteenth centuries, with a fine fourteenth-century wine cellar, and now contains a most interesting wine museum. The history of Burgundian vineyards and of wine-making is presented excellently on the ground floor. On the first floor are some fascinating pitchers, bottles, wine-tasting glasses and *tastevin*, the low silver cups used by Burgundian *vignerons* for smelling, judging the colour and tasting wine from the barrels or vats in their cellars. I once saw a man solemnly *drinking* his Beaune from a *tastevin*, and I am sorry to say that he was an English writer! The room I love is the headquarters of the Ambassade des Vins de

France, which contains two big and beautiful Aubusson tapestries – one by Michel Tourlière and the other by one of my very favourite artists and the great rejuvenator of the tapestry art, Jean Lurçat. In the cellar is a collection of wine presses and vats.

The old Charity hospital, Hôtel Dieu (*see* Wine, page 36), is indeed a wonderful and remarkable building. From the street it looks austere and dull – a simple façade with a tall, steeply sloped slate roof with dormer windows. The wrought iron canopy over the gate is the only ornament. Step into the Court of Honour and you are surrounded by a most beautiful mansion, with a magnificent roof of glazed tiles, ablaze with colour and in rich complex geometric patterns – Flemish splendour in Burgundy – a lovely timbered gallery around the first floor, and charming arcades of slim pillars around the ground floor. It is indeed 'more like the house of a prince than a hospital for the poor'. Perhaps, despite his life of greed and grabbing, its founder Nicolas Rodin did just about deserve to buy himself a mansion in Heaven, as he intended.

Hôtel Dieu

Nicolas Rodin was Chancellor to both Dukes John the Fearless and Philip the Good and, as the Ducal chronicler Chastellain wrote of him, he governed, managed and looked after Burgundy's business affairs in peace and war on his own. 'He always harvested on earth as if the earth was his abode for ever.' Rodin became fabulously rich, gaining much of his wealth by dubious methods. Growing older, he began to think of his future. When he founded Hôtel Dieu in 1443 as an alms house and hospital for the poor of Beaune, he wrote quite openly, 'I set aside all mortal cares and consider nothing but my salvation, wishing by a happy transaction to exchange for heavenly riches those earthly ones bestowed on me by God's favour, so to make transient riches eternal.' Louis XI of France put it another way, 'It is only right that he who made so many destitute in his life should build them an alms house before he died.'

Inside, the huge hall of the Paupers' Ward is 52 metres (171 feet) long and has a great timber roof like an upturned ship, supported by chestnut tie beams carved in the shape of monsters' heads and throats. The four-poster beds with side tables and chairs are much like the originals, which were destroyed in the Revolution though the originals were half as wide again – just as well, as two sick people slept in each, and in times of epidemics there were four to a bed. The sexes were mixed indiscriminately until Louis XIV visited the hospital in 1658. The Sun King, so addicted to sharing the beds of women, was shocked by such a scandalous arrangement and commanded that the women should be banished to another ward. This ward (Grand Chambre des Pôvres) was used until 1948 when doctors insisted that the patients should be moved to a more modern hospital for treatment.

Patients were not allowed to forget that they would face Judgement Day. The beds were all lined up so that they could see the altar in the chapel at the end of the ward. Over the altar was a truly remarkable picture – a nine-panel polyptych (a painting of four or more panels) by Roger van der Weyden, renowned as a portrait painter. So the sick and old looking down the ward from their beds saw frightening scenes of the final Judgement, with the Just being escorted to the Gates of Heaven and the Damned hurled screaming into the eternal sulphurous pit. The picture is a masterpiece and must have brought many a tough Burgundian transgressor to repentance. It is no longer on the altar. It was hidden in a loft from Revolutionary destroyers and put back in 1836. The nudity of the risen dead scandalized the nineteenth-century sisters who had them clothed in sackcloth, though happily this was done in water-colour and was removed by Paris restorers in 1877. The picture was hidden again in the cellars of La Rochepot Château in 1940. When it returned, it was hung in the small Chambre du Roi, where Charles IX and Louis XIV slept on their visits to Hôtel Dieu. I saw it there and through a magnifying glass was shown the extraordinarily careful detail by the great Flemish master – he has painted every button and jewel exquisitely. But experts said that the room, crowded with visitors, was too humid, so a special museum room was built with automatic temperature, humidity and light controls, and that is where you will find it now.

Almost inevitably, the high arched window in the chapel shows Nicolas Rodin himself with two Dukes, Philip the Good and his son Charles the Rash. The floor tiles and walls are decorated with Rodin's motto, *Seule*, followed by a star. Romantics say that it signified to his wife that he loved only her, but in view of his reputation as a womanizer and his lone control over the Duchy, it seems much more likely that he himself was the 'Only Star'. Powerful men of his time adopted the most arrogant mottoes.

Hôtel Dieu is still a rest home for 240 elderly people of Beaune, and the same old kitchen makes their meals – but with modern equipment. You can still see an interesting automatic spit made by a Beaune clockmaker in 1698.

The collection of pewter vessels, bronze mortars and Nevers pottery from the eighteenth century in the pharmacy is remarkable.

To provide income for the hospice, Nicolas Rodin endowed it with the income of a salt-works at Salins which his wife Guigone de Salins had brought with her as her dowry. It soon proved insufficient, and Nicolas got the Duke's permission to do some fund-raising. Inevitably, he put the squeeze on the *vignerons*, who donated vineyards. Through the years others followed Rodin's example of investing in their heavenly fortune by leaving more vineyards in their wills. So now the hospice owns 2000 acres, of which 125 acres produce great wine of the Côte de Beaune. The famous auction of these wines on the third Sunday in November used to take place in the Hôtel Dieu in the cuverie, but now only the tasting takes place there. The auction is held in the Market Hall. The most recent donation to the hospice was a vineyard producing Mazis-Chambertin, from the Côte de Nuits, first auctioned in 1977. A white wine, a Corton-Charlemagne, usually fetches the highest price.

There are so many old houses in Beaune that you are sure to see some of them. A fine sixteenth-century group is in rue Lorraine (numbers 18–24).

Beaune's Collegiate Church of Our Lady, begun about 1120 by the Cluny monks, contains some magnificent tapestries of the life of the Virgin Mary. Made in wool and silk, the five panels were woven from cartoons of a local artist Pierre Spicre, commissioned in 1474 by Rodin's stepson Cardinal Jean Rodin. Incidentally, Chancellor Nicolas Rodin had a picture painted by the great Van Eyck showing himself with the Madonna! It is now in the Louvre. The Cardinal donated corn-land to the hospice in return for the sisters' prayers for his soul.

Beaune's ramparts are almost continuous for 2 kilometres, but much is privately owned and other parts are hidden behind greenery or houses. There are eight bastions. The double bastion of St Jean beside boulevard Maréchal Joffre is the old castle. The moat is now mostly gardens or orchards, with some tennis courts. Following boulevard Joffre north-west to rue de Lorraine you pass St Jean, Tour Blondeau and Bastion Notre Dame. At rue Lorraine you reach the eighteenth-century town gate of St Nicolas.

The town hall, just off rue Lorraine, is in a seventeenth-century former Ursuline convent. It has two museums. The Beaux Arts museum contains sixteenth- and seventeenth-century Flemish and Dutch paintings, works of Picasso, Fernand Léger and Marc Chagall, and a number by Félix Ziem (1821–1911) who, although born in Beaune, was known for his high-key seascapes in the manner of Turner and, like Turner, for his paintings of Venice. His sunsets are splendid.

The other museum is devoted to Étienne-Jules Marey

(1830–1904), local doctor and physiologist who took the first motion pictures with a single camera. He called it Chronophotography. He was an experimental scientist making several inventions, including a gun-camera which you can see with some of his films made from 1888 onwards. He was interested in photographing animal movements, which he studied, and he designed cameras which reduced exposure time to 1/250,000 of a second to photograph insects in flight. (Museum closed Tuesday and 1 December–end March.)

Do try to see the vineyards of Montagne de Beaune. Take D970 west and a road branching right leads to the top, where there is a Libération statue, war memorial and a viewing table. The view spreads from the brown-tile roofs of the town to the vineyards and south to the Mâconnais mountains.

Four miles south of Beaune by D18 Chalon road, then left on D23 towards Merceuil is the new Archéodrome, in a service area lying alongside A6 motorway. It shows a panorama of Burgundy through prehistory to Gallo-Roman times. This is more interesting than it sounds. Stone Age huts have been reproduced, as have burial cairns, a Gallic house, a Roman villa and huge defence works showing a reproduction of Caesar's camp in 52BC when he defeated the Gauls at Alesia (now Alise-Ste-Reine, page 98).

TOURIST INFORMATION Tourist Office, opposite Hôtel Dieu (80.22.24.51).
MARKETS Thursday, Saturday.
FESTIVALS Son-et-Lumière, Hospice April–October; Fair, early June; Classical Music Festival, end June; Folk Festival, September.

HOTELS

Central, 2 rue Victor Millot (80.24.77.24): my old favourite, where you could always find true Burgundian and classical cooking. Locals eat here. Conveniently around the corner from Hôtel Dieu, the tourist office and the market. ROOMS D–F.

MEALS D–G. Shut 5–25 January. Restaurant shut Wednesday, Sunday evening in winter.

Poste, 1 boul. Georges-Clemenceau (80.22.08.11): classical hotel and cooking. Very expensive rooms and meals. ROOMS G. MEALS G. Shut end November–end March.

Auberge Bourguignonne, 4 place Madeleine (80.22.23.53): near station. Very agreeable; good value regional dishes. ROOMS C–D. MEALS B–E. Shut mid-December–mid-January; Monday.

Ermitage de Corton at Chorey-lès-Beaune (4km along route Dijon), (80.22.05.28): opulent, Hollywood décor, sumptuous meals, outrageous prices. ROOMS G. MEALS F–G. Shut mid-January–mid-February. Restaurant shut Sunday evening, Monday.

La Paix, 47 faubourg Madeleine (80.22.33.33): good restaurant with rôtisserie. Hideaway across courtyard in town centre. ROOMS D–E. MEALS C–F. Shut March. Restaurant shut Tuesday lunch, Monday.

RESTAURANTS

Relais de Saulx, 6 rue Very (80.22.01.35): of Beaune's Michelin-starred restaurants, my readers have found this the most interesting, with several dishes personalized by Jean-Louis Monnoir and a good choice of menus and wines. MEALS Ḋ–G. Shut 15–30 June; 15–31 December; Sunday evening, Monday.

Maxime, 3 place Madeleine (80.22.17.82): excellent value, good regional cooking; shady terrace. MEALS A–D. Shut 6–27 January; Monday.

Auberge St Vincent, place Halle (80.22.42.34): seventeenth-century building, convenient for sightseers. Open every day. Reasonable prices. MEALS C–F.

Chalon-sur-Saône

[MAP 3, page 273]

Chalon has been an important and busy town since Julius Caesar's conquest of Gaul. It is still an important centre for industry and business and a market town for farming, stock-rearing and the vineyards of the Côte Chalonnaise. Yet, being in Burgundy, it does not seem to hurry. If you sit by the river you might mistake it for a holiday town, for pleasure boats are replacing the barges which for so long served the Schneider heavy engineering and arms factories, and even the Canal du Centre, which joins it to the old Schneider 'City of Steel' Le Creusot (*see* page 157), is used for pleasure craft.

Chalon's great carnival in March, lasting eight days, draws people from far beyond Burgundy. Its two pelt and fur fairs in February and June, les Foires Internationales des Sauvagines, draw people from even further away. Although furs are no longer acceptable in some countries, the conservation lobby has not been so successful in most parts of the world, including Italy and Germany, so the business still thrives. In the middle ages the two fur fairs lasted for a month each.

The two islands in the river, easily defendable in those days, encouraged Caesar to use Chalon as an important base. The three Roman roads from Boulogne, Trier and Strasbourg met at the town. Not until 1794, when Le Creusot became a steel town, was the Canal du Centre finished as a vital artery serving industrial centres. The Schneider brothers, who were expanding in Le Creusot into one of the most important steel and arms companies in the world, set up a Chalon subsidiary in 1839 called Petit Le Creusot, now part of Creusot-Loire group.

Modern industries include a company making equipment for the nuclear power industry. As a result of industry, Chalon is not an attractive-looking town, but it has some charming old houses, especially half-timbered ones in place St Vincent and rue St Vincent. Above all, Chalon has a pleasant atmosphere.

The area around place St Vincent has been made into a

pedestrian precinct, giving it a most surprising medieval appearance. Alas, the former cathedral of St Vincent, named so fittingly for the patron saint of wine, and built from the eleventh century in a variety of styles, was given a rather hideous neo-Gothic façade last century. Its fifteenth-century cloisters have been restored and at their entrance a chapel has a very attractive early sixteenth-century tapestry. St Vincent was built on the site of a temple to Baco, a Boar god from whom we get the word 'bacon'.

Across the river in the suburb of St Marcel-lès-Chalon is the simple early-Gothic church of the old priory which was attached to the great abbey of Cluny. In a side-chapel is the very well into which the Romans tossed St Marcellus to his death. Peter the Venerable, Abbot of Cluny, sent Peter Abelard, the great thinker and bold theologian, to the old priory to die in comfort and peace, which he duly did in 1142. It was Abbot Peter who had saved him from excommunication when his adversary, the bigoted Bernard of Clairvaux (St Bernard), had had him declared a heretic by the Pope at the Council of Sens. Abelard had caused a great scandal earlier in his life by running off with a seventeen-year-old pupil Héloïse, daughter of a Canon of Notre Dame, and presenting her with a son. When he died, Héloïse, now Abbess of a convent at Paraclete, had his body exhumed from the monks' cemetery at St Marcel and reburied at her convent, where she was later buried beside him.

Denon Museum, in an eighteenth-century building in place Hôtel-de-Ville, is named after Vivant Denon, who organized the museum system, including the Louvre, for Napoleon. He was called Grand Purveyor and Organizer of the Museums of France. An Egyptian scholar, he had accompanied Napoleon on his abortive Egyptian campaign. The museum has a large collection of good but not great paintings, mostly Dutch and French. The best is 'Study of a Negro' by Théodore Géricault (1791–1824), founder of the anti-classical realist school, who fled to England after harsh criticism of his work. There are also archaeological collections in the museum and interesting wine-growers tools and implements. (Shut Tuesday.)

On the banks of the Saône, in the eighteenth-century Hôtel des Messageries, is a museum devoted to Joseph Nicéphore-

Niepce 'father of photography', born at Chalon in 1765. After fighting in the Revolutionary Army, he became a research scientist. He invented a marine engine on the same principle as the jet, and a bicycle. Then in 1822 he succeeded in fixing on a glass plate an image previously obtained in a dark room. Unlike Fox-Talbot, he did not produce a 'fixer' for his pictures, so it was impossible to reproduce in large numbers. He took his invention to Paris to enlist the support of Daguerre, who owned a magic lantern entertainment called the Diorama. They became partners, but before he had made any money from his expensive experiments, Niepce died of a stroke. His widow died destitute.

Daguerre got a hearing from the Académie des Sciences and gained a large pension for himself and Niepce's son by selling the patent to the French State. There is a statue to Niepce on quai Gambetta and in the museum are very interesting cameras which he used, as well as later equipment used by Daguerre, early colour pictures, and equipment of the Lumière brothers, who produced a ciné-camera in 1893. On the ground floor is a fascinating display of old cameras. (Museum shut Tuesday.) Alas, Niepce's very first photograph is in the Gernsheim Collection at the University of Texas – a long way for French amateurs of photography to go.

Pont St Laurent joins the two river islands to Chalon. On the corner of the first big island is the fifteenth-century Tour du Doyenné (Deanery Tower), moved there in 1907 from its original position by the cathedral. Continue over both islands, then turn left into rue Julien-Lenouveu and you reach the great rose trail (Roseraie St-Nicolas) which is 5 kilometres long. It winds through a rose garden laid out in a loop of the Saône beyond the golf course and despite the long walk is well worth visiting any time from June to September. It has 25,000 rose trees set among huge lawns shaded by conifers and apple trees. In June and July the beds are a mass of colour. The September-flowering roses are in separate beds, and there is a rockery of rare plants, an arboretum, bulbs (iris, geraniums), a water-plant and a heather garden. You don't have to walk the *whole* trail but it is rewarding. And if you want further exercise, there is a 1½-mile keep-fit track. (Open early June–early October, for times ask Tourist Office, *see overleaf.*)

TOURIST INFORMATION square Chabas, boul.
République (85.48.37.97).
MARKETS Wednesday, Friday, Sunday (poultry).
FESTIVALS Carnival (parades, fairs, children's fancy-
dress ball), eight days in March; Foires Sauvagines (pelt
and fur fairs), end February and late June; National
Festival of Street Artists, July. October Fair.

HOTELS

St Georges, 32 ave J. Jaurès (85.48.27.05): best hotel in town with
best restaurant. ROOMS D–E. MEALS C–G. Restaurant shut Sat-
urday lunch.
St Régis, 22 boul. République (85.48.07.28): classic; town centre.
Spacious rooms double-glazed for sound, air-conditioned.
ROOMS C–E. MEALS B–F. Restaurant shut Sunday.

RESTAURANTS

Bourgogne, 28 rue Strasbourg (85.48.89.18): seventeenth century; eat in restaurant or wine cellar. Local favourite. Local and
regional dishes. Menus excellent value. MEALS B–F. Shut mid-
November–early December; Sunday evening except July,
August.
Gourmets, 15 ave J. Jaurès (85.48.37.25): good classical cooking:
big price variation; good value. MEALS B–E. Shut spring
holidays; Saturday.
Huchette, 33 rue Lyon (85.48.28.22): cheap, simple, good
regional dishes. MEALS A–D. Shut 23 December–mid-January;
1–21 August; Saturday lunch, Sunday.
Moulin de Martorey, at St Rémy, 4km SW by N6, N80, local road
(85.48.12.98): very pleasant. Young chef uses local products well
and deserves a Michelin star. MEALS D–G. Shut most of August;
February holidays; Sunday evening, Monday.

Dijon

[MAP 2, page 271]

Dijon is a delightful town – busy by Burgundian standards, as befits the capital of Burgundy. It is a wine centre, with many fêtes and fairs; it has delightful old buildings, and is a wonderful place to eat – not quite so good as Lyon but not so self-conscious about its gastronomic delights, either.

From the Ducal Palace to the delicious little fifteenth-century mansion of a Mayor of Dijon – now the headquarters of the illustrious wine-lovers society, Compagnie Bourguignonne des Oenophiles and their restaurant 'Toison d'Or' – Dijon is rich in truly beautiful old houses. 'Oh, what a beautiful town!' said François I of France when he saw its bell-towers and treasures. But I love, too, its open spaces, little parks and flower beds. Green space has grown within my memory.

Certainly it is deeply proud of its past and was one of the first towns to protect its old areas by turning many of them into pedestrian precincts. But it is also a forward-looking town, with new industries, which are certainly not obvious to the visitor. Anyway, they are of little consequence beside the main industries of Dijon: food and wine. In fact these are more than industries: they are hobbies and a religion.

There is only one great problem in Dijon, caused by its ancient narrow streets and pedestrian areas: the one-way traffic system makes driving hell for strangers. Walk whenever you can.

When the first of the Valois Dukes, Philip the Bold, took over in 1364, he moved the Burgundian capital from Beaune to Dijon and Dijon's period of greatness began, not only as titular capital of the great Burgundian Empire (*see* Beaune, pages 65–7) but as a centre of learning and art, with Flemish painters and craftsmen coming to the lovely city François so admired. After the last Duke, Charles, was killed and the French took over Burgundy at the end of the fifteenth century, Dijon lost much of its importance and gradually slumbered as an attractive small

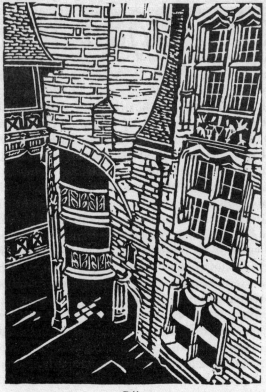

Dijon

provincial town, dealing in wine but overshadowed in the business by Beaune.

Then came the railways. In fact, then came the moment when Dijon's corporation and its chief engineer, Henri Darcy, *grabbed* the railway. The original Paris–Lyon line was routed direct through Auxerre and Beaune, but the corporation voted a huge fund to fight for it to go through Dijon. Darcy drew up a plan for a line via Montbard, and on 1 June 1851 the first train came to the town. Dijon became the main junction in Eastern France and its population doubled in about forty years.

Much the same happened when the fast TGV service was planned in the 1970s. Originally the service from Paris to Lausanne and Berne in Switzerland was to go through Beaune but was quickly changed to Dijon, with a side-line to Beaune, putting Dijon within 1 hour 35 minutes of Paris, with fifteen services a day, while Beaune and Chalon-sur-Saône have only three daily services. The result is a big boost to commercial activity between Dijon and Paris, and the growth in numbers of weekend commuters, returning to second homes in and around Dijon on Friday nights.

The engineer Darcy also brought the first modern water supply to Dijon, and refused any extra fees, so he has been honoured with the name of the centre of modern Dijon, place Darcy, and a very pleasant garden with fountains. Beside the garden is the elegant, renowned hotel of Dijon, La Cloche, a national monument, with a restaurant which is itself a gastronomic landmark, named now after its quiet, unassuming young chef Jean-Pierre Billoux. Opposite is the eighteenth-century Porte Guillaume, which replaced an ancient town gate. From the gate, rue de la Liberté (once called rue Royale) leads to place de la Libération (place Royale), and the Palais des Ducs – the Dukes' Palace. Place de la Libération is an attractive semi-circular 'square', designed by Jules Hardouin Mansart, designer of part of Versailles, around 1686. Its arcades, topped by a stone balustrade, prolong the Court of Honour which was enclosed by the king's apartments. Originally, a great bronze statue of Louis XIV stood in place Royale, so big that it took thirty years to bring it from Paris. Sixty years later during the Revolution it was pulled down and melted.

The old Dukes' Palace became empty and neglected when the French took over but was rebuilt and enlarged towards the end of the seventeenth century. Philip the Bold's tower remains from the old Ducal building and so do the medieval kitchens, with massive fireplaces on three sides to prepare great Burgundian feasts. The chef, I am told, sat on a big stool in the middle with a huge ladle, to taste the dishes brought to him and to thump tardy underlings.

In the tower Philip the Good imprisoned 'good King René' – the peace-loving René d'Anjou, Duke of Bar and Lorraine, Count of Province and of Anjou and titular King of Sicily, the scholar and lover of the arts who preferred poetry to the pomp of being a ruler. The tower was called 'Bar' after his title and the courtyard beside it is called Cour de Bar. A delightful seventeenth-century staircase leads up the tower.

Part of the palace is used as the town hall. Much of the rest is used for the Beaux Arts museum and I must say that some of the rooms are so splendid that I find myself admiring them more than the exhibits. Salle des Gardes, the guard room built by Philip the Good, is exceptionally beautiful, with its Flamboyant chimney-piece and lovely Renaissance gallery. It was used as a banqueting hall on special occasions. The Beaux Arts has been described as one of the best museums outside Paris.

In Salle des Gardes' minstrels' gallery there are two very ornate but majestic tombs of Philip the Bold, whose recumbant figure is protected by two gold-winged angels, and of John the Fearless and his wife Margaret of Bavaria with similar kneeling angels and figures, their feet resting on lions. It was virtually a copy of the older tomb. They were moved here from Chartreuse de Champmol (*see* page 83).

Among many treasures on the ground floor are religious paintings by Veronese ('Assumption') and Rubens ('Virgin and St Francis') and interesting sculptures by Rude and Carnova. François Rude (1784–1855) was a Dijon man who was devoted to Napoleon and fled to Brussels on the Emperor's abdication. He was brilliant at getting a look of movement into his sculptures. On the second floor a room is devoted to another Burgundian sculptor, François Pompon (1855–1933), who was a pupil and assistant to Rodin but only became famous late in life with magnificent animal sculptures.

Many great artists and sculptors are represented in the museum, including Géricault, Delacroix, Daumier, Courbet, Millet, Rodin, Bourdelle, more painters Manet, Monet, Boudin, Georges de la Tour, Picasso, Braque, a strange abstract 'Football Players' by Nicolas de Staël, and a most colourful impression of Venice, 'Coucher de Soleil sur les Doges', by Charles Lapicque.

Among the Dutch paintings are an excellent Franz Hals 'Portrait of a Gentleman' and a typical 'Portrait of a Burgomeister' by Ter Borch. (Museum shut Tuesday.)

At the other end of the Cour d'Honneur from the museum is Salle des États, the great hall of the States General of Burgundy which has a superb ceiling and a magnificent staircase designed in 1735 by Jacques Gabriel. Through the hall is the Cour de Flore, with decorations glorifying the Prince of Condé, Governor of Burgundy. From the court a passage leads to rue des Forges, with fine old buildings, a typical street of old Dijon. Look for number 34 (Hôtel Chambellan), a Flamboyant Gothic mansion built for a draper, with a magnificent interior court-yard and fine spiral staircase. It now houses the Syndicat d'Initiative and a tourist information office. Number 38 has a decorated Renaissance façade. Number 40, with a thirteenth-century façade, belonged to bankers in medieval times and Dijon's bankers and traders deposited their reserves, in many currencies, in the vaults, which could be reached only through pavement-level windows. It was named after a fourteenth-century banker Guillaume Aubriot, whose son, a Provost of Paris who hated priests, built the Bastille. Numbers 52, 54 and 56 were once a single house belonging to Philip the Good's adviser, Jean Morel.

The church of Notre Dame just behind rue des Forges is beautiful and strange. Built in the thirteenth century, it must have given the architect a headache for it was confined by mansions into a cramped space. The monumental façade which faces the pedestrian rue Musette is original – a flat wall between two beautiful bell turrets, with two thin arcades and three tiers of false gargoyles clamped on as ornament. The present gar-goyles representing lost souls and demons were added by a nineteenth-century sculptor. The originals had started to fall off centuries before and had been removed for safety reasons. The local story is that a money-lender and his bride stopped outside the church before entering and a gargoyle fell down and killed them – the offending gargoyle represented a usurer with a bag of gold. So the frightened bankers of Dijon paid the Corpor-ation to destroy the other gargoyles. The sculptures on the doorways were destroyed by an apothecary who chiselled them away after the Revolution.

The right-hand bell-tower is home to one of Dijon's most popular families – the Jacquemarts. In 1382 Philip the Bold marched to Flanders with an army which included 1000 Dijon-nais to put down a revolt of the Flemings of Ghent and Courtrai, who were objecting to paying punitive taxes to fund the Duke's

ostentatious life-style. To punish the people of Courtrai, Philip
cut the top off their clock tower and sent it by ox cart to Dijon. It
contained a pipe-smoking automaton who struck the hours and
he settled into his new home contentedly. The people called him
Jacquemart.

Then one day in 1610 he went on strike and stopped
striking. The people decided that he was lonely and gave him a
wife. Next century a local wit composed a lament for their
sterility and, sure enough, a son was born to strike the half-
hours. In 1881 the family was completed with a little girl who
strikes the quarter-hours.

Inside the church is a twelfth-century Black Virgin statue,
Our Lady of Good Hope, much venerated as the Protectress of
Dijon. When the Swiss siege was raised on 11 September 1513,
with the help of barrels of wine (*see* page 10), Our Lady of Good
Hope received the credit rather than St Vincent, and a tapestry
given at the time is now in the Beaux Arts museum. Another
Gobelins tapestry, given after Dijon was liberated from German
occupation on 11 September 1944, is in the church. There are
superb medieval stained-glass windows, too. In rue Chouette is
Hôtel de Vogüé, an early seventeenth-century mansion with
colourful tiled roof and Renaissance doorway leading to a courtyard. It is now the town architect's offices.

Rue des Forges and rue de la Liberté both run into place
François Rude, named after the local sculptor. A very attractive
square, it contains the secularized former Cathedral St Étienne,
now the stock exchange and also containing a museum with
reproductions of Rude's work, including a huge relief for Arc de
Triomphe in Paris. Local people call the square place du
Bareuzai, Burgundian word for *vigneron*, after the statue of a
naked vineyard worker treading grapes.

Close to the rue de la Liberté and place Darcy is the market,
an unusually interesting and animated market area very much
for local people and quite unconscious of tourists.

In the streets across rue de la Liberté is the old cathedral of
St Benignus, thirteenth to fourteenth century, with a 93-metre
(305-feet) high tower rebuilt in 1896. The remains of the tomb
of St Benignus, who is said to have converted much of Burgundy and was martyred in AD187, still lures pilgrims on

20 November. The present church in huge, severe Gothic, was built in 1280. The crypt is interesting. The abbey of St Bénigne was very rich. The only remaining building (the monks' dormitory) houses an archaeological museum, which includes a superb head of Christ by the medieval sculptor Claus Sluter. The head belonged to a monument called the Well of Moses in the Chartreuse de Champmol (*see below*). The fifteenth-century painted Holy Family is charming.

To the east of Palais des Ducs is St Michel's church with a spectacularly ornate Renaissance façade and a most unusual central doorway. It was started in the fifteenth century in Flamboyant style, then completed in glorious Renaissance style after the French brought back their understandable enthusiasm for this style after losing a war in Italy. Inside, the church is sober Gothic. The four paintings are by an eighteenth-century German artist Franz Kraus.

South of Palais des Ducs is the Palais de Justice (Law Courts), the old Burgundy parliament building with a Renaissance façade. The chamber of the civil courts has kept its original sixteenth-century decoration and the huge lobby has a superb panelled ceiling. It was once lined with stalls and refreshment bars and fashionable people met there to gossip and parade.

On the west edge of Dijon at 1 boulevard Chanoine-Kir, near the lovely Arquebuse gardens, is a huge psychiatric hospital on the site of the old Chartreuse de Champmol, destroyed shamefully in the Revolution. The first Dukes of Burgundy were buried at Cîteaux abbey but Philip the Bold as a true Valois wanted a more royal burial place for himself and his heirs, so in 1383 he founded this little monastery, using the best artists of his time to decorate it lavishly. The tombs of him and John the Fearless in the Beaux Arts museum came from here. There still remains Puits de Moïse (Well of Moses), the many-coloured base of a massive Calvary with six great statues of Moses and the prophets David, Jeremiah, Zachariah, Daniel and Isaiah. There is a replica of the whole Calvary in the Beaux Arts. The Calvary was the work of Claus Sluter, and has been called one of the most important sculptural works of the late middle ages. Certainly it was considered important at the time. The Pope offered an indulgence to anyone who went to see it in a pious spirit.

Among many other fine old buildings in Dijon, the Municipal Library is worth visiting. Apart from its superb illuminated manuscripts, large rooms have been luxuriously arranged with eighteenth-century furnishings and a reading room made from the chapel of a seventeenth-century Jesuit college. In the courtyard is an old Puits d'Amour (Well of Love).

The fifteenth-century Mayor's House in rue Ste Anne, near place Wilson, which I mentioned earlier, is my favourite old house in Dijon, not only for its superb Toison d'Or restaurant serving true old Burgundian dishes, nor because it is headquarters of the Company of Burgundian Wine-lovers, but for its charming atmosphere, its Gothic courtyard where you can drink your Kir and its little museum of wine-making and superb figurines in authentic old costumes. Needless to say, it has a superb wine-cellar, with wines chosen at special tastings of the Compagnie.

On N5 west, past the Arquebuse Gardens, a lake was constructed in the 1960s at the suggestion of Canon Kir, and it is named after him. It is a very popular centre for swimming and watersports. Unfortunately characterless modern apartment blocks have been built around it.

Dijon has become a good place to shop, especially, of course, for food and mustard. Dijon not only supplies half of France's mustard but exports a lot, too. It was introduced by the Romans (important because meat did not keep so well then) but at that time it was granular – the grains were just crushed enough to bring out the flavour. That is sold now as *moutarde à l'ancienne*. In the thirteenth century cinnamon and cloves were added. The smooth paste which most of us use now came in the eighteenth century. The firm of Grey-Poupon, established in 1777, developed a recipe using white wine instead of vinegar or *verjus* (unfermented grape juice). The company's shop at 32 rue de la Liberté, still run by the family, has a number of superb old mustard pots on display and some fine replicas and more modern pots which you can buy. Rue de la Liberté is the top shopping street, including many fashionable shops, and there are also very interesting shops around the market. Simone Porcheret has her wonderful cheese shop and maturing cellars at 18 rue Bannelier.

TOURIST INFORMATION Office de Tourisme, place
Darcy (80.43.42.12) and 34 rue Forges (80.30.35.39).
MARKETS every morning, plus Tuesday, Thursday,
Friday special markets.
FESTIVALS Florissmo (exotic plant show), every three
years mid-March (1993, 1996, etc). Music Festival, July.
Bell-ringing Festival, August. Fêtes des Vignes (Wine
Festival) and International Folklore Olympiad, early
September. Flea Market, September. International
Gastronomic Fair, fortnight in early November. Paulée,
Wine harvest dinner, bring your own wine, early
December.

HOTELS

La Cloche, 14 place Darcy (80.30.12.32): fine old hotel, national
monument, in very centre. For restaurant *see* Jean-Pierre
Billoux below. ROOMS F–G.
Chapeau Rouge, 5 rue Michelet (80.30.28.10): comfortable, with
character; convenient position. Excellent cooking. Slightly mod-
ernized regional dishes. ROOMS E–G. MEALS D–F.
Nord and Restaurant Porte Guillaume, place Darcy (80.30.58.58):
friendly, pleasant, high-standard family hotel run by Franchot
family for four generations, with fifth-generation son winning
the Student Chef of Burgundy award in 1990. Lovely traditional
Burgundian dishes the way they should taste. Superb wine list.
Wine bar in cellars. ROOMS C–E. MEALS C–E. Shut 23
December–10 January.
Jacquemart, 32 rue Verrerie (80.73.39.74): in lovely old street
near Palais des Ducs. No restaurant. ROOMS B–D.

RESTAURANTS

J. P. Billoux, Hotel La Cloche, 14 place Darcy (80.30.11.00): run
separately from hotel. Unassuming, brilliant young chef. Modern versions of classic dishes and of carefully researched old
recipes. One of the best restaurants in Burgundy. Expensive.
MEALS F–G. Shut two weeks early August; part February; Sunday evening, Monday.

Toison d'Or, 18 rue Ste Anne, near place Wilson (80.30.73.52): (*see* page 84). Superb surroundings; excellent classic and regional cooking. Local favourite. Superb wine list. MEALS C–G. Shut Sunday evening except in school holidays.

Petit Vatel, 73 rue Auxonne (80.65.80.64): excellent value menus; good cooking. MEALS B (lunch), C–E. Shut mid-July–mid-August.

Mâcon

[MAP 3, page 272]

Mâcon has always been a people's town. Dukes and Counts never made it their capital, and it had no excessively rich merchants to leave a heritage of beautiful palaces, public buildings and big mansions. The people of Mâcon welcomed the Revolution with great enthusiasm, demolishing their cathedral of St Vincent, the great historic abbey of Cluny nearby, and eleven other churches.

So Mâcon is not a lovely old town, though it has a handsome river front on the Saône and its roofs of rounded tiles give it a southern look – as if it is the outskirts of Provence. It was always the commercial centre for the wine business of the Chalonnais, but was overshadowed by Lyon industrially and commercially, and it had closer links with Lyon, through river, road and rail connections, than with Dijon. During the post-World War II boom, a number of Lyon enterprises expanded into Mâcon. The TGV trains came and Mâcon was well on the map. Dijon, with an excellent service to Paris, was put on the route to Switzerland, and Mâcon on the new route from Paris to Chambéry and Modane, a route to Italy and, more important, on the Paris–Lyon route to St Étienne, a great bonus for the town, for Paris is now only 1 hour 40 minutes away and Lyon only 15 minutes.

Mâcon's most important annual event is the French National

Wine Fair in the last two weeks of May. It is the ambition of almost every French wine-maker, from Roussillon and Bergerac to the Rhône and Alsace, to stick on his bottles a gold and red label marked 'Concours des Grands Vins de France – Mâcon Médaille d'Or, 1992' – or even 'Médaille d'Argent' or 'Médaille de Bronze'. That means that their wine is adjudged best in its category. After the efforts of Claude Brosse, the giant *vigneron* of Charnay-lès-Mâcon, to sell Mâcon wine at Louis XIV's Court, Mâcon deserves to hold the National Concours.

Mâcon is still obsessed with a local lad born there in 1790, the poet Alphonse de Lamartine (*see* page 15). He is admired not only for his poetry, but for his political career as a typical Burgundian – Independent Radical, totally opposed to the little dictator Napoleon III – and for his life-style of good wine and bad women. Mâcon has a quai Lamartine, a rue Lamartine, and a statue of him on the promenade. There is a Lamartine museum of documents and souvenirs in Hôtel Senecé, an eighteenth-century mansion, along with period paintings, tapestries and furnishings left from the years when the house was the seat of the Arts Academy of Mâcon. The poet was its president for several years. Then there is the Lamartine Heritage Trail – 69 kilometres of it to Monceau Château (page 188), Milly-Lamartine (page 188), Berzé-le-Châtel, St Point (page 118), Pierreclos, where Mlle de Milly (Laurence in *Jocelyn*) lived in the seventeenth-century château, and Bussières where Lamartine's tutor and friend, who appears in *Jocelyn* is buried by the little church.

Lamartine's old family house, Hôtel d'Ozenay, 15 rue Lamartine, is where the poet lived until his marriage. After all that, though he lived his last days in respectable poverty in Mâcon, he died in Paris.

The seventeenth-century convent of the Ursulines – a school for daughters of the well-off and well-connected, was saved in the Revolution by becoming a prison. Now it is a museum. It has a room with remarkable exhibits of Burgundian pre-history, including local excavations at the famous Solutré site (8 kilometres south-west, page oo), and other rooms with relics of Celtic, Gallo-Roman times and the middle ages. Paintings are interesting rather than great, but there are superb ceramics and porcelain of Delft, Italy, Nevers, Lyon, Rouen, Dresden and Sèvres.

A room of works of local artists has some interesting paintings by Gaston Bussière, who remained traditional through all the flashy changes in art fashions from the 1890s to 1920s. I liked his sensuous 'Salammbo', inspired by Flaubert's novel. (Museum closed Tuesday.)

In the eighteenth-century Hôtel-Dieu hospital is a Louis XV dispensary with splendid pottery.

To taste Mâcon wine and learn more about it, do visit the Comité Interprofessionel des Vins de Bourgogne et Mâcon at 484 avenue Maréchal-de-Lattre-de-Tassigny (85.38.36.70) and Le Cellier des Cordeliers, rue Dufour (85.38.91.05) – Tuesday– Friday 10.30 a.m.–12.30 p.m., 4 p.m.–8 p.m. Saturday 9.30 a.m.–12.30 p.m., 2.30 p.m.–8 p.m. Sunday 10.30 a.m.–12.30 p.m.). Le Cellier is in a seventeenth-century cellar and offers a choice of many Burgundy wines.

There is a wonderful drive through vineyards and photogenic country of La Montagne from Mâcon north-west, then east to Tournus. Here you are in a world away from the direct roads A6 and N6.

Take D103 north-west from Mâcon through vineyards to Clessé and Azé (page 115), then D82 north to Bissy-la-Mâconnaise. Here turn left on D187 through La Pistole Pass, after which a steep road on the right takes you up Mont St Romain. Back to the route where D446 takes you through the forest of Goulaine to the delightful village of Blanot (page 122). Follow D146 north through Grison river valley to Prayes, then D282 to Chissey-lès-Mâcon, a hamlet with a twelfth-century church with a fine belfry, and Chapaize (page 132). Turn right on D14 to Brancion (page 123), through Brancion Pass (Col de Brancion) to Ozenay, with a small château and twelfth-century church, then through the Beaufer Pass and downhill to Tournus, with fine views on the last stretch.

TOURIST INFORMATION 187 rue Carnot (85.39.71.37).
Département Tourist Office – 189 ave Maréchal-Lattre-de-Tassigny (85.39.47.47)
MARKET Saturday (regional).

FESTIVALS International Fair of French Wines, third or
fourth week of May (eight days).

Bellevue, 416 quai Lamartine (85.38.05.07): excellent bedrooms.
Chef's personalized menus and classic dishes à la carte. ROOMS
E–F. MEALS D–G. Restaurant shut end November–mid-
December; Tuesday.

Altéa Mâcon, Restaurant St Vincent, 26 rue Coubertin, 500 metres
north of town (85.38.28.06): modern, in a fine position among
greenery beside the Saône river with a restaurant terrace open in
summer. Good value meals. ROOMS E–F. MEALS B–F.

Grand Hôtel de Bourgogne et Restaurant La Perdrix, 6 rue Victor-
Hugo (85.38.36.57): town centre, sound-proofed, totally
renovated. ROOMS C–D. MEALS B–E. Restaurant shut 23–29
December.

At Crèches-sur-Saône, 8km SW by N6, *Château de la Barge*
(85.37.12.04): pretty 300-year-old mansion in big park. Large
rooms; meals excellent value. ROOMS C. MEALS B–E. Shut 25
October–3 November; 20 December–5 January; Saturday, Sunday in winter.

Nevers

[MAP 5, page 275]

Nevers is a pleasant, seemingly contented town of 45,000 people,
a nice size, and an attractive place once you pass its modern
suburbs and find the old city, where parts of the medieval walls
remain. It was capital of the old County and Dukedom of
Nivernais, the virtual enemy of the Dukes of Burgundy. Then

John the Fearless of Burgundy was made Count of Nevers, but François I made it a separate Duchy until it was incorporated into Burgundy after the Revolution – something of a mystery to the local people, as Nevers is on the Loire river, which runs along the west border of Nièvre, and even the wine is called 'Loire'. Nevertheless, Nièvre is still one of the four *départements* of Burgundy and Nevers is its capital. For centuries it was world famous for pottery and some is still made there. The local countryside is rich, particularly good for grain, and Nevers is lively on agricultural market days. Charolais cattle are bred in the nearby pastures.

From the big reddish-brown bridge carrying the N7 over the Loire, you can see the old town, with the narrow towers of the Ducal Palace and the high square tower and flying buttresses of the cathedral rising above the steep roofs.

The Ducal Palace, now part of the Law Courts, is a lovely example of elegant Renaissance architecture. In warm ochre stone, it has a slender central tower carrying the main staircase. On its façade are reliefs showing the legend of the Knight of the Swan, based on an ancestor of the House of Clèves, who inspired the story of Lohengrin. A plaque reminds the people of Nivernais that two daughters of Dukes became queens of Poland. The tower ends in a pointed roof topped by a delicate bell-tower. Two other slim towers are at the corners of the façade.

The palace was begun in the sixteenth-century by the Clèves family and their kinsmen, the Gonzagas. Louis de Gonzaga, son of the Duke of Mantua, became Duke of Nevers in 1565, and brought artists and artisans from Italy to develop glass and artistic pottery industries. By 1650 there were twelve pottery workshops with 1800 workers. The Revolution destroyed the industry by beheading the main customers. But there are still three pottery workshops.

You can see a fine collection of pottery in the Municipal Museum, tracing its development through the centuries. There are interesting examples of spun glass and enamel work, too, and Flemish tapestry exhibits. Surprisingly, the museum has a collection of modern art, including works of the remarkable French painter Suzanne Valadon, who died in 1938. She became an artists' model after an accident ended her young career as an acrobat. She gave birth at the age of sixteen to Utrillo, whom she later persuaded to take up painting to distract him from drinking and to give him a reason for life. She was a friend of many Impressionists, became Renoir's mistress and a life-long friend of Degas. Toulouse-Lautrec, Degas and Cézanne encouraged her to start painting and she became well known for painting nudes and figures, though her two best known works in the Luxembourg are of flowers. (Museum shut Tuesday.)

Round the corner from the palace is the strange cathedral of St Cyr and Ste Juliette, once beautiful, I am told, but cruelly treated. One end is Romanesque (mid-twelfth century), the other end Gothic, after a fire, and the middle rebuilt around 1951, after damage by shellfire in World War II. Inside, the nave is enormous. Narrow streets lead west from here to the very handsome Porte du Croux, a town gate from the fourteenth century – a fine square tower with a high steep roof and pointed defence turrets, which houses an archaeological museum with a collection of Romanesque sculptures. Below the town walls a walk through pleasant gardens takes you past several original rampart towers to the riverside road. Nevers has pleasant green open spaces, including gardens from the Ducal Palace to terraces above the roofs of the old town, called Montée des Princes, from which are good views over the Loire.

The church of St Étienne, built in the eleventh century, is a great joy to lovers of Romanesque architecture, though its towers were destroyed in the Revolution.

The Convent of St Gildard has a more modern fame. This is where Bernadette Soubirous, the girl who claimed visitations at Lourdes, entered as a novice. It seems that she was not very popular with the older nuns, who believed that she was a hysterical young girl, and she was quite badly treated. But the Convent has made much of her since she became a saint. She died here in 1879 and her mummified body, hands and face coated in wax, is displayed in a lit glass coffin. Thousands of pilgrims visit it each year. They can visit, too, a church built in 1966 called Ste Bernadette-du-Banlay which is rather like a warehouse from outside.

Earlier nuns of Nevers had a traumatic experience with a

parrot called Vert-Vert. They brought him up to be well behaved and religious. His fame spread to Nantes, where the nuns pleaded that he should visit them for a few days. Alas, on the river boat, sailors and dragoons taught Vert-Vert some very irreligious words. The horrified nuns of Nantes sent him straight back. At Nevers he was brought before the Mother Superior and Council and sentenced to a long period of fasting, solitude and silence. At the end of his sentence, the other nuns were so pleased to have him back that they stuffed him with sugar, wine and sweets. He died happy, of over-indulgence. That is how the rest of France has seen Burgundians.

There are river cruises in season from Nevers on the Loire aboard a river barge from Port de la Junction, with lunch on board if you want it, and on Nivernais Canal (Nièvre Tourisme, 3 rue du Sort (83.36.37.01).

Magny-Cours motor circuit and driving school are 3.5 kilometres south. In some years the French Grand Prix is held there (page 180).

TOURIST INFORMATION 31 rue du Rempart
(86.59.07.03).
MARKET daily.
FESTIVALS Bi-annual Festival of Pottery, March.
Fair-Exposition, March. Spring Fair, May.

HOTELS

Loire, quai de Médine (86.61.50.92): pleasant classic hotel with modernized bedrooms beside the Loire. ROOMS D–E. MEALS C–F. Restaurant shut mid-December–mid-January; Saturday.
Morvan, 26 rue Mouësse (86.61.14.16): Logis with good classic and regional meals. Good value. ROOMS B–D. MEALS B–E. Restaurant shut Tuesday evening, Wednesday.
Château Rocherie, at Varennes-Vauzelles, 5km N by N7, then private road (86.38.07.21): Napoleon III house in quiet centuries-old park. Good value meals, big price range. ROOMS C–D. MEALS B–F. Shut 1–11 November.

RESTAURANTS

Auberge Porte du Croux, 17 rue Porte du Croux (86.57.12.71): lovely house, two bedrooms, good classic cooking, excellent value menus. Fish direct from La Rochelle. ROOMS C. MEALS B–F. Shut 10–31 August; Friday evening, Sunday.

Les Voûtes, 21 rue St Étienne (86.61.19.28): in vaulted thirteenth-century chapel. Excellent value. MEALS B–E. Shut Sunday evening, Monday.

Sens

[MAP 4, page 274]

It is difficult to believe that Sens is in Burgundy. It is in the north-east of Yonne, a mere 118 kilometres from Paris, and we tend to think of it as a town east of Fontainebleau. To add confusion it was once in Champagne.

Sens has had moments of great power. The Senones, a Gallic tribe, marched to Rome in 390BC and captured it. They might well have destroyed it but for the honking of the holy geese in the Capitol, which awoke the Romans from slumber. The Gallic invaders only agreed to go home after being paid a ransom in gold that left Rome poor for a long time. The Senones leader, Brennus, son of the King of Sens, flung his sword on the scales on which the Roman ransom was being weighed, saying: 'Woe to the conquered.'

The Romans, of course, got their own back – in gold, according to legend – when they conquered Sens on their way through Gaul. But they made Sens capital of a Gallo-Roman province called Senonia and gave it such strong ramparts that they were not destroyed entirely until the nineteenth century. An oval of boulevards replaced the ramparts and they now surround the town.

Cathedral of St Etienne

It was under the Church that Sens gained its later power, and the old church buildings make it such an impressive town today.

For seven hundred years from the ninth century, Sens was a centre of great power. Its archbishop was called Primate of the Gauls and of Germania, and had authority over Paris, Chartres, Orléans and Meaux, as well as Auxerre, Nevers and Troyes. This power waned, however, when Paris became an Archbishopric in 1622.

The cathedral of St Étienne was begun in 1130, one of the first great Gothic churches in France, and though battered in wars it is still beautiful. For me, it is not possible to explain its beauty, for the great west façade is lop-sided, with one tower uncompleted above roof height, while the other soars to 78 metres, topped by a Renaissance bell-tower housing two massive bells weighing just under 14 and 16 tons. The original tower fell down in the thirteenth century – a fate that happened to a number of medieval buildings whose architects were too ambitious. It is lucky it did not fall about thirty years earlier when Louis IX (St Louis) was marrying Marguerite of Provence there.

The doorways and windows of Sens Cathedral have a lovely look of harmony, despite so many of the statues having had their heads knocked off during the Revolution. The Revolutionaries spared the original statue of St Étienne (St Stephen), merely decorating him with their symbol, a red bonnet. He still stands on a pillar of the central doorway.

Inside, the pillars are charmingly carved and the windows are magnificent. They range from the twelfth to seventeenth century and they include impressive rose windows with tracery like flames. Four of the windows show scenes in the life of Thomas à Becket, the murdered Archbishop of Canterbury. They depict Thomas and Henry II of England striving to be reconciled, Becket's return to England, his welcome, and his murder by four knights at Canterbury Cathedral. Becket stayed in Sens and then in nearby Columba Abbey when in exile. He lived in a house in the canon's cloister near the north tower of the cathedral. His murder shocked the people of Sens as much as it did the English.

True experts in church architecture can see similarities between Sens and Canterbury cathedrals. The head mason at Sens when the cathedral was started was William of Sens (Guillaume de Sens). After a fire destroyed the choir and other parts of Canterbury Cathedral in 1140, William was chosen to rebuild it. He finished the work at Canterbury in five years but unfortunately fell from scaffolding, receiving injuries from which he later died.

Part of Becket's vestments are among the remarkable

collection in Sens Cathedral's treasury on the first floor of the Henri II wing to the right of the choir. Ivories and tapestries are also on show in one of the richest church treasuries in France. Strangely, one of the finest pieces is an Islamic casket of the twelfth century.

Attached to the cathedral at the front end is the beautiful thirteenth-century Synodal Palace, restored in the nineteenth century by Viollet-le-Duc, who restored Notre Dame in Paris, the Château of Pierrefonds and Amiens Cathedral. The Ecclesiastical Tribunal sat in the great vaulted chamber, and the bishops met in the magnificent first-floor hall.

It was in 1234 that King Louis IX, the crusader who became St Louis and patron saint of France (until ousted by St Joan of Arc in 1920) married Marguerite of Provence in Sens Cathedral. In the Chapter House in 1140, a church court, egged on by St Bernard of Cîteaux Abbey, condemned the writings of Peter Abelard as heretical. Abelard was saved from excommunication and almost certain death by the powerful old Abbot of Cluny, Peter the Venerable. St Bernard was a fervent and bigoted man, who practised and preached the strictly ascetic life of prayer, fasting and little sleep, and he was infuriated by the beautiful decoration in Sens Cathedral. Happily for us, the Archbishop of Sens, Henri Sanglier, went ahead with the decoration of the cathedral despite the powerful preaching of St Bernard.

Pope Alexander III, the man from Siena who was not recognized by the Emperor Frederick Barbarossa, spent a year of virtual exile in Sens in 1163–4. There he was involved in the quarrel between Becket and Henry II of England – on Becket's side, of course, for the quarrel was really one of Church and kings.

Along the pedestrianized Grande Rue, the main street of the old town, and in the back streets you can find interesting old timber or stone houses, many built with stone from Roman fortifications and buildings. Look especially for the sixteenth-century Maison Abraham in rue République opposite the front of the cathedral.

TOURIST INFORMATION place Jean-Jaurès
(86.65.19.49).
MARKETS most days.
FESTIVALS Fair-Exposition – end April–early May.

HOTELS

Paris et Poste, 97 rue République, opposite Town Hall
(86.65.17.43): traditional old hotel of Sens. Fine old dishes from
recipes passed from father to son. Parisians used to drive here to
dinner (118km). ROOMS E–F. MEALS D–F.
Relais de Villeroy, at Villeroy, 6km W on D81 Nemours road
(86.88.81.77): 8 comfortable rooms offered now at this good
relais, serving seasonal dishes, classic cooking. Good menu
range. ROOMS C–D. MEALS C–F. Shut Monday (except hotel),
Sunday evening.

RESTAURANTS

Auberge de la Vanne, 176 ave Senigallia (take Auxerre direction)
(86.65.13.63): in greenery beside river Vanne. Outside terrace.
Traditional cooking. Big choice. MEALS B–F. Shut first week
September; mid-December–2 January; Thursday evening,
Friday.
Potinière, rue Cecile de Marsagny (86.66.31.08): owned by same
family as Poste Hotel (*see above*). Modern regional cooking.
MEALS C–F. Shut part February; Monday evening, Tuesday.

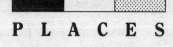
ALISE-STE-REINE
[Côte d'Or]

Mont Auxois rises 407 metres in the centre of a ring of hills 16km NE of Semur-en-Auxois, way to the east of Avallon. Beside it is Alise-Ste-Reine, a little town named after St Reine (St Reina), a young Christian girl beheaded in the fourth century for refusing to go to bed with a Roman governor (aptly named Olibrius), and Alesia, the camp where Julius Caesar very nearly suffered a defeat that might have changed the history of the world – and history dominates the little town.

When Caesar had over-run Gaul in 56BC and sailed to conquer Britain, Gallic tribes began many revolts. He was busily putting them down when a crisis arose in Rome. To cap his troubles, the Gauls joined together in a co-ordinated revolt under a chieftain called Vercingetorix. Caesar attacked their stronghold near Clermont-Ferrand, failed to take it and had to retreat northwards with Vercingetorix chasing him. The Gauls were very strong in cavalry, but Caesar met up with his other forces fighting around Paris and Sens, and regrouped.

The tribes of Burgundy joined the revolt. To the Gauls, Caesar's defeat seemed inevitable. He started to march towards the river Saône, as if he was trying to flee to the south. Vercingetorix, with a vastly bigger army, decided to attack him near Valesia. The Gauls were crushed and Vercingetorix took the remnants of his army to his camp at Valesia. With picks and shovels Caesar's legions built a double line of trenches, palisades, stakes and towers – one to keep the Gauls besieged, the other facing outwards to stop relief forces breaking in. The outer line was 12 miles round. A Gallic army, 250,000 strong, arrived to save Vercingetorix, but failed to break through the Roman lines. The Gallic commanders went home and Vercingetorix surrendered. Six years later, when Caesar celebrated his triumph in Rome, the Gaulish chieftain was paraded through the streets in chains, then thrown in a Roman prison where he was strangled to death.

Last century a new battle broke out over the site at Alise-Ste-Reine. Some historians claimed that it actually took place at Alaise, a village in Doubs *département* south of Besançon. In an attempt to end the argument, Napoleon III had excavations carried out at Alise-Ste-Reine from 1861–5. These revealed extensive trenches around Mont Auxois: bones of men and horses, silver coins, weapons and broken weapons. Napoleon's interest was to provide material for the life of Caesar he was writing. Like Mussolini later, he fancied himself as a new Caesar and drew parallels between the Roman leader and himself, even translating freely a speech Caesar is supposed to have made to Vercingetorix: 'A united Gaul, forming a single nation, moved by the same spirit, could defy the universe.' The words must have seemed hollow to Frenchmen after Napoleon III's débâcle at the hands of the Prussians.

After the digging at Alise-Ste-Reine, a bronze statue of Vercingetorix by Aimé Millet, 23 feet high, was erected on Mont Auxois on a stone plinth by Viollet-le-Duc. It gives a good viewpoint over the site of the Roman earthworks and plain of Les Laumes. Local old ladies once thought the statue was of St Gétorix and crossed themselves when they passed.

The statue did not stop the argument over Alesia, kept alive by Georges Colomb (author of *Savant Cosinus* and other classics for young people) until his death in 1945. His supporters, backing the village of Alaise as site of the battle, claimed that medieval monks had made the earthworks as drainage ditches. Now some archaeologists are claiming that the battle was fought in the Jura! But at the new archaeological Archéodrome (*see* Beaune, page 71) Alesia is recreated and located here at Alise.

Excavations still continue and you can visit the site, but the major finds are in Musée Alésia in Alise-Ste-Reine (open mid-February–1 November daily). The excavations themselves do include remains of a basilica dedicated to St Reine and a second-century tiered Gallo-Roman theatre. Near the statue is Théâtre des Roches built in 1945 on the ancient model. It holds four thousand people, and is used particularly for a mystery play on the weekend nearest 7 September, when a pilgrimage to St Reina includes a procession through the streets with people dressed in Gallic and Gallo-Roman clothes. The pilgrimage is to the Fontaine St Reine, a fountain said to have gushed from the spot where St Reina was sentenced to death and believed until the eighteenth century to have miraculous powers of healing. It is near Hospice St Reine, founded in 1660 by St Vincent de Paul for sick pilgrims. Half of the hospice was pulled down to make a modern hospital. In the chapel are paintings of the life and death of St Reina. But the seventh- to tenth-century church of the village is dedicated to St Léger.

ALOXE-CORTON
[CÔTE D'OR – *see* Wines, pages 34–5]

ANCY-LE-FRANC – Château d'
[YONNE]

The château of Ancy-le-Franc is a family house and an extremely elegant one, with magnificent decorations inside. It was built in 1544–6 when François I, deeply influenced by Italian Renaissance building and art, had brought French Renaissance into flower, and it was designed by an Italian, Sebastiano Serlio, who had come to François's Court. Antoine de Clermont, Comte de Tonnerre, Grand Master of Waters and Forest, built it. He was the husband of Anne-Françoise de Poitiers, sister of the cultivated and intelligent Diane de Poitiers, mistress of Henri II, and I am certain that they must have loved their house. It is in that classical Renaissance style, with a quite simple, almost austere face hiding the most beautiful decoration. The huge galleried inner courtyard is a Renaissance masterpiece. On each wall is the motto of the Clermont family '*Si omnes, ego non*' ('If all desert you, not I'), which harks back to the twelfth century when a Clermont stood by the Burgundian Pope Calixtus II, elected at Cluny, during one of those many squabbles and intrigues over the papal throne, which had more to do with power than religion.

The inside was decorated by Il Primaticcio, who had come to France from Italy to help François I decorate Fontainebleau, and by his pupils, including Niccolo dell' Abbate, who was better known for his landscapes. The furniture, mostly from the sixteenth to nineteenth centuries, is superb; so are the ceilings and panelling. The frescoes in the Salle des Nudités and Chambre de Diane are very interesting. The model for the goddess Diana in the Diane room and for the Huntress Diana painting above the fireplace in the floral bedroom was *not* Diane de Poitiers, who was painted as the goddess several times, but a girl from the Clermont-Tonnerre family. Diane de Poitiers does appear in the Judith and Holsfernes room with François I.

The paintings, panelling and frescoes are not only sumptuous and mostly beautiful, but often surprising. The long Gallery of the Sacrifices is named after nineteenth-century wall panels depicting Roman sacrifices, in great contrast to the Pharsalus Gallery with vast sixteenth-century murals showing Julius Caesar's defeat of Pompey at Pharsalus during their fight for power in 48BC. The fight seems to have taken place largely in the nude. The most charming room is the Flower Bedroom with delicate pictures of flowers and the goddess Diana over the fireplace.

The desk belonging to Madame de Sévigné, the brilliant seventeenth-century writer of barbed, witty gossip, is in the château because she was a close friend of the wife of the owner, Marquis de Louvois, Louis XIV's war minister, and often stayed at Ancy.

Louvois, who had wanted the château since he had visited it ten years earlier, bought it in 1683 because the Count of Clermont-Tonnerre had sent himself bankrupt buying Tonnerre County. Louvois had outhouses built and commissioned Le Nôtre of Versailles fame to lay out the gardens. He had little time to visit it, but his wife lived there. Louis XIV did stay there on his way back from the 'conquest' of Franche Comté in 1678. In 1845 the Clermont-Tonnerre family reclaimed the château. When the last count died, he was succeeded by his nephew, the Prince of Mérode.

The chapel has some excellent panelling by a Burgundian painter of talent, André Ménassier. In the outbuildings are veteran cars, including a Truffault of 1900, Renault and Dion Bouton of 1905, with about sixty carriages. (Château and Car Museum open end March–early November. Tours precisely on the hour, 10 a.m.–6 p.m. Park also open.)

TOURIST INFORMATION Mairie (mid-April–30 September, 86.75.13.21).

HOTEL

Centre (86.75.15.11): ROOMS C–D. MEALS A–E. Shut 2–20 January.

ANZY-LE-DUC
[SAÔNE-ET-LOIRE]

The Brionnais region which stretches along the right bank of the Loire in the SW corner of Burgundy is of low hills from which you have nice views of the Loire valley. It is known for cattle and for fine old churches of local yellow stone. The most beautiful and famous is the eleventh-century Romanesque priory church at Anzy-le-Duc, which is said to have inspired the builders of Vézelay. It has a magnificent octagonal three-storey bell-tower, pierced with bays.

The priory, founded around 876, has gone. There is a farm in its outbuildings, with a square tower.

APPOIGNY
[YONNE]

A small town on the river Yonne and N6, 8km N of Auxerre. Not very interesting, but it has a thirteenth-century collegiate church, a sixteenth-century tower, and four modern, functional hotels, including one of those 'Formula 1' cheap, comfortable sleeping pads in which every room is exactly the same down to the last ashtray – they look like cabinets for filing people 'away for the night (tel. 86.53.25.34).

RESTAURANT
Auberge les Rouliers (86.53.20.09): MEALS B–E.

ARCY-SUR-CURE
[YONNE]

The river Cure, which runs strongly through the Morvan to join the Yonne, and is loved by canoeists, cuts the village of Arcy in two, joined by a hump-backed bridge from which you have attractive river views. You can also see Manoir du Chastenay. Built in 1349 and once owned by the Knights Templars, it was a resting place on the pilgrim route to the shrine of St James at Santiago-de-Compostella in Spain. It is in the hamlet of Val-Ste-Marie, and has an elegant façade with a five-sided stairway tower and turret. Its sculptures include symbols of alchemy. It is owned by Count Gabriel de la Varende and used sometimes for concerts, exhibitions and conferences. (Open daily July, August, except Sunday morning. Rest of year open weekends except Sunday morning.)

Eight hundred metres along a narrow road from the manor, great limestone cliffs on the west bank of the Cure are pierced with caves used by prehistoric man. The Great Cave is open, although you can visit only 900 metres (½ mile) of its 2.5km length. Chambers and galleries are filled with stalactites, stalagmites and curiously shaped concretions. There are two small lakes, too. From outside the cave a pathway along the river bank passes many more caves which are not open to the public – a pity, because they contain wall drawings by prehistoric man of horses, mammoths and hyenas. (Guided ¾-hour tours of the Great Cave take place from March–November.)

HOTEL
Grottes (86.81.91.47): simple Logis. ROOMS B–C. MEALS A–D. Shut 20 December–25 January; Wednesday low season.

ARLEUF
[NIÈVRE]

Village east of Château Chinon on the D978, a winding, attractive road with hamlets in terraces on the hillside. To the east through the Morvan forest, with views of the high Anost forest, a road southward, D179, cuts through Canches Gorge. Arleuf's houses are protected by slates against rain on the western end.

Arleuf holds a market fair on the 17th of each month except August.

ARNAY-LE-DUC
(CÔTE D'OR)

This little town at the meeting of N6 and N81, between Dijon and Autun, looks rather tired and depressed if you drive through at the bottom of the hill. But climb to the top and you find pleasant roads and squares of old buildings and tiny shops. You could be fooled, too, by the outside of its superb hotel-restaurant, Chez Camille, which looks like a small-town commercial hotel from the outside, but is superbly furnished and well run, and serves wonderful meals.

Always important as a major crossroads, in 1570 Arnay was the scene of young Henri of Navarre's (later Henri IV) first victory for his Protestant forces in the Wars of Religion. Arnay became an important stage-coach relay post, and in the Revolution the aunts of Louis XVI, Adelaide and Victorie, were caught there trying to flee to Italy. After they had been accused of abandoning the kingdom at a moment of crisis, the authorities, at the insistence of the local people, allowed them to continue towards Italy.

The town is known for its tableware and the seventeenth-century hospice has become Maison des Arts de la Table – a fascinating show of pottery, crystal, silver and pewter. In the kitchens is a splendid eighteenth-century dresser and pottery dating back to the sixteenth century. (Open mid-April–mid-October; shut Tuesday, also Monday except July, August.)

Place Bonaventure-des-Perriers, named after a local poet who was the protégé of the brilliant writer and scholar Marguerite of Navarre, grandmother of Henri IV, has attractive buildings, including the town hall and a turreted house.

TOURIST INFORMATION 15 rue St Jacques
(80.90.11.59).
MARKET Thursday.

HOTELS

Chez Camille, 1 place Édouard-Herriot (80.90.01.38): *see* text. Armand and Monique Poinsot have made a delicious little hotel from an unlikely building. Superb cooking with regional undertones. Delightful bedrooms. Excellent service. ROOMS/SUITES E–G. MEALS D–G.

Terminus, 2 rue Arquebuse (N6) (80.90.00.33): simple, good-value Logis. ROOMS B–C. MEALS A–E. Shut 6 January–6 February; 1–15 October; Wednesday.

AUTUN
(SAÔNE-ET-LOIRE]

Who could believe that this little town dozing among hills under its beautiful cathedral only 20km from the Morvan Forest could have once been called 'sister and rival of Rome' or that until 1957 it produced so much oil from shale that it exported to the United States?

A Gaulish tribe called Aedui had a capital, Bibracte, on Mont Beuvray, south of what is now Château Chinon. They rebelled against the Romans. To control them and to assert Roman authority in the whole area of Gaul, Augustus Caesar decided to build a real Roman city to the east. He called it Augustodunum, and it became a great centre of Roman law and civilization, with 100,000 people, 12,000 of them students. It boasted that it was the Rome of the Western Roman Empire. Agrippa's Way, the road from Lyon to Boulogne, ran through it. It flourished in education and commerce, but as Rome's power lessened under attacks from Northern tribes, it was inevitable that Augustodunum would come under attack from 'Barbarians' seeking loot. It never recovered from being sacked in AD270.

Little is left of Autun's days of Roman glory. Porte-St-Andre, with two tall arches for vehicles and two smaller arches for pedestrians, is topped by a gallery of ten arches. Its guard room alongside was saved by its conversion into a church in the middle ages. The gate was restored last century by Viollet-le-Duc. Senonica Gate (now Porte Arroux), the entrance from Agrippa's Way, is better preserved. The decoration on the gallery at the top was copied by the architects of Cluny Abbey and then used extensively in Burgundy. The gate was built in the time of the Emperor Constantine. The Roman theatre at the eastern end of the town under the medieval ramparts has been extensively restored. It held 15,000 people and is used for summer festivals. Across the river Arroux in a field is a 24-metre-high square tower of which only two walls remain, part of a defence work now wrongly called Temple de Janus.

An accident of birth made Autun prosperous again in the fifteenth century – in 1376 Nicolas Rolin was born there. As Chancellor to the Dukes of Burgundy, he became enormously powerful and rich by dubious means, and built the hospice at Beaune to try to buy his way into Paradise (*see* Beaune, pages 67–8). Then his son, Cardinal Rolin, became Bishop of Autun and made it a great religious centre. It already had a famous cathedral, St Lazarus, with sculptures so superb that they are regarded as some of the finest in Europe.

In 1079 Gérard de Roussillon brought the bones of St Lazarus from Marseille and gave them to the church of St Nazaire in Autun. No one did anything with them for 140 years, then in 1120 Bishop Stephen of Bagé began a new church alongside the old one to house them. The two churches took it in turns to be the cathedral – six months each. St Lazare eventually took over, probably because it became rich from pilgrims, and St Nazaire was demolished in 1783.

Unlike most church sculptors of the middle ages, the sculptor of St Lazare left his name on his work. He was Gislebertus from Rome and he worked, too, on the great church at Vézelay. He is sometimes called Gilbertis France. His masterpiece at St Lazare is the tympanum over the west door, which is

Adam and Eve, *St Lazare*

of the Last Judgement and one that must have frightened even the toughest medieval peasant into praying for redemption. The evil grimace of Satan trying to cheat St Michael out of a soul, the fiend pushing terror-struck sinners into the flames of hell, the prostitute being devoured by serpents, the talons seizing the head of a man – it is all worthy of the gruesome advertisements for horror films. But it is magnificent. Beneath the feet of Christ in Majesty is the inscription '*Gislebertus hoc fecit*' ('Gislebertus made this').

The capitals inside, too, show imaginative scenes from the

Bible and history. Some are funny. You need to get a plan at
the church to follow them. In one Joseph sleeps through the
Nativity, in another Simon the Sorcerer tries to fly up to Heaven,
key in hand, but, to St Peter's obvious delight, is next seen
plunging to earth looking very scared, as one would be without a
parachute.

The wonderful tympanum sculptures were saved from
mutilation or destruction by the lack of taste of the cathedral's
hierarchy. In 1766 they decided that Gislebertus's work was
barbarian and crude, and covered the tympanum with plaster,
but because Christ's head stuck out they chopped it off with a
chisel. The plaster was taken off in 1837. In 1948 someone
noticed that a fine head of Christ in the Rolin Museum was the
one missing from the doorway, so it was replaced.

The cathedral canons of 1766 also covered the apse and
choir with marble, which was not removed until 1939, and broke
up the big medieval tomb of Lazarus. His bones are now in a
casket under the altar. On the left as you enter the nave is a
painting by Ingres of the martyrdom of St Symphorian at the
gate of St André.

From the outside the cathedral has lost some of its Romanesque character. The belfry and spire fell down in the fifteenth
century when hit by lightning, and Cardinal Rolin replaced
them with an 80-metre-high belfry in Flamboyant Gothic style.
Climb the 230 steps to the top for views over the rooftops to the
outline of the Morvan hills. The two large white slagheaps that
you can see are from the schist mines which produced shale oil.

The two towers over the main doorway were added by
Viollet-le-Duc when he restored the cathedral last century. He
could rarely resist adding *something* to old buildings, but we do
owe him a lot for his restorations of Amiens Cathedral and
Notre Dame in Paris.

Rolin Museum is in a wing of Nicolas Rolin's fifteenth-
century mansion and a nineteenth-century house next door. It
contains Gallo-Roman exhibits, including good mosaics, and
Romanesque statuary, including a superb statue of Eve by
Gislebertus, saved from St Lazarus's tomb, and showing Eve in
her true colours as a slim, nude girl lying among the trees and
bushes, plucking the apple nonchalantly. It was rediscovered in

1866, built into a wall. Alas, the other half showing Adam is missing.

On the upper floors are paintings of interest, mostly nineteenth-century French, including one of Anne Boleyn in the Tower by Cibot. (Museum closed Tuesdays.)

Autun is not only a very pleasant town but a good base for sorties into the Morvan forest and hills. See also Sully Château 15km NE (page 246).

TOURIST INFORMATION 3 ave Charles-de-Gaulle (85.52.20.34).

MARKETS Wednesday, Friday.

FESTIVALS Son-et-Lumière: daily except Sunday, Monday in July, August, September; Friday, Saturday only mid-May–end June. Morvan Music: Fridays, Saturdays mid-July–mid-August.

HOTELS

Vieux Moulin, porte d'Arroux (85.52.10.90): old mill, working until 1958, with a flower garden beside the river. ROOMS C–D. MEALS D–F. Shut mid-December –1 February; Sunday evening, Monday low season.

St Louis, 6 rue l'Arbalète, near town hall (85.52.21.03): seventeenth-century post relais. Summer terrace. Wide range of menus. ROOMS C–D. MEALS B–E. Shut 20 December–end January.

RESTAURANT

Chalet Bleu, 3 rue Jeannin (85.86.27.30): classic cooking, very good value. MEALS B–E. Shut February; Monday evening, Tuesday.

AUXERRE

[YONNE – *see* Major Towns, pages 60–5]

AUXEY-DURESSES

[*See* Wine, page 41]

AUXOIS MONT
[*See* Alise-Ste-Reine, page 98]

AUXONNE
[CÔTE D'OR]

In the days of the Dukes of Burgundy, the Saône river was the frontier with Franche Comté, and Auxonne was a vital frontier town. Its fortifications were kept up to date through the centuries and it was still an important garrison town when 2nd Lieutenant Napoleon Bonaparte, aged eighteen, arrived in June 1788. Serious, hard-working but broke, he fell in love with and wanted to marry the daughter of a rich timber-merchant but her father scorned a puny, penniless Corsican with no prospects, so Napoleon's dreams of a wife and a prosperous career in the timber trade were squashed. In 1791 he was posted back to Valence to join the Grenoble Regiment as a full lieutenant and decided to stick to soldiering as a career. His brother Louis served at Auxonne, too.

Now Auxonne is a market town, centre of an area SE of Dijon famous for leeks and asparagus from the market gardens near the river, and a centre, too, for canoeing, sailing and windsurfing on the river. Fishing is also good – the Saône is rich in pike, perch, carp and eels, almost as far as Mâcon, and this is a good area to taste pochouse, the stew of freshwater fish in white wine and *marc*. There are pleasant shaded walks by the river, but the old N5 road, which is still a main road to Geneva, passes through the town, so it is hardly sleepy. In a quiet square just off N5 is Notre Dame church with interesting sculptures. It is finely decorated with gargoyles.

Napoleon, of course, gets a museum. Called Musée Bonaparte, and founded in 1863, it takes up three rooms of the largest tower of the fifteenth-century castle which overlooks the Saône. Only one is devoted to Napoleonic souvenirs, presented by Napoleon III and General Vaillart, and including a marble statue of Napoleon by Pietreli. Other rooms are devoted to

Gallo-Roman discoveries and local folklore and history. (Open 1 May–15 October, afternoons only except July, August.)

Near the church is another statue of Napoleon (nineteenth century by François Jouffroy) in place d'Armes, facing the fifteenth-century town hall. Some seventeenth-century fortifications exist and an artillery arsenal built by Vauban.

TOURIST INFORMATION Porte du Comté (80.37.34.46).

MARKETS Wednesday, Friday.

FESTIVALS Carnival early March. Son-et-Lumière end July–early August. Grand Fair (centuries old) end October.

HOTEL

Corbeau, 1 rue Berbis (80.31.11.88): 2-chimney Logis. ROOMS C–D. MEALS B–E. Restaurant shut Sunday evening, Monday.

AVALLON
[YONNE]

Perched on a granite spur between two ravines, Avallon must have been a lovely old town in the days of the horse – it has not quite come to terms with the motor car. It is a busy little commercial centre and as its narrow streets and ramparts attract tourists from spring to autumn, cars tend to take over. Grande-Rue Aristide Briand, the main shopping street which runs from the centre, place Vauban, past the ancient church to the Promenade de la Petite Porte, high above the valley of the river Cousin, is marked 'Priority for Pedestrians'. Not all motorists give way. To be sure of avoiding them, you must take to the old ramparts.

Avallon was very heavily fortified from the middle ages, but in 1432 it still fell to a band of freebooters in the pay of Charles VII of France and under the command of Jacques d'Espailly, known as Fortépice. He had captured many castles in Burgundy, and had even threatened Dijon, but the people of Avallon had great faith in their defences and slept soundly behind them. One December night Fortépice and some of his men surprised the guard, scaled the ramparts, and sacked the town. He, too, was impressed by the town's walls and decided to strengthen Avallon and use it as a base.

Philip the Good, Duke of Burgundy, was furious. He rushed from Flanders to regain his town. He brought with him a *bombarde*, a machine for hurling great rocks. It knocked a hole in the walls and the Burgundian soldiers tried to rush through. They were thrown back by Fortépice's two hundred men. Philip then sent for more knights and cross-bowmen. Fortépice realized that he could not win, so he treated the townspeople of Avallon to a feast. While they were drinking and dancing he slipped away under cover of darkness, leaving his men to face the Duke's army.

Vauban, the great military architect, who was born about 30km away at St Léger, redesigned the defences for Louis XIV. Then Louis decided that Avallon no longer needed defending and gave the ramparts to the town. He was undoubtedly trying to save money – foreign wars, his own extravagance and the cost of Versailles had made him virtually bankrupt. Vauban's statue is in place Vauban alongside the road to Paris. Grande-Rue Aristide Briand passes the town hall, the old house of the Princes of Condé and Tour Escalier, the thirteenth-century home of the Dukes of Burgundy. It then runs beneath Tour de l'Horloge, a fifteenth-century gate and tower with a fine clock and turret and a slender belfry. The tower was used as a lookout and a meeting place for the town's aldermen. The information centre is alongside. Go in and get a map of the old town and ramparts. Further along on the left in a cobbled square is the interesting but slightly battered church of St Lazare. Underneath it is the original fourth-century crypt of a church dedicated to St Mary. The supposed skull of Lazarus was given to the eleventh-century church by a Duke of Burgundy, Henri le Grand, and it was venerated by people who believed that it could ward off or even cure leprosy. So many pilgrims arrived that a new church was built, consecrated by a Pope in 1106, but it was soon too small and the front was moved 28 metres forward fifty years later. The north tower caught fire several times and collapsed finally in 1633, taking part of the façade with it. The tympana of the two surviving doorways of the façade from 1150 are the great attraction, but they have been so mutilated that, although you can see that they must have been spectacular, it takes an ardent amateur of Burgundy Romanesque sculpture to appreciate them now. But I love the carving on the arches above them, especially above the small doorway. Here is a flower garden in stone – rose blossoms, arum lilies, stock and twining vines. The inside is impressive, with a charming rose window and several seventeenth-century painted wooden statues.

At the end of the road, the wide Promenade de la Petite Porte is shaded by tall old lime trees. From the wall you look almost vertically 100 metres down to the Cousin valley. The road from La Petite Porte runs through the ramparts and takes a hair-pin bend by terraced gardens to lead you into a lovely drive through the river Cousin valley.

You can stroll around the ramparts, beginning either way from La Petite Porte, although you run into traffic from the bastion at Porte Auxerroise along the Terreaux Vauban promenade and right to Tour Beurdelaine. You will pass many towers and interesting old buildings, including Tour du Chapitre (1450), Éperon Gally (a spur flanked by a 1591 watchtower with steps down to a terrace), Beurdelaine Tower (the oldest, built by John the Fearless in 1404 and strengthened in 1590 with a bastion), and Tour de l'Escharguet (the Elected), also called Tour Vachère because it was once the cow-herd's tower.

In the side streets of the old town within the ramparts are many fine buildings including fifteenth-century houses with turrets, and sixteenth- to eighteenth-century townhouses. There are also good restaurants.

When Napoleon had escaped from Elba and was marching from the south towards Paris, he stayed a night at the Poste Hotel at 13 place Vauban, which was already over one hundred years old. His old general, Marshal Ney, was approaching with a big army from Paris, sworn 'to bring Napoleon back in a cage'. They met the next day at Auxerre and Ney switched sides with his army. That cost him his head after Napoleon's defeat at Waterloo. The hotel has been renovated recently. For a long time, when the chef was René Huré, it had two Michelin stars. Champérard described it as 'one of the grand temples of French gastronomy' and *Gault Millau* called it 'a paradise of French gastronomy and hotellerie'. Now the last two offer faint praise and in 1991 Michelin didn't mention it at all. The new chef is a young American. When I last heard, there was talk of restoration.

TOURIST INFORMATION 6 rue Bocquillot (86.34.14.19).

MARKETS Thursday, Saturday.

FESTIVALS Fair-Exposition early May.

HOTELS

Poste, 13 place Vauban (86.34.06.12): *see* text. ROOMS E–G. MEALS D–G.

Capucins, 6 ave P. Doumer (86.34.06.52): like a small country house in town. Very good traditional Burgundian dishes. ROOMS D. MEALS C–F. Shut mid-November–mid-January; Tuesday evening low season; Wednesday.

Moulin des Ruats, in Cousin valley, 6km on D427 (86.34.07.14): lovely old flour mill with flower-decked balconies hidden in a lush green valley beside the little Cousin river. In summer you can eat on the river bank under trees within casting distance of the trout. Meals are pricey. ROOMS D–G. MEALS F–G. Shut 20 November–20 December; mid-January–early February; Tuesday lunch, Monday in winter.

RESTAURANTS

Morvan, 7 route de Paris N6 (86.34.18.20): jolly Jean Breton cooks excellent Burgundian specialities as well as ever. Good value. Surrounds of his old mansion looked drab last time I saw it. MEALS C–F. Shut a week in November; early January–end February; Sunday evening, Monday.

Les Fleurs, at Pontaubert, 5km W by D957 (86.34.13.81): restaurant with 7 rooms. In country. Regional dishes. Good value cheap menus. ROOMS C–D. MEALS B–E. Shut mid-November–early January; Thursday lunch in winter; Wednesday.

AZÉ
[Saône-et-Loire]

Village in the Mâconnais, 30km NW of Mâcon by D103, the same distance SW of Tournus. It has caves which were home to prehistoric man and wild animals, especially bears, then were used later as a hiding place for the Eduen tribe when fighting the Romans and for Gallo-Romans after the Roman Legions had left. The first cave is 208 metres long, the second 800 metres with an underground river that you can walk alongside. The museum has more than two thousand local finds from diggings and the caves.

Azé is on the winding, attractive Montagne route of the Mâconnais from Tournus to Mâcon through Forêt de Goulaine.

BARD-LE-RÉGULIER
[Côte d'Or]

The unusual name of this hamlet 18km S of Saulieu on D15 came from its ancient ownership by the Augustinian Canons Regular. Now it is known for its unusual twelfth-century church, with round-headed arches, narrow windows and a floor on three levels to beat the slope of the site. A delicately carved figure of St John the Divine from the fifteenth century is attributed to the great sculptor Jean de la Huerta, who worked at the Duke of Burgundy's Court. The celebrated choir stalls of the fourteenth century have interesting carvings, including strange beasts on the arm-rests.

From the Bard Signal Station, 1km E, then a fifteen-minute walk to 554 metres (1818 feet), are fine views of the Morvan and the Auxois region. Arnay-le-Duc is 17km E by the D17 road.

BAZOCHES
[Nièvre – *See* St-Léger-Vauban, page 229]

BEAUJEU
[BEAUJOLAIS]

This little town, 26km NW of Villefranche, strung along the
Ardières valley, and 13km W of Belleville, was the ancient capital of the Beaujolais, founded in the ninth century. Its Sires
owned a large area between Lyon and Mâcon, and it acted as a
buffer when the two were fighting each other. The Dukes of
Burgundy owned it in the fourteenth century and one of them,
Pierre de Bourbon, married the daughter of Louis XI who
became known as Anne of Beaujeu. Ironically, it was she who
took away Beaujeu's title as Capital of Beaujolais in favour of
Villefranche. The last Sire of Beaujolais was the Duke of
Orléans who joined the French Revolution and called himself
'Philippe Égalité' (Philip Equality) – but he was still guillotined
by Robespierre. His son became King Louis-Philippe, friend of
Queen Victoria.

Beaujeu inevitably lives by selling wine, but it is known, too,
for its unusual Museum Marius-Audin in the town hall. Marius-
Audin, a publisher who died in 1951, left to the town his superb
collection of dolls, dolls' houses, dolls' furniture and all household goods and chattels of the nineteenth century, with dolls in
costumes from different areas of France and Italy. Another
section of the museum shows the inside of a peasant's house in
the nineteenth century, and old tools of various trades from
shoe-making to wine-making. (Museum open Easter–1 November afternoons only, all day Sunday; rest of year open Sunday
only.)

Below is a cave, the Temple of Bacchus, where you can taste
wines of Beaujolais Villages. In December, Beaujolais wines are
sold for the hospice, a lesser Beaune-type sale.

TOURIST INFORMATION Syndicat d'Initiative,
4 Grand'Han (end March–mid-December, afternoons
only except July–October. 74.69.22.88).
FESTIVALS Exposition of Beaujolais Villages wines
through December.

HOTEL
Anne de Beaujeu (74.04.87.58): ROOMS C. MEALS C–G. Shut first
fortnight August; 23 December–25 January; Sunday evening,
Monday.

BEAUMONT-SUR-VINGEANNE
[CÔTE D'OR]

Around 1724, Abbot Claude Jolyot built himself a delicious little
château in this village on the river, NE of Mirebeau and Dijon, to
hide from the junketings, intrigues and back-stabbings of Versailles and the Court – he was chaplain to King Louis XV. The
château, standing in a 15-acre park, with terraces, is beautifully
proportioned, elegant but rather rustic, with round-headed windows. The main rooms are beautifully panelled. Under the
garden terrace there is a large vaulted chamber, which has
caused some speculation as to what the abbot used it for. It could
have been a chapel or just a store for gardening tools; some say it
was an orangerie. I should like to live there – and I should use
the chamber as a wine-tasting room.

BEAUNE
[CÔTE D'OR – *see* Major Towns, pages 65–72]

BELLEVILLE
[BEAUJOLAIS]

Belleville is an important little town to lovers of Beaujolais wine,
for it is the main wine centre for distribution and sales. It is on
the Saône river, along which the wine used to travel, and beside
the A6 motorway, by which it travels now. On N6, 3½km NW at
St Jean d'Ardières, is the renowned Maison de Beaujolais, where
you can taste the whole range of Grands Crus wines and local

specialities. Unlike much of Burgundy, the Beaujolais produces excellent lamb. (Shut Monday evening, Tuesday, 74.66.16.46.)

Belleville is a good alternative to Villefranche as a base for Beaujolais wine villages. You could tour the northern vineyards on the first day, the southern on the second.

Belleville has an interesting twelfth-century church from a former Augustinian abbey.

Château de Pizay near St Jean d'Ardières is a fourteenth-century manor with a handsome French-style formal garden by Le Nôtre (*see* Hotels).

TOURIST INFORMATION Mairie (74.66.17.10).

MARKET Tuesday

HOTELS

Ange Couronné, 18 rue République (74.66.42.00): ROOMS B–D. MEALS A–E. Shut part November; part February; Sunday evening from 15 September–Easter. Restaurant shut Sunday evening, Monday.

Château de Pizay, at St Jean d'Ardières, 5km NW by D18, D69 (74.66.51.41): *see* text. Big bedrooms; park with swimming pool. Attractive Le Donjon restaurant. Among vineyards. ROOMS F. MEALS E–G.

RESTAURANT

Beaujolais, 40 rue Maréchal Foch (74.66.05.31): a winner for hearty appetites and good wine. Generous, well-cooked regional dishes. Five menus. Very good cellar. Rooms possible (telephone). MEALS A–E.

BERZÉ-LA-VILLE and BERZÉ-LE-CHÂTEL
[SAÔNE-ET-LOIRE]

In its great and powerful days, the Abbey of Cluny (*see* page 151) kept a country house for its pupils called Château des Moines, 12km SE of Cluny. Its great abbot, St Hugh of Cluny, who died in 1109, used it as his country seat near the end of his life. One night while he was there a terrible thunderstorm broke, the house was hit by lightning and burned down. The abbot was saved from the flames and immediately started to rebuild. Now there is only the little Romanesque chapel among a farmyard and barns, but it contains paintings which are a clue to what the decorations of Cluny itself must have been like. By a fluke, the chapel's frescoes were whitewashed and hidden until 1887. Then the curé of Berzé, Father Jolivet, saw an outline that puzzled him. He scraped some paint away with a penknife and revealed the head of Christ. Carefully he cleaned the rest and found a painting of Christ in Majesty 4 metres high, with the apostles and the deacons St Laurence and St Vincent. Preserved by whitewash, the colours, ochre and purple, with blue background, are incredibly bright for paintings eight hundred years old. These and paintings of martyrs on the base of windows and sides of the apse, have a definite Byzantine appearance, like the mosaics of Ravenna, and art historians trace the flowering of Byzantine trends in wall paintings and manuscript illuminations through this period. On the left of the apse is the legend of St Blaise, with a widow bringing to him in prison the trotters and head of her pig he had rescued from a wolf, followed by the scene of the saint's beheading. On the right is the martyrdom of a saint by roasting alive – most say that it is St Laurence, but there is a good argument for it being St Vincent of Saragossa, who became patron saint of wine merchants and *vignerons*.

Ironically, the chapel was decorated on the orders of Cardinal-Abbot Pons de Melgeuil, described by his detractors as 'a barbarian baron masquerading as a priest' (*see* Cluny, page 151). Having been forced by the Pope to resign as Abbot of Cluny because of scandal and extravagance, he staged a coup with armed men and when in control of the abbey again, melted down many of its treasures, including gold crosses, chalices and candlesticks, to pay his soldiers. Arrested by the Pope, he died in prison, but Cluny's finances never recovered.

Five kilometres to the north of Berzé-la-Ville, in a magnificent position among vineyards, is the formidable castle of Berzé-le-Châtel, protector in old times of the southern approaches of Cluny.

A grey feudal fortress with round and square towers and strong surrounding walls, it was the seat of the old barony of Mâconnais. From the middle ages, a local legend spread that one Baron of Berzé had locked up a man and an ox just to find out which would starve to death first. The result was never recorded, but when the ruins of the castle were being restored last century a human skeleton and some ox bones were found on different floors of a tower.

This is the countryside of the poet-politician Lamartine (*see* pages 15–17) who wrote that the ruined castle added 'solemnity of past ages and a touch of melancholy to the cheerful and varied aspect of the landscape'. It looks bright enough now that it has been carefully restored.

The sixteenth-century garden was restored very pleasantly with the castle, and you can visit the garden terrace from early April to early November.

BEUVRAY – Mount
[SAÔNE-ET-LOIRE]

On the top of this hill (31km SW of Autun) was situated the Gallic village of Bibracte, capital of the Eduens tribe and a fortified village used as a refuge. Here the Gallic leader Vercingetorix called a Council of War of tribes which had risen against Julius Caesar in 52BC, and led them in the campaign against the Romans which nearly toppled Caesar (*see* Alise-Ste-Reine, page 98). In 12BC Augustus Caesar abandoned Beuvray to build Augustodunum (now Autun, *see* page 105).

The site was excavated last century but the ruins found were reburied. Every spring the Gallic people met here to worship a god of new life, and fairs were held at this festival until the sixteenth century. From the summit is a fine panorama of the Autun countryside, and I am told that on fine days people have seen the Juras and Mont Blanc.

BÈZE
(CÔTE D'OR]

This charming little market town at the source of the river Bèze, 26km NE of Dijon by D70 and D960, was the site of a priory which gave its name to Clos de Bèze, the vineyards adjoining Chambertin producing the first Grand Cru wine on the Côte de Nuits. All that is left of the priory is a tower at the river's edge and the fourteenth-century belfry of the church, which has a sundial.

Today Bèze is known for water. The 'source' of the river Bèze, a tributary of the Saône, is now believed to be a resurgence of two smaller rivers, the Tille and Venelle, meeting underground. The spring is no tiny trickle but a magnificent fountain gushing out at anything from 300 to 2000 litres a second! A series of caves made by the underground river Tille have been linked to form a swift-flowing underground river along which you can travel by boat for 300 metres. You can drink the crystal clear waters from the 80-metre (260-feet) deep lake. (Open May–September except Tuesday morning and Monday. In April weekends only.)

HOTELS

Relais, 2 place Verdun (80.75.30.62): renowned for fine traditional Burgundian dishes at bargain prices. Five generations of the Chambrette family have run it. Excellent wines. Simple bedrooms, 4 with bathroom, WC. ROOMS B–C. MEALS A–D. Shut Wednesday low season.

Auberge Quatr'Heurie (80.75.30.13): 2-chimney, 2-star Logis. ROOMS B–D. MEALS B–E.

Bourguinon, rue de la Porte de Bessey (80.75.34.51): another 2-chimney Logis. ROOMS C–D. MEALS A–E. Shut 20–30 December.

BLANOT
[Saône-et-Loire]

Hamlet of 160 people living in old houses surrounded by dry stone walls in a delightful setting below Mont St Romain, 10km NE of Cluny. The fortified fourteenth-century priory and the late eleventh-century church with an unusual Romanesque belfry once belonged to Cluny. The priory has one polygon and one round tower. Past the hamlet of Fougnières N on D446 is a network of caves 80 metres (260 feet) underground and 1km long stretching to Mont St Romain. There are steep stairs and low ceilings. In the twenty-one chambers you can visit are some big stalactites and stalagmites. Two are massive but one of them has fallen because of its weight. (Open March–late October.)

BOURBILLY – Château
[Côte d'Or]

In the Serein valley, 9km SW of Semur-en-Auxois by D954 and D9, is this vast château with four round towers. Originally it was a fortified manor which belonged to Jane de Chantal (Jeanne Françoise Fremyot), who helped St Francis of Sales found the order of nuns called the Order of Visitation. Her orphaned grandchild, Madame de Sévigné, the writer, lived there as a child and often visited it later. The manor was damaged in the Revolution. Last century the present château was built around it. It was burned badly in 1952 but was rebuilt.

BOURBON-LANCY
[Saône-et-Loire]

Small hilltop spa overlooking the Loire valley and the Allier plain, 36km E of Moulins. Four springs gush out here at temperatures from 46°C to 58°C (115°F to 136°F), giving 88,000 gallons a day. The thermal establishment in a fine old park has been modernized. It is used to alleviate rheumatism and circulation problems. The eleventh-century church of St Nazaire, founded by a prior from Cluny, is now a museum displaying paintings and sculptures. Among fifteenth-century buildings are an unusual wooden house and a fortified gateway with a clock tower. Agricultural machinery is made in the town.

TOURIST INFORMATION place Aligre (shut mornings in winter, 85.89.18.27).

MARKET Saturday.

HOTELS

Grand (85.89.08.87): ROOMS B–C. MEALS B–D. Open mid-April–mid-October.

Villa Vieux Puits, 7 rue Bel Air (85.89.04.04): good Burgundian dishes; good-value menus. Simple rooms. ROOMS B–C. MEALS B–F. Open Easter–mid-December.

Manoir de Sornat, allée des Platanes, route to Moulins (85.89.17.39): Gérard Raymond moved to this romantic old manor house in 1989. Classic cooking. ROOMS D–G. MEALS D–F. Shut 15–31 January. Restaurant shut Monday in winter.

BRANCION
[SAÔNE-ET-LOIRE]

A superb medieval fortified village perched on a spur overlooking two rivers, 14km W of Tournus, in the middle of the Mâconnais, it has its ruins of ramparts with a fourteenth-century gateway. Inside are imposing ruins of a castle dating back to the tenth century, narrow streets lined with medieval houses, mostly well restored, an old covered market and, on the end of the spur, a church from 1150 in Romanesque style with a square belfry. From the church terrace are splendid views, and inside are fourteenth- to fifteenth-century wall paintings, which have deteriorated badly, and the effigy of an owner of the town who died as a crusader fighting with his cousin St Louis at the defeat of El Mansurah in Egypt in 1252.

The castle was enlarged in the fourteenth century by Duke Philip the Bold of Burgundy, and the Dukes sometimes stayed there. It was destroyed by the Catholic League in the sixteenth-century Wars of Religion, but the keep has been restored. Eighty-seven steps to the top of the keep give you a view of the town and even to the hills of Charollais and the Morvan.

Many of the fine old houses have flowered balconies and stone staircases outside.

BROCHON
[Côte d'Or]

Village at the boundary of the Dijon and Côte de Nuits vineyards between Fixin and Gevrey-Chambertin, on D122. It produces an ordinary Bourgogne Rouge wine. Its château was built in 1900 by a journalist and poet Stephen Liégeard, who invented the phrase 'Côte d'Azur' for the Mediterranean coast of Provence. The poem won him an award from the Académie Française. The name is international; the poet and his writings are forgotten.

BUSSIÈRES
[Beaujolais]

Abbot Dumont, the poet Lamartine's first master, who became his great friend, was curé of this hamlet west of Mâcon by N79 and D45. He is buried by the chevet of the little church. Nearby is Pierreclos Château (see page 202) where Mademoiselle de Milly lived. Lamartine's love story *Jocelyn*, in which she was 'Laurence', is based on their lives.

MARKET Thursday.

BUSSY-RABUTIN – Château
[CÔTE D'OR]

Two kilometres S of the village of Bussy-le-Grand and 8km N of Alise-Ste-Reine (*see* page 98) is this fascinating château of a true eccentric, Roger de Rabutin, Count of Bussy (1618–93). It has some of the most sophisticated graffiti in history.

While his cousin Madame de Sévigné was writing wittily if bitchily about the Court of Louis XIV, Bussy's amusing but biting couplets were getting him into all sorts of trouble. As a young and very successful army officer he was said to have hinted that he, a mere lieutenant colonel, was the equal of the great commander Henri de la Tour d'Auvergne, Viscount of Turenne. Turenne was not pleased, and he described Bussy to Louis XIV as 'the best officer in your army – for poems'.

Next Bussy took part in the notorious 'debauch of Roissy' during Holy Week, when a future Cardinal baptised a frog, and he and other rakes sang obscene songs to hymn tunes. He was exiled to Burgundy and he took with him his mistress, the Marquise de Montglas. There, for her amusement, he wrote *Histoire Amoureuse des Gaules* (*A Love History of Gaul*), satirizing the love affairs of the Court.

Bussy was allowed back at Court, where his *Histoire* was doing the rounds. The king asked to see one. As there was nothing in it which libelled Louis himself, he and his new mistress, Mademoiselle de La Vallière, thought it very funny. Thanks to this and another of Bussy's writings, *Maximes d'Amour*, the king gave consent for Bussy-Rabutin to be elected to the Académie Française.

Like so many wits, Bussy could not resist a witticism even at the expense of those closest to him. He loved his cousin Madame de Sévigné, but painted a cruel, malicious portrait of her (though it is said to have been true) that marred their great friendship for years. Almost fatally, he included the Prince of Condé among his victims – the very man who had backed him in his successful military career. Condé, who was very powerful and arrogant, threatened to assassinate Bussy in the street, then he and his friends bribed a hack to write satirical couplets about the king, claiming to Louis that Bussy had written them.

Bussy was sent to the Bastille on Louis' orders and when he came out, he was exiled once again to his château in Burgundy.

It is difficult for us to understand why it should have been such a punishment to be rusticated from Versailles, which was so overcrowded it was dangerously unsanitary and so cold and draughty that the wine froze in the decanters, to a château among beautiful countryside like the Loire valley or Burgundy, where the wine was much better and could be served at the right temperature. Surely the presence of the megalomaniac Sun King was not all *that* attractive? Perhaps they missed the licentious ladies Bussy described in his *Histoire*. Even his beloved mistress forsook him for Versailles and another lover.

He spent most of the rest of his days rebuilding his château and redecorating it as a remarkable picture gallery of his life, loves and of the women who appeared in his *Histoire*. For each picture he composed a caption – many were in verse and often witty and biting.

He sent to Paris for the pictures – most were copies, apart from one of himself by Le Febvre, pupil of Charles Lebrun, Louis XIV's own artist-decorator and furnisher for Versailles, and a few by Pierre Mignard, the painter of historic scenes and portraits of people in allegorical trappings. Several of the pictures were of the Marquise de Montglas, his former mistress. She was represented as the moon 'with more than one face', as a rainbow, as Zephyr 'lighter than air', and as a swallow who 'flees the bad weather'.

The château is in the woodlands, with trees on three sides, and on the fourth a balustraded terrace overlooking Bussy-le-Grand village. Its main building in limestone has a tower at each end, and two delicately decorated lower wings in Renaissance style are built at right angles to form a Court of Honour, leading to two more towers with conical roofs. One is a keep, the other a chapel.

Inside, the dining room, called Cabinet des Devises (Room of Mottoes), shows views of the Royal châteaux as they were at the time, which are fascinating for architects and historians. Below are allegorical paintings and over the fireplace Bussy himself, by

Le Febvre. On the first floor the Salon des Grands Hommes de Guerre is crowded with sixty-five portraits of great warriors from Du Guesclin to Condé and Turenne; Bussy shamelessly included himself. Most were French but Oliver Cromwell was included – an accolade, no doubt, for Cromwell's Ironsides having helped the French beat the Spanish in Flanders, and take Dunkirk and save Louis from losing Flanders and Picardy.

Portraits of the kings of France decorate an adjoining wing. Bussy's bedroom has pictures of twenty-five women, including Royal mistresses such as Henri IV's Gabrielle d'Estrées, Louis XIV's Madame de Maintenon and the courtesan Ninon de Leclos, with Bussy's second wife, and his cousin Madame de Sévigné with her daughter. Bussy was in love with his cousin, and foolishly had once written asking her to be his mistress, but her husband had intercepted the letter, and he was banned from her house. Her husband, a dissolute rake, was later killed in a duel.

In the round Tour Dorée (Gilded Tower) Bussy excelled himself. The room is covered in paintings. He himself appears again with Louis XIII and Louis XIV, but mostly they are allegorical pictures of the ladies of Louis' Court, with barbed captions. The notorious Comtesse d'Olonne was 'less celebrated by her beauty than by the use she made of it', and of Madame de la Baume, who had borrowed the *Histoire* and had a copy made, he wrote rather magnanimously, 'The most amiable and prettiest, if she had not been the most unfaithful.' All the Court wanted to know what was written under these pictures, and no doubt found out.

Bussy did finally make peace with Madame de Sévigné, and they wrote to each other regularly. He died in 1693 and three years later volumes of his letters were published. They were regarded as a model of the best French style. Some of Madame de Sévigné's letters were published with them, which were also praised and more of her correspondence was published, mostly letters to her daughter. It was so witty and amusingly bitchy that her reputation gradually excelled Bussy's, so that now he has sunk into near obscurity.

The château is open daily April to September, except Tuesdays; late morning and early afternoon the rest of the year except Tuesdays, Wednesdays and Sundays. It has belonged to the State since 1929 and you must wait to join a guided tour (¾ hour). It is an amusing and rewarding visit.

Bussy-le-Grand is a pleasant village of brown-roofed houses and a twelfth-century church, dull outside, interesting within.

BUXY
[Saône-et-Loire]

Very pleasant small town on D981 Chalonnaise wine road, centre for the white wines of Montagny, named after a village 3km W (*see* Wine, page 46). Montagny wines from the Chardonnay grape are still very good value but becoming more popular. You can taste them with snacks and buy them at La Tour Rouge cave in Buxy village centre. Cave de Buxy on the edge of the village is a good place to buy most Burgundy wines, especially Montagny and other Chalonnaise.

MARKET Thursday.

HOTEL

Relais du Montagny, place de la Gare (85.92.04.04): 2-chimney Logis offering Burgundian dishes. ROOMS B–E. MEALS B–E.

CHABLIS
[Yonne]

For its wine, I can forgive Chablis anything, even the new ugly filing cabinet apartments on the fringe and the constant noise of lorries pounding through on the D965 between Auxerre and Tonnerre, but I do wish that it had a bypass.

There are plenty of caves offering *dégustations* (tastings) and it is very wise to take them up on the offer. Chablis wines had almost cornered the good quality Chardonnay market until recently. Americans and then Japanese were bidding so high at auction that it was regarded as a wine for special occasions, the Premiers Crus wines for very special occasions and Grands Crus

St Martin's

only if someone rich was paying. Now South-West France produces quaffable Chardonnay at very reasonable prices, California is producing good Chardonnays and Australia and New Zealand are producing superb wines. So the prices of Chablis have remained stable while other wines have shot up. Ten million bottles are produced each year, and a lot of fake Chablis, too – it is said to be the most faked label in the world. It is worth tasting in Chablis, not only to choose the one you like best, but to find out how much better most of them are than some Chablis we are offered in Britain.

For more about the wines and places to taste, see Wine, pages 55–7. Another producer, Guy Robin, 13 rue Marcelin Berthelot offers visits 'all day, every day' and the Robins are very friendly (tel. 86.42.12.63). They have been *vignerons* for three generations. My own favourite producers Simmonet-Febvre, have been producing wine for more than 150 years. In fact, I have a bottle of their 150th anniversary Premier Cru wine of 1990, a double magnum (four bottles in one). It will do nicely to bring in the new century, if I can wait that long.

The little river Serein runs through the town and there is a nice walk along it under old trees called Promenade du Patis. Alas, the river was very low in the summer of 1991.

The church of St Martin (twelfth century) was started by the canons of St Martin-de-Tours, who brought the relics of their saint when fleeing the Normans. Horse-shoes nailed to the door are ex-voto offerings from pilgrims. One is said to have been left by Joan of Arc.

MARKET Sunday morning.

FESTIVALS Wine Fair, fourth weekend in November.

Feast of St Vincent end January.

HOTELS

Hostellerie des Clos (86.42.10.63): Michel Vignaud was given a Michelin star in 1986 before his hotel opened because of his reputation. Modern cooking if not nouvelle. Old house with a wine bar in an eighteenth-century chapel. Carte prices are very high. ROOMS C–G. MEALS D–G. Shut mid-January–mid-December; Thursday lunch and Wednesday in winter.

Étoile, 4 rue Moulins (86.42.10.50): for long the main hotel of the area. New young owner offers traditional Burgundian dishes. Good-value menus. Most rooms without bathrooms. ROOMS A–C. MEALS A–E. Shut mid–end January; Monday evening, Tuesday in winter.

CHAGNY
[Saône-et-Loire]

A small industrial town on N6 where the Côte d'Or meets the Chalonnaise. It was the headquarters in 1365 of the army of soldiers who had been discharged and had no work. Calling themselves 'les Grandes Compagnies' they laid waste the Burgundy countryside, robbing, killing, raping, burning. To fight them, the great soldier Du Guesclin was ransomed from captivity in England. He did not fight them, instead he signed them up to join him in fighting the Spanish.

For travellers not interested in local industry or commerce, Chagny is known as a good place for a meal – especially at Lameloise Hotel and Restaurant, a Relais et Châteaux hotel in a lovely fifteenth-century Burgundian house. The cooking rates three Michelin stars.

TOURIST INFORMATION 2 rue Halles (shut January, February – 85.87.25.95).

FESTIVAL Wine and Food Fair mid-August.

HOTELS

Lameloise, 36 place d'Armes (85.87.08.85): *see* text. Splendid and very expensive. Book for meals. ROOMS E–G. MEALS G. Shut 18 December–25 January; Thursday lunch, Wednesday.

Hostellerie du Château de Bellecroix, 2km on N6 to Chalon, then a lane (85.87.13.86): in a lovely park. Château of twelfth to fifteenth centuries which belonged to the Knights of Malta. Delightful rooms. Good cooking, regional bias. Pool. ROOMS F–G. MEALS E–F. Shut 20 December–1 February; Wednesday except July, August.

CHAILLY-SUR-ARMANÇON
[Côte d'Or]

Hamlet on D977bis, 6km W of Pouilly-en-Auxois, which has a fine château with attractively decorated Renaissance façade said to be one of the first in Burgundy. It is now a splendid hotel where, when I saw it, they were building a golf course.

HOTEL

Château de Chailly (80.90.30.30): *see* text. Two restaurants. Rooms extremely expensive. Pool. ROOMS G. Meals in Le Rabillon C; in L'Armançon F–G.

CHALON-SUR-SAÔNE
[SAÔNE-ET-LOIRE – *See* Major Towns, pages 73–6]

CHAMBOLLE-MUSIGNY
[CÔTE D'OR]

Not surprising that this village which produces such delicately flavoured wine should have its houses beautifully decorated with flowers and that its two best-known vineyards should be called Les Amoureuses and Les Charmes. It is on the slopes over-looking Clos de Vougeot and it is recorded that in 1110 a parcel of land called Musigny was given to the abbey of Cîteaux, owners of Vougeot. Since 1766 the Vogüé family – diplomats, archaeologists, writers – have been a major force in the development of wines here. It is a photogenic village at the mouth of a gorge down which a stream runs fiercely in spring rain.

CHAPAIZE
[SAÔNE-ET-LOIRE]

Hamlet 19km W of Tournus with a beautiful and remarkable church, in the style of Lombardy. Its tall square belfry tower, 35 metres high and tapering, stands above quite a jumble of irregularly shaped buildings under roofs at different levels. It is beautiful and charming, and was built between the eleventh century and the early thirteenth.

CHARENTAY
[BEAUJOLAIS]

Charentay may sell its wine as Brouilly but its village has a character of its own and some interesting buildings. On a hillside is an old chapel of St Peter where pilgrims once flocked to cure 'fevers'. In Domaine de Combe there is a big nineteenth-century tower like a lighthouse, 35 metres high. It is said to have been built by a mother-in-law so that she could spy on her daughter's husband.

The most interesting building is the decaying Château d'Arginy. Much of it now dates from the sixteenth century, but there is a tall brick tower dating from the twelfth or thirteenth century, which was once one of twenty-two when the castle was a place of splendour owned by the Order of the Knights Templars and was surrounded by deep moats with three drawbridges. In the Tower of the Seven Beatitudes, new knights were initiated into the order with ceremonies still not known. It was also called the Tower of Alchemy.

The Knights Templars Order was formed to fight the 'Infidel' – the Moslems in the Middle East – and to take the Holy City of Jerusalem which, of course, was a Holy City to them, too. Only the younger sons of Europe's aristocratic families could join. But it deteriorated from being a Holy Order to an independent military force, meddling in politics, owning great wealth and huge areas of land, rivalling the Jewish families as 'moneylenders', and held in fear by the peasants around them. They lived in great luxury and were accused of the abduction of women, of occult rites, and of orgies. Then Philip the Fair of France, who wasn't at all fair in his dealings, fell out with the Pope over the taxation of clergy, imprisoned him and replaced him with the French Pope Clement V at Avignon. In 1312 he more or less compelled Clement to abolish the Order of Knights Templars to the great relief of many European peasants. Condemned Templars were burned and Philip appropriated their wealth. Later he did the same to the Jews.

A lot of people in Beaujolais, including Arginy's owners, believe that the Templars' treasure is still hidden there. It is said to be hidden in three chambers, protected by booby traps operated by huge stones, and mostly it is in the form of gold.

LA CHARITÉ-SUR-LOIRE
[NIÈVRE]

The Loire is broad and stately here as it sweeps past this peaceful little town which was once an important river port. From the photogenic hump-backed bridge of the sixteenth century there is a fine view of the town, showing signs of its old glory. It was called Seyr, town of the Sun, until the monks of the eleventh century got such a reputation for kindness to poor travellers and pilgrims that more and more people accepted advice to 'Go to La Charité' and the name gradually changed.

It is difficult to think of it as being in Burgundy, for it seems to be a Loire town. In the argument between the Burgundians and the Armagnacs, who supported Joan of Arc's Charles VII of France in the Hundred Years War, a commander in the service of both the Burgundians and the English, Perrinet Gressard, took the town. Joan of Arc came to besiege it, but failed, probably because Charles did not give her enough troops. Perrinet Gressard kept the town, then sold it back to the French under the Treaty of Arras for a large ransom and a job for himself as Governor.

The church that the charitable monks left behind was called one of the greatest examples of Romanesque architecture in Burgundy. When it was built it was the largest church in France next to Cluny and was called 'Eldest daughter of Cluny'. It is still impressive but in great decay. It had five naves, of which four survive. Cottages stand where the rest of the nave stood. Only one of the two towers survives. It looks as if it has been cut in two.

The oldest and most attractive houses are near the river. On the river bank south of the town is a delightful grass promenade shaded by plane trees.

TOURIST INFORMATION place Ste Croix (86.70.16.12)
MARKET Saturday.

FESTIVALS Prize Poultry Fair, December.

HOTELS

Grand Monarque, 33 quai Clemenceau (86.70.21.73): super site beside the Loire. Good old-style but thoughtful cooking. 9 rooms C–D. MEALS B–F. Shut part February; Friday in winter.
Terminus, 23 ave Gambetta (86.70.09.61): traditional hotel with garden. ROOMS B–C. MEALS A–E. Shut 22 December–22 January; Thursday in winter.

CHAROLLES
[SAÔNE-ET-LOIRE]

A small town in South Burgundy 13km E of Paray-le-Monial, which has given its name to a world-famous breed of beef-cattle, (usually spelt with one 'l' – Charolais – while the area is called Charollais) (*see* pages 2 and 19). Massive and completely white, the cattle are now seen not only all over France, but in many other countries where they are often crossed with local breeds. Although they are the leading French breed for beef, three Normandy dairy cattle breeds surpass them in numbers. The French are quite sure that Charolais beef is the best in the world but the Scots, Canadians and Argentinians disagree! As do some chefs and gastronomes. Glyn Christian, for instance, wrote in his book *Edible France*, 'The appeal is more to the breeder and producer than the eater, for the flavour of the huge amounts of flesh each animal produces is pretty inferior.'

The animals are put out to grass in April, and from then to December are sold at weekly markets or fairs which are well worth seeing. These markets are held at Charolles and nearby Paray-le-Monial, and at St Christophe-en-Brionnais, but the biggest are now held at Sancoins in Cher.

Charolles itself is a delightful town in very green meadow and woodland country. The Arconce and Semence rivers, which meet here, turn and twist like sinuous dancers, so there are thirty bridges in the town. There are also good views from the little park in which the ruins of the castle of the Counts of

Charollais stand. The last Count was Charles de Bourbon-Condé who relieved the boredom of his rustic life by shooting at the tilers who worked on the roofs of houses within range of his castle. He injured or killed several. Being both a Bourbon and a Condé, such powerful families through history, he assumed that the easy-going, 'fun-loving' Louis XV would pardon his little eccentricity. But Louis tired of complaints and told him: 'I have signed a pardon for whoever kills *you* in reprisal.' The main building of the château is now the town hall.

Charolles was known for pottery from 1845, but cattle have rather overshadowed the industry. It still produces finely decorated pieces.

Sixteen kilometres NE by N79, D983 and D7 is the Château of Chaumont – not quite so spectacular as its namesake in the Loire – which has a Renaissance façade but was 'modernized' last century. It was built by Pierre de la Guiche, who negotiated the marriage between Henri II and Catherine de' Medici. His grandson, Grand Master of the Ordnance, finished it in 1584. The Grand Master's daughter Nanette, Duchess of Angoulême, built the huge stables in 1648, a superb 'hotel' for ninety-nine horses – her husband was Commander of the Light Cavalry in France. Only the king could have one hundred horses in his stable, so the hundredth is in stone, carrying in its saddle her father. The château has a grand double staircase leading to the guard room.

TOURIST INFORMATION Ancien Couvent des Clarisses, rue Baudinot (85.24.05.95).

MARKET Wednesday.

FESTIVALS Bull Fair, fourth Wednesday in October. Folklorique, first Saturday, Sunday in August. Chamber Music in July.

HOTELS

Poste, ave Libération (85.24.11.32): very good traditional dishes; several menus. 9 rooms with bathroom, WC. ROOMS C–D. MEALS C–G. Shut mid-November–mid-December; Sunday evening, Monday.

Moderne, ave Gare (85.24.07.02): garden, pool. Cooking balanced between modern and traditional. Logis, 3 chimneys.

ROOMS C–E. MEALS C–F. Shut end December–1 February;
Sunday evening, Monday except summer.

CHASSELAS
[BEAUJOLAIS]

Village SW of Pouilly and Fuissé which produces grapes from
the south-facing walls of the *vignerons'* houses, which are eaten as
a dessert. At the 'other' Pouilly (sur Loire) and in the Savoy and
Alsace, the Chasselas grape is used to make a sweet wine, drunk
young. There is also a Mâcon Chasselas.

Vineyards of Chasselas

CHASTELLUX-SUR-CURE – Château
[YONNE]

The château stands in a truly picturesque setting in the Morvan forest, overlooking a gorge of the river Cure south of Avallon just off D944. You can see it well from the D944 viaduct over the Cure, clinging to a rocky slope. Claude de Beauvoir, Baron of Chastellux, born here in 1386, was the man who, as Marshal to John the Fearless, won the Battle of Cravant in 1423, which gave him and his descendants the right to attend services at Auxerre Cathedral in full armour, with his falcon (*see* Auxerre, pages 60–5).

The waters of the river Cure are dammed just downstream where it meets the Chalaux. The dam is 37 metres high, 330 metres long and is used to generate electricity and even, via the Yonne river, to help control the flow of the Seine.

Alas, the château, which has been in the Chastellux family for one thousand years, is not open to the public.

CHÂTEAU CHINON
[NIÈVRE]

The capital of the Morvan and one of the best bases for the Morvan National Park. Through history, the rocky hill above it, 600 metres high, has been an important strategic site. The Gauls and Romans used it as a defence fort and there are traces of a medieval fortress. Now there is a simple cross and orientation table. Battles and sieges dogged the town through centuries, and the town's motto became 'Petite Ville, Grand Renom' ('Little Town, Great Renown').

You can drive along the side of the hill on a road that circles the town, with rewarding glimpses of the countryside and gorges of the infant Yonne, but the view from the Calvary is the best. To the east is the Yonne valley, west you can sometimes see to the Loire valley, and to the south-east are Mount Preneley – 855 metres (2800 feet) – and Haut-Folin – 901 metres (2950 feet). To the north is the great lake formed by the Pannesière-

Chaumard dam, starting only 10km away. Further NE is Lac des Settons (*see* page 245), a reservoir with a granite dam built last century. You can take boat trips on the reservoir from Easter to 1 November – a pleasant trip, for the lake is surrounded by pretty, deciduous trees, low hills and small beaches. (M. Bosset, tel. 85.52.30.21.)

In Château Chinon are two unusual museums. Musée du Costume in a fine old house in rue du Château has a most interesting collection of regional costumes from the seventeenth to twentieth centuries, a cottage-weaver's workshop and souvenirs of Napoleon III, including his two-cornered hat (like Napoleon I's), and the Empress Eugénie's sleigh. Septennot Museum in the same road shows gifts given to President François Mitterand during his days as president. Mitterand was Château Chinon's mayor when he stood for (and lost) the Presidency in 1974.

The town is becoming more and more industrialized. It rains there about 180 days in a year, but there is enough snow to make Haut-Folin, southward, a ski resort. It's ski-lift is along a forest road reached from D500 or D179.

TOURIST INFORMATION rue Champlain (86.85.06.58).

MARKET Second Monday of each month.

FESTIVALS Fête of the Morvan and Fair, 15 August.

HOTELS

Vieux Morvan, 8 place Gudin (86.85.05.01): superb views. Fine country cooking. Good value. 2-star Logis. ROOMS C–D. MEALS B–E.

Lion d'Or, 10 rue Fossés (86.85.13.56): simpler Logis. ROOMS B–C. MEALS A–D. Shut Sunday evening, Monday.

CHÂTEAUNEUF
[SAÔNE-ET-LOIRE]

Hamlet SE of Semur-en-Brionnais, in the Loire valley, in the SW corner of Burgundy, with a simple country Burgundian Romanesque church and Château de Banchet (part sixteenth

century) in an attractive woodland setting on the river Sornin.
Seven kilometres W of Chauffailles by D8.

Fontaine (85.26.26.87): MEALS B–F. Shut 20 January–20 February; 10–19 June; Tuesday evening, Wednesday.

CHÂTEAUNEUF-EN-AUXOIS
[CÔTE D'OR]

This old fortified market town has only sixty inhabitants, but its
castle once commanded the road from Dijon to Autun and the
country around, and belonged to the powerful Philippe Pot,
Seneschal of Burgundy.

It is a truly imposing fortress of the twelfth century, standing high on rocks surrounded by vineyards, with a moat, massive
walls, great round gateway towers and a drawbridge. The views
are magnificent, especially from a round chamber inside, and it
has been used for films including *Partir, Revenir* by Claude
Lelouche. You can see it from the A6 about 10km SE of the A38
intersection or even from the Burgundy canal there. You can
reach it from the village of Sombernon, W of Dijon, by taking
D977 SW and following the signs.

Built in the twelfth century for his son by the owner of
Chaudenay Castle, which stands in ruins 6km S, it was altered
and enlarged by Philippe Pot in the fifteenth century. Pot was
given it by Philip the Good in 1456 after Catherine de
Châteauneuf, wife of the owner, had murdered her husband by
giving him poisoned cakes. Her crime had been discovered
through the death of a kitchen maid, who had helped herself to
one of the cakes. Catherine was drawn on a hurdle through the
streets of Paris and burned at the stake. The castle was 'the finest
military ruin in Burgundy' when the Comte de Vogüé partly
restored it and gave it to the nation in 1936.

Guided tours of the castle (¾ hour) every day April–
September; shut Tuesday, Wednesday.

An old Châteauneuf superstition says that the first person

you greet in the New Year must be a man or catastrophe will follow. So people hide behind their shutters until a man passes, rush out and wish him best wishes for 365 days.

The church of Vandenesse-en-Auxois (thirteenth–fourteenth century) 2½km W has several stone tombs of Seigneurs of Châteauneuf.

Château de Commarin, with two squat towers of the fourteenth century protecting its lovely seventeenth- to eighteenth-century wings, is in a valley 6km N beside the great Panthier reservoir which supplies the Canal de Bourgogne. It is one of the nicest châteaux in Burgundy. Reached by a long avenue, it has a moat filled with water among birch trees. In the left wing, which you can visit, the 1759 furnishings and décor are still intact in the great room. The picture of Charles X by François Gérard was given to the Marquis de Damas, the owner, by the king. The superb series of heraldic tapestries (fifteenth to sixteenth centuries) in the antechamber belonged to the Veine family, through whom Damas inherited the château. (Open 1 April–1 November, except Tuesday.)

Henri Vincenot, the best-selling novelist (1912–85) who described nineteenth-century peasant life in Burgundy in his book *Le Billebaude* was born in Dijon but lived in Châteauneuf between the world wars. His grandfather was the blacksmith. *Le Billebaude* is an autobiographical novel about hunting in the Morvan, gargantuan Christmas celebrations and other local feasts.

HOTEL

Hostellerie du Château (80.49.22.00): peaceful, good views. Straightforward cooking, regional dishes. ROOMS C–F. MEALS C–F. Shut end November–31 January; Monday evening, Tuesday except midsummer.

CHÂTILLON-EN-BAZOIS
[Nìevre]

Once an important inland waterway port on the Nivernais canal between Decize and the little lakes of Baye, it is on both the canal and the river Aron. It still has boat yards, and a château built in the thirteenth to fourteenth centuries, altered in the eighteenth century. (Open by appointment 86.84.12.15.)

Châtillon is on a stretch of the canal popular for pleasure boating. It is very attractive and has practically no barges any more. You can hire boats at Baye (58110 Bazolles) from Amica Tours (tel. 86.38.90.70). Baye is at the canal's highest point, and there is quite a water staircase down to Châtillon.

TOURIST INFORMATION Mairie (86.84.14.76).

HOTEL

Auberge de la France, 29 rue Charles Duret (86.84.13.10): Logis. ROOMS B–C. MEALS C–E. Shut mid-December–1 February; Sunday evening off season.

CHÂTILLON-SUR-SEINE
[Côte d'Or]

A charming little town through which the young river Seine, little more than a stream, wanders in a double loop, dividing and rejoining. It is joined by the river Douix, which spouts out from under a rock at anything from 600 to 3000 litres a second, making a pleasant pond, but it flows into the Seine within 200 metres. The pool was once believed to be haunted and bread was thrown in at Candlemas.

Sheep are bred on the plateaux around, but Châtillon itself now lives largely from tourists, which is not surprising for it is a nice place to stay for a night or two.

Almost halfway between Dijon and Troyes (on the N71), it has had its share of war troubles. In September 1914 when the Germans were driving the French back, General Joffre,

Châtillon-sur-Seine

Commander-in-Chief of the French Armies, set up head-quarters in the little town and sent out his famous message to all ranks: 'We are about to engage in a battle on which the fate of our country depends and it is important to remind all ranks that the moment has passed for looking to the rear.' The Germans were stopped – the French won a victory on the Marne, where the German army was marched right across the French front and attacked in the flank.

In 1940, the Germans bombed the town with incendiaries and destroyed the centre, but the scars have now healed. Long before that it was an important outpost fort of the Dukes of Burgundy.

In 1814, when Napoleon was hard pressed by Allied troops marching towards Paris, a Napoleonic deputation met Allied representatives (Austrian, Russian, English and Prussian) at Châtillon to discuss peace terms. Napoleon thought the terms too harsh, he fought on, but soon gave in and abdicated at Fontainebleau.

In 1953, on a low hill called Mont Lassois at Vix, 6km N of Châtillon towards the Champagne border, the archaeologist René Joffroy and his team excavated a hill fort and made a most extraordinary discovery. In a burial chamber beneath a barrow 137 feet in diameter they found the body of a woman between thirty and thirty-five lying on the debris of a chariot and surrounded by amber beads, Greek pottery and other artifacts. She was clearly a princess, either Celtic or Gallic, from her bracelet, earrings and other fine jewellery, and especially from her superb golden tiara. Around her were other gold objects, silver and bronze goblets and a huge decorated bronze wine jar with lid made by craftsmen of Lacedemonia Sparta, the Greek province. At 1.8 metres (6 feet) high and weighing 208 kilograms (459 pounds), it holds about 1200 litres. It is decorated with a frieze of Greek armoured chariots and plumed and helmeted soldiers on the march and the two huge handles are of gorgons' heads. It is said to date from around 500BC and to resemble the description given by Herodotus of a vase presented to Croesus, King of Lydia, by the Lacedemonians. No one knows how it got to Gaul. Now it is on show in the Châtillon museum, in a Renaissance mansion called Philandrier, with a round staircase tower. The Princess's diadem is a brilliant copy as the original was stolen. The museum also contains a rare portrait of Napoleon's son, the Duke of Reichstadt, who died aged twenty-one. Napoleonic followers called him Napoleon II. It was presented by Marshal Marmont, Duke of Ragusa, the Napoleonic general who was born and buried in the town. He later backed the Bourbon monarchy. (Open daily except mid-

November–mid-March when it is open Wednesday and weekends.)

Perched on a bluff overlooking the town is the church of St Vorles, built in the eleventh century, much altered, but still with a thirteenth-century belfry, and an original underground chapel where it is said that St Bernard prayed as a child.

Across place Marmont, the central square, are the remains of the Abbey of Notre Dame, scene of great scandals in the seventeenth century. The abbey housed both monks and nuns and the abbess kept her nuns and the young women that were sent to her to be educated happy by holding balls and masques. The young ladies were even allowed to have visits in the convent from their lovers. The abbot, a lay abbot appointed by Richelieu, liked to gamble and eventually lost all the abbey's money so that the townspeople had to pay to keep the whole establishment from starvation! St Bernard would *not* have approved.

The Seine is especially attractive where it runs through Marmont park, past the abbey.

TOURIST INFORMATION place Marmont (80.91.13.19).
MARKET Saturday.
FESTIVALS Agricultural Fairs, end April, September.
'Flea Market' (Brocante) Fair, May.

HOTEL

Côte d'Or, rue Charles Ronot (80.91.13.29): old-style hostelry with modernized rooms. Very good traditional dishes of Burgundy. ROOMS C–G. MEALS B–F.

CHAZAY-D'AZERGUES
[SAÔNE-ET-LOIRE]

A fortified medieval town above the river Azergues south of Villefranche by D70 and D30, the remains of a crenellated triple wall surround a fifteenth-century château and two old churches. The château was the residence of the abbots of Ainay whose abbey brought great prosperity to the little town until the sixteenth century. In the cave of Baboin near the château are frescoes showing the legend of a clown who, in 1364, disguised as a bear, saved the niece of the châtelain of the castle from a fire, married her, and so later became Seigneur.

CHÉNAS
[BEAUJOLAIS]

Near the north of Beaujolais, the oaks (*chênes*) have long since given way to vines and two wines are produced: Moulin-à-Vent, named after the now vaneless old windmill which stands high on the hill on the Chénas–Romanèche-Thorins road; and Chénas, lighter and cheaper, though better when kept three years or so. Moulin-à-Vent is a big, strong, dark Beaujolais wine, rather like a Burgundy. Fruity and tannic when young, it becomes more elegant with age, but not like the flowery light wines now fashionable. Best drunk after three to four years.

The Chénas Co-operative is in a Louis XIV château and it is a good place to taste the difference between Chénas and Moulin-à-Vent (open for tastings Monday–Saturday midday; and Saturday afternoons 1 April–30 October). Some 250 growers belong to the Co-operative and its vaulted cave is the biggest in Beaujolais.

RESTAURANT

Daniel Robin, les Deschamps (85.36.72.67): 'Relais des Crus' – restaurant in the vines. Robin is also a producer. Taste his wines on the garden terrace. MEALS E–G. Shut 15 February–15 March and evenings except Friday, Saturday.

CHIROUBLES
[BEAUJOLAIS]

The wine is light and tasty; very popular with young Parisian Nouvelle Cuisine enthusiasts. Alas, they are drinking it as early as February and March, so you are lucky to find it in summer to go with salad snacks.

The D26 N from Beaujeu through marvellous Beaujolais hill country passes on the left Terrasse des Chiroubles, 750 metres high with one of the most magnificent views in France. Eight kilometres from Beaujeu, a little winding road to the right takes you to Chiroubles village. But first go to the top of the Terrasse, for there the *vignerons* of Chiroubles have a chalet for tasting their wine, which is open every afternoon. In the village, too, is a Maison des Vignerons, where you are invited to taste 'la Tassée de l'Amitié' ('Cup of Friendship').

To plant each vine very high on a rocky hillside, the *vignerons* have had to make individual holes in the granite to plant each vine. All Europe's winegrowers owe a debt to a man from the village, Victor Pulliat (1827–96). When the dread phylloxera had destroyed most of the vines in 1880, Pulliat, a vine scientist, made researches which led to the cure by grafting French slips on to American root stocks. He planted the first of these hybrids. In the village main square, opposite the church and a curious seventeenth-century clock tower, is his statue.

After Easter, Chiroubles holds a Fête des Crus – a wine festival at which the Victor Pulliat cup is given to the Beaujolais judged best by a jury of *négociants* and *vignerons*.

CÎTEAUX – Abbey
[CÔTE D'OR]

Fourteen kilometres E of Nuits-St-Georges. A rival to Cluny Abbey (*see* page 151) but never so influential although St Bernard, who joined in 1113 and later became abbot, made it world famous. Robert, Abbot of Molesme, founded this Order of Cistercians in 1098 as a breakaway from Cluny. They sought a desolate place where they would have no contact with the outside world and chose this spot among the marshes of the Saône. They started a life of privation, hard labour, much prayer and little sleep. The abbey was collapsing in 1113 when Bernard of Fontaine (later St Bernard) joined with thirty-one companions.

He made it the driving force of militant, unbending Christianity. By 1200 the Cistercians controlled one thousand abbeys and priories. Their rivalry with Cluny was almost a religious war. Now, the Cistercian house remembered best by most people in Europe is Clos de Vougeot – because of its part in developing wines in Burgundy! (*See* Wine, page 31) As at Cluny, the monks gave up hard labour, leaving it to hired hands – the hard schedule of prayer was blamed.

In 1790 the abbey was suppressed. All that remains is a ruined library. But in 1898, eight hundred years after the foundation of the abbey, the monks returned. They are Trappists and, I am told, live a very hard life. They produce a good cheese on sale at the abbey gate. Their modern buildings are of little interest.

CLAMECY
[Nièvre]

A fine old town with narrow winding streets, sitting on a spur overlooking the meeting of the Yonne and Beuvron rivers in the NW of the Morvan, it was for long the centre of the Morvan timber trade. In the sixteenth century a timber merchant from Paris, Jean Rouvet, started running logs by water from Burgundy to Paris. When the logs were felled, they were dragged by horses or oxen to the banks of the rivers Cure and Yonne, where they were stacked and given an owner's mark. On a given date the river sluices were opened to give a rush of water and the logs were pushed in. Those from the upper Yonne floated down to Clamecy, where they were stopped by a dam, pulled ashore by men with long hooks and sorted. When the spring floods came in mid-March, the logs were trussed into rafts which were joined to make huge 'trains' of logs. These were loaded with various cargoes and directed down the Yonne into the Seine and on to Paris. I wonder how many innocent fishermen, boat and ferry men were hit and sunk by this formidable armada of rafts? Running logs reached its peak at the beginning of the nineteenth century. In 1861 a large dam was built on Lac des Settons to help the process on the river Cure. But in 1834 the Nivernais canal was opened from Decize on the Loire to the Yonne near Auxerre and barges could get nearer to the logging camps. Then came the railways. For cheapness, the *flottage* lasted a while. The last logging 'train' left Clamecy in 1923; the carbon plant, the largest in France, lasted until 1983.

On the Bethléhem bridge is a statue to the loggers, upstream on a point overlooking the river and canal is a bust dedicated in 1849 to Jean Rouvet. The face may look familiar. The sculptor was David d'Angers and it seems that he was very busy when he got the order – so busy that he sent an old bust that was lying around his workshop. He felt certain that no one in Clamecy would have any idea what Rouvet had looked like. But some people did spot the familiar features – the bust was of Napoleon I. By then, David had been paid.

Across the Pont de Bethléhem lies an area called Judaea. In 1168 Duke William IV of Nevers died of the plague at Acre on a crusade. In his will he asked to be buried at Bethlehem and he bequeathed a property at Clamecy to serve as a refuge for the Bishop of Bethlehem if Palestine fell into the hands of the Moslems. When Jerusalem fell, the Bethlehem bishop did take refuge in Clamecy. Fifty succeeding bishops did the same, ruling their non-existent see of Bethlehem from this little French town. Their little chapel (now gone) was upgraded to a cathedral. In 1801 the see of Bethlehem was abolished by the Pope, although the last bishop refused to resign. The title was revived in 1840, but is now held, for some reason, by a bishop in Valais, Switzerland. In 1927 a modern chapel called Notre Dame de Bethléhem was built on the spot where the old chapel stood.

Clamecy has many old houses, a twelfth-century church and a museum in a mansion which belonged to the Duc de Belle-garde, with a room devoted to the log *flottage*, paintings by Breughel and Vernet, and interesting Art Deco posters of the 1920s and 1930s, including well-known advertisements.

Outside the museum is a bust of Roman Rolland (1866–1944) writer and musical critic who was born here. Rolland won the Nobel Prize for Literature in 1915 with his ten-volume novel *Jean-Christophe*, the hero of which is a musician – the author being a Professor of Music History at the Sorbonne. In World

War I he became unpopular for his writings from Switzerland criticizing the war, and in the 1930s and 1940s he was the mouthpiece of opposition to the Fascists and Nazis. He wrote a play on the French Revolution, and many biographies, including one on Gandhi and two on Beethoven. He was an idealist biographer, always seeking to show the greatness of humanity and hope for the future. He called Clamecy 'the town of beautiful reflections and graceful hills', and there are still peaceful walks on those hillsides.

TOURIST INFORMATION Grand Marché (86.27.02.51).

FESTIVAL Joutes de l'Eau (Water Jousting), July.

HOTEL

Hostellerie la Poste, 9 place Émile-Zola (86.27.01.55): traditional inn with good-value meals. 3-chimney Logis. ROOMS C–D. MEALS B–D.

LA CLAYETTE

[SAÔNE-ET-LOIRE]

To a Burgundian La Clayette means horse-racing. Pronounced 'La Clette', it started as a toll-house on the road from the Mâconnais to the Brionnais, 57km W of Mâcon, then in the thirteenth century a fortress was built. In the fifteenth century it was owned by the Chantemerles family, powerful at the Court of the Dukes of Burgundy, and it was almost certainly their name which was used in the fictional village of Clochemerle, which lives in the heart of every Frenchman. For Gabriel Chevallier (see Writers, page 17), author of *Clochemerle* and its sequels, lived in La Clayette and took his holidays in the wine villages of the Beaujolais.

La Clayette used to breed war horses. Henri IV rode a white charger from La Clayette when he beat the Catholic Leaguers at Ivry in 1590. Now they breed racehorses and show-jumpers, and hold race meetings. Its Tote is said to take more money per head of the population than any in France.

The château standing on a terrace above the fast-flowing

river Genette, which forms a shaded lake, was built to defend
Burgundy against the French king, who held Mâcon. It is magnificent, with its tall slim turrets, machicolated walls and deep
moat rich in carp, and has fooled many people, including eru-
dite travel writers. For this fairy-tale 'fourteenth-century' castle
was built last century on the remains of the original, and it is
superb.

The Château of Drée, 4km N by D193, is *not* a fake. It was
built in 1620 by a man determined to marry his way into wealth
and grand title. A man with a name like Charles de Blanchefort
de Créquy deserved to succeed as a fortune-hunter. He thought
he had done so when he married the daughter of a Constable of
France, de Lesdiguières, but his wife Madeleine died before her
father. So de Lesdiguières's heiress was now Françoise, his legit-
imized child by the daughter of a furrier from Grenoble. Un-
abashed, Créquy married her, but this time he took no chances,
marrying off his son by his first marriage to Madeleine, Françoise's young sister.

La Clayette has an exhibition of old cars in the outbuildings
of the castle, part of a bigger show at Chauffailles, 13km S.

TOURIST INFORMATION place Fossé (afternoons May–
mid-September; all day July, August. 85.28.16.35).

HOTEL
Gare, 38 ave Gare (85.28.01.65): high standard Logis. Pool.
ROOMS C–D. MEALS B–F. Shut Friday evening, Sunday
evening, Monday, September–May; Monday lunch.

CLUNY
[SAÔNE-ET-LOIRE]

Seeing this little medieval town 26km NW of Mâcon today and
the remains of its abbey and church, it is difficult to understand
what power it had, not only in religion, but learning and art and
architecture in what was called the Dark Ages. 'Wherever the
wind blows, the abbey of Cluny holds riches,' was the saying.
'You are the light of the world,' said Pope Urban II in 1098. Its

church, built between 1088 and 1130, was the largest in Christendom for five hundred years, until St Peter's in Rome was built just 9 metres longer. Its abbot was often as powerful as the Pope, and kings sought his advice or his judgement in disputes. Young scholars came to study from all over Europe. Given the right by the Pope to take other abbeys and priories under its wing, it grew until there were six hundred monks at Cluny itself and 10,000 under its authority in its dependencies which spread through France, Italy, Germany, England, Spain, Switzerland and Poland.

All this had started in AD910 when Abbot Berno of Baume was given a farm and a chapel in the valley of the Grosne, a little tributary of the Saône, by Duke William of Aquitaine to start an abbey which was to rid itself of the unworldliness of the medieval monasteries. Monks must renounce the world as poor men, bringing nothing with them but their good will. The Duke journeyed to Rome to put the abbey under the Holy See, to make sure that no bishop or civil authority could interfere with it. It grew in size, power and fame until the wooden buildings had been replaced by a great religious palace, with marble columns brought from afar along rivers for the cloister and the enormous church. Gifts poured in. In 1114 the Emperor Henry II gave to the abbey his coronation sceptre, orb and crown and a great cross of gold. The monks gave up their Benedictine duties of seven hours manual labour a day, which was thereafter done by hired hands or serfs, to devote themselves to intellectual pursuits. Even the great abbot Peter the Venerable expressed the abbey's new dictum: 'It is more noble to set one's hand to the pen than to the plough, to trace divine letters on the page than furrows in the fields. Sow on the page the seed of the Word of God.' So much for the rules of St Benedict himself!

Cluny was at the height of its influence and intellectual glory while St Hugh was abbot (1049–1109), but the monks became too rich and powerful. The abbots had a magnificent mansion in Paris, Hôtel de Cluny, where they spent a lot of time. It is now a museum. Their mansion at Cluny was often used by kings of France. St Bernard may have been a bigot, but he was probably not exaggerating much when he said that the bishops at Cluny 'cannot go four leagues from their house without trailing a retinue of sixty horses. Will the light of Cluny only shine if it is in a candelabrum of gold or silver?'

Cluny was a natural target for the Huguenots in the Wars of Religion. Its abbey and church were ransacked, the library was robbed of its most precious manuscripts, gloriously illuminated in gold, no doubt, but also of great historical importance. At the Revolution, the people of nearby Mâcon were very ardent in their revolutionary fervour. The abbey was suppressed, even the great church was sold to a demolition contractor for its stone. By 1823 nothing remained except what we can see now. Of the church there remains the arms of the two transepts, the big octagonal belfry, Clocher de l'Eau Bénite, which is lovely, and the smaller Clocher de l'Horloge. From the abbey, the cloister is still there, surrounded by eighteenth-century buildings, now used as a technical college. Two great stone stairways with wrought-iron balustrades and a fine sundial are in the cloisters. In the gardens is a centuries-old lime tree called the 'tree of Abelard', who took refuge at Cluny from the zealous attacks of St Bernard just before he died.

Various pieces from the abbey are in the Ochier Museum next door to the town hall, both of which are in the mansion of the abbots which was built at the end of the sixteenth century at the same period as Hôtel de Cluny in Paris.

You can get a good view over the site of the abbey by climbing 120 steps up the Tour des Fromages (open mid-March–mid-October – rest of year afternoons only. Entrance through Tourist Office).

The National Stud (Haras National) near to the abbey was built from stone taken from it. Most of the one hundred stallions are away 'at work' from March to July (guided tours mid-February–late June). There is a display of carriage driving and of the stud's stallions on the last Sunday in August.

Cluny still has some Romanesque houses, and St Marcel church with a three-storey Romanesque belfry topped by a fine fifteenth-century brick spire, 42 metres (138 feet) high.

The old fortifications are now the promenade Fouettin under old lime trees and a terrace with good views over the river Grosne valley from the southern end.

TOURIST INFORMATION rue Mercière (85.59.05.34).

FESTIVALS Grandes Heures concerts, August. Horse display (*see* text) last Sunday in August.

HOTELS

Bourgogne, place l'Abbaye (85.59.00.58): Good choice of menus. Michelin star. ROOMS F. MEALS D–G. Shut mid-December–mid-February; Tuesday (except evening midsummer), Wednesday lunch.

Moderne, 1km SE at Pont de l'Étang (85.59.05.65): tastefully modernized old Burgundian house on banks of Grosne river. Riverside terrace. Pleasant. ROOMS C–D. MEALS C–F. Restaurant shut February; mid–end November; Thursday lunch, Wednesday.

COMMARIN
[CÔTE D'OR – *See* Châteauneuf-en-Auxois, page 140]

CORBIGNY
[NIÈVRE]

Small cattle market town NW of Château Chinon on the Anguison river, at the borders of Morvan and the Nivernais regions, it holds a lot of local fairs. Four kilometres W is Château de Chitry, built in the sixteenth to eighteenth centuries with an Italian gallery (open afternoons 15 June–1 October).

MARKET Friday.

RESTAURANT

Grange aux Loups, 2 rue Briou, crossroads to Avallon and Saulieu (86.20.01.86): excellent value. MEALS B–E. Shut Sunday evening, Monday except July, August.

CORCELLES-EN-BEAUJOLAIS
[BEAUJOLAIS]

Wine-tasting in the grand manner. The restored fifteenth-century fortress Château de Corcelles has a seventeenth-century Grand Cuvier 80 metres long, with Beaujolais Villages AOC wines maturing in huge casks. It is a beautiful sight. The château entrance is surmounted by the arms of the de Ragny family. The inner court has Renaissance galleries. In the chapel are fine woodcarvings.

Corcelles is just outside Vieux Bourg on D9, 4km E of the wine village of Villié-Morgon. The château was built to defend Beaujolais from Burgundy, but made into a more comfortable home in the sixteenth century. It is open for tastings in the afternoons (for mornings, telephone 74.66.00.24).

CORMATIN
[SAÔNE-ET-LOIRE]

Village 13km N of Cluny in the Grosne valley has a magnificently furnished and decorated château well worth visiting. Sculptured or gilded French-style ceilings, Louis XIII period furniture, sumptuous baroque decorations and fine paintings are all so rich and magnificent that they are almost overpowering. The attractive Renaissance château is reflected in the moat and beyond is a charming park with ornamental pools, formal gardens, a maze and a walk along the river bank.

The château was built in 1605–8 for the Governor of Chalon, Antoine du Blé. (Open daily 15 June–1 November; Saturday, Sunday 1 April–15 June.) It belonged later to Pierre Dezoteux, who called himself 'Baron de Cormatin' and took part in the US War of Independence. Later his daughter Nina Dezoteux, wife of Guillaume de Pierreclaux and childhood friend of Lamartine, had an affair with the writer and in 1813 had a son by him, Léon de Pierreclaux. No wonder Lamartine called Cormatin alluring, artistic and delightful.

In 1888 the author Jacques de Lacretelle whose best work, *Les Hauts Ponts*, about the decline of a family, was born in the château. At the turn of the century it was owned by Raoul Gunsbourg, director of the Monte Carlo Opera, who built up the fame of the great singer Caruso. He entertained all the great opera, ballet and stage personalities, including Diaghilev, the composer Fauré and the actress Cécile Sorel, who had her own bedroom at the château.

Cormatin was in a sorry state by 1981, when four enthusiasts bought and restored it and its lovely seventeenth-century gardens.

COSNE-SUR-LOIRE
[Nièvre]

A small industrial town on the east bank of the Loire, N of La Charité and on the border of Burgundy and Loire. Since it was bypassed by the N7 it has become pleasant, and has an interesting museum of shipping on the Loire through the centuries (open afternoons July, August, except Monday, Tuesday). In the eighteenth century it had a famous arsenal, owned by Baron de la Chaussade, making cannons, muskets and sea anchors. Louis XVI decided to buy it in 1781 but he never paid the baron, who died almost penniless. The forges were moved in 1782 to Guérigny in Nièvre.

Two kilometres E at St Père is a former Knights Templars mansion Commanderie de Villemoisin (twelfth to sixteenth century). (Open daily in August; Saturday, Sunday morning in June, July, September.) Four kilometres N is Château La Motte Josserand, medieval fortress remodelled in the seventeenth century (open July, August).

TOURIST INFORMATION place Hôtel-de-Ville
(86.28.11.85).

HOTEL
St Christophe, place Gare (86.28.02.01): good-value meals. ROOMS C. MEALS A–D. Shut first three weeks August; Monday (except hotel), Sunday evening.

LE CREUSOT
[Saône-et-Loire]

The Schneider brothers, forge masters, set themselves up at Le Creusot in 1836 and their company turned the little town into one of the greatest steel and arms towns in the world. They chose it because iron deposits and coal were mined in this area west of Chalon and because of good water connections with the nearby Canal du Centre joining the Saône at Chalon to the Loire at Digoin. The population of the town soon grew tenfold, especially after the company produced steam and marine engines and the power hammer, invented by an employee, and after the introduction of steel in 1867. The Schneiders at Le Creusot rivalled the Krupps at Essen.

In 1924 the old 100-ton power hammer, which now stands symbolically at the southern edge of the town, was replaced by great hydraulic presses. In the heady days after World War II, when steel production was believed to be the magic key to national prosperity all over the world, and Germany, France and Britain were competing to build bigger and better steel works, the Creusot steel empire (Schneider factories) expanded in Le Creusot and set up more factories at Breuil, Torcy and Montchanin. In 1970 it amalgamated with another big steel company to form Creusot-Loire. I can remember Le Creusot in the late sixties with its steel mills going flat out and looking very dark and satanic! The steel bubble had burst by 1984; the world was producing too much. Creusot-Loire looked for new products and industries and they have had great international success with cooking pans and equipment. Most of the old mills have gone, replaced by modern factories. The canal barges have been joined by pleasure boats, and Château La Verrerie, home of the Schneiders and named for the former Queen's Crystal Works which shut in 1833, is now an industrial heritage centre, recalling the former glories of the steel business, and – wait for it – a centre for creativity in the *plastic* arts! (Museum closed Monday, Saturday and Sunday morning.) In a courtyard are two old conical glass-ovens which were converted into a chapel and a theatre. Behind the château is its magnificent park.

The countryside around Le Creusot is delightful away from the mining centres such as Montceau-lès-Mines.

TOURIST INFORMATION 1 rue Maréchal Foch
(85.55.02.46).

MARKETS Tuesday, Thursday, Friday, Saturday.

HOTEL

Petite Verrerie, 4 rue Jules-Guesde (85.55.31.44): next to the Château Verrerie, in the house where the Schneiders put up their guests. Elegant rooms. ROOMS D–E. MEALS B–E.

RESTAURANT

St Laurent, 42 rue Edith Cavell (85.55.31.14): intimate dining room opening on to park. Good chef. Very good value. MEALS B–E.

DECIZE

[NIÈVRE]

A delightful town on a rocky island of the Loire where it is joined by the Aron river and the end of the attractive Nivernais canal where it flows into the Loire Lateral canal. The Nivernais canal was built in stretches between 1784 and 1842 and winds its way 170km between Auxerre and Decize. There is little barge traffic now and it has become a favourite waterway for cruising and watersports. It runs through wild stretches and countryside of exceptional beauty. You can hire boats from several companies in Decize: one is Champvert-Plaisance (86.25.38.43), and Crown-Blue Line have boats at Decize which you can hire in Britain (Hoseasons, Sunway House, Lowestoft, Suffolk NR32 3LT. Tel. 0502 500555). The Water Fête (Fête Nautique) is held in July.

The high rock at Decize was once the site of a château of the Counts of Nevers. The eleventh-century church built on a crypt of the seventh century is dedicated to St Aré, Bishop of Nevers, who asked that when he died his body should be put in a boat which should be pushed into the Loire. It grounded at Decize.

Tourist Information Mairie (86.25.03.23).
Market Friday.
Festivals Lamb Fair, June. Grand Fête, June. Water
Festival, July. Secondhand and Antique Fair end
August.

HOTEL

Grand Hotel du Commerce, 1 place Champ de Foire (86.25.05.31):
simple Logis but comfortable; good value. Terrace opposite the
Loire. Rooms A–E. Meals A–E. Shut mid-December–mid-
January; Saturday evening, Sunday low season.

DIGOIN
[Saône-et-Loire]

Several valleys meet here – Loire, Arconce, Arroux and Bourbince – as well as the Canal du Centre from Saône. Many
tributaries flow into the rivers a few kilometres away. It is right
on the borders of Burgundy and the Loire, so it is quite an
important junction and an angler's paradise. The Pont Canal is
carried across the Loire on an aqueduct of sixteen arches.
Tourist Information 1 rue Guillemont
(85.53.00.81).
Markets Friday, Sunday.

HOTEL

Gare, Restaurant J. P. Mathieu, 79 ave de Gaulle (85.53.03.04):
made its name when the brilliant young Jean-Pierre Billoux
(now in Dijon) cooked there. His successor, too, offers modern
regional dishes. Rooms D. Meals C–G. Shut mid-January–mid-
February; Wednesday except July, August.

DIGOINE – Château
[Saône-et-Loire]

Lovely eighteenth-century mansion 15km NE of Paray-le-Monial, built to replace an old fortress. You can see it from D128 or from the other side of the Canal du Centre from D974. It is in the valley of the Bourbince. The château seems to have two façades: one faces a courtyard and is flanked by two pavilions, the other faces the park and has domed round towers at each end. The pavilion was made into a little theatre where the great Sarah Bernhardt performed. Unfortunately you cannot go inside.

DIJON
[Côte d'Or – see Major Towns, pages 77–86]

DRÉE – Château
[Saône-et-Loire– see La Clayette, page 150]

DRUYES-LES-BELLES-FONTAINES
[Yonne]

The twelfth-century castle of Druyes is a ruin but impressive. It is 33km SW of Auxerre by N151 to Courson-les-Carrières, then the very attractive D104 through Frétoy forest. You pass under a fourteenth-century fortified gateway to reach the castle, of which the outer walls are mainly intact. Near the twelfth-century Romanesque church is the source of the Druyes river in an attractive setting.

ÉPOISSES
[CÔTE D'OR]

To most of us, Époisses is the name of the cheese which the gastronome Brillat-Savarin called the King of Cheeses and which is still compared, not unfavourably, with Brie. But the pleasant village on the plateau of Auxois, 12km W of Semur-en-Auxois, is said to be the oldest continuously fortified place in Burgundy. In AD598 it was a Royal seat – where the degenerate King of the Franks, Thierry II (Theodoric), lived with his odious grandmother Queen Brunhilda (known to the French as 'la reine Brunehaut'). Thrown out of the kingdom of her other grandson, King of Austrasia, Brunhilda took refuge in Burgundy and got power over Thierry by pandering to his depraved tastes. The Irish monk Columban was an outspoken critic of Thierry's debaucheries and when summoned from the monasteries he had founded in the Vosges to bless Thierry's bastards, he refused to eat the banquet prepared in his honour. The dishes mysteriously shattered. Queen Brunhilda was not amused, and Columban had to flee to Switzerland and then Lombardy in Italy where he founded the monastery of Bobbio.

The château, which is outside the village, has four towers. The keep is the gatehouse. The Condé tower of brick and stone is named after the Prince of Condé, who once stayed there. The octagonal tower is from the fourteenth century, the Bourdillon Tower from the tenth century. It is all protected by two heavily fortified lines of ramparts and two moats, now dry. Between them you can walk round the outside of the château. In an outer courtyard is a twelfth-century chapel and a sixteenth-century dovecote; inside the walls is a balustraded terrace, then comes the main courtyard with an iron-topped well. The Guitaut family have owned the château since Guillaume de Guitaut acquired it by marriage in 1661.

Inside the château Renaissance paintings are set into panelling and there are richly painted ceilings, as in the room of Madame de Sévigné, who stayed here with her friends because her own château nearby, Bourbilly (*see* page 122), was damaged during the Revolution. The King's Bedroom is said to have been used by Henri IV. I was glad to see among the portraits in the vestibule Henri IV's friend the Duc d'Épernon. The château's irregularity was caused when Revolutionaries knocked down part of it. (You can walk round the outside any day, but the inside opens only in July, August daily except Tuesday.)

The meadows around Époisses are a sanctuary for pied-red cattle in a world of white Charolais beef. From their milk is produced small cylinder-shaped cheese which is traditionally ripened on straw and washed regularly with white wine and *marc*. Their rind turns orange-red, the softish inside is yellow. In the summer it is creamy and pleasant, but left to mature until November, then kept in ashes over the winter it becomes powerfully savoury, fit to eat with a good Beaune or a Pommard. It has a powerful smell, too! The cheese died out among farmers in World War II and was made only in a factory, but Robert Berthaut, a farmer, and his wife now make it the way of their ancestors and you can buy it at their Fromagerie de la Perrière in place-de-Foire, Époisses.

LA FERTÉ-LOUPIÈRE
[Yonne]

Right up in the NW of Burgundy, 18km SW of Joigny, but if you are going that way do take a detour to see the murals in the church. They were painted in the sixteenth century, covered later with distemper and not revealed again until 1910, which accounts for their good condition. They stretch right along the left wall above the arches, and have the usual warning messages for the late medieval congregation, most of whom could not read. There is the old French story of the three young roistering gallants meeting three walking corpses, who tell them of their own carefree life and that death is always just around the corner. The other story is the Danse Macabre, the dance of death, showing people from all stations of life, from popes and kings, archbishops and courtiers to farmhands and serfs, facing the inevitable death. Death, the great leveller.

Detail from the Dance of Death mural

FIXIN
[CÔTE D'OR]

Fixin, on D122, 11km S of Dijon, is one of only two villages producing Côte de Nuits-Villages wine which is allowed to use its own village name – deservedly, for when kept four to six years Fixin is a lovely and largely underestimated red wine – gutsy but fruity, and its Premier Cru wine will keep ten years. The best Premiers Crus vineyards are Clos du Chapitre and La Perrière.

There are several simple inns offering good-value meals, plus Chez Jeannette, where the *vignerons* eat and which is especially good for food; there are eleven simple rooms.

Fixin is a pleasant little place, almost totally devoted to vineyards and wine. From the village centre take rue Noisot to the car park and follow an avenue of firs to Parc Noisot. Here Claude Noisot, major of the Grenadiers in Napoleon's Army, who followed his idol into captivity in Elba, retired after the defeat at Waterloo. He laid out a park, complete with a replica of the fort of St Helena. Then he approached François Rude, the great sculptor who was equally dedicated to Napoleon and had fled from Paris to Brussels after Waterloo. Noisot wanted a statue of Napoleon. 'I'll do you an Emperor,' said Rude and charged him nothing for it. He produced 'Napoleon Awakening to Immortality', and you can see it at the top of the hill in the park, reached by steps. Napoleon is leaning on a rock, presumably St Helena, dressed in his cloak with the Imperial Eagle on the ground. He is just raising himself on one elbow. A path leads to a belvedere with Noisot's tomb. He is buried standing, with his sabre, facing towards his Emperor.

There are good views of the Saône valley from the belvedere. The park attendant's house has a small museum of Napoleonic souvenirs, and a path from there leads to fountains and one hundred steps, built by Noisot to symbolize the hundred days between Napoleon's escape from Elba and his second abdication after Waterloo. (Park closed on Tuesdays.)

HOTEL

Chez Jeannette (80.52.45.49): *see* text. Traditional inn; good cooking of regional dishes. ROOMS A–C. MEALS B–D. Shut 23 December–25 January; Thursday.

FLAVIGNY-SUR-OZERAIN
[CÔTE D'OR]

In a delightful spot on top of a rock, surrounded by the Ozerain river and two of its tributaries, it stands just east of the D905 and 12km SE of Alise-Ste-Reine (page 98), and it looks so impressive from the little valley road D9 that the writer Châteaubriand compared it to Jerusalem. Perhaps he was influenced by the old Benedictine abbey which had been there since the eighth century, for the lush Burgundy countryside hardly looks Middle-Eastern. The whole town had fallen into disrepair when I first saw it, its lovely old mansions with turrets, spiral staircases and sculptures almost in ruins in its narrow streets. Some had long been used as cattle stables. The abbey buildings housed an anis factory, the aniseed spirit which here flavours little sweets. The recipe was brought by Ursulines who arrived from Langres in the seventeenth century. A background smell of anis still floats across the town. This factory was the main sign of life in the town – the *vignerons* fled after the phylloxera struck in the 1880s and the town refused to allow passage for the Paris–Dijon railway. Then, in the late 1970s, Flavigny was declared a national monument. House restorers moved in, selling the rescued houses as quiet and quaint second-home hideaways to the richer citizens of Dijon, Beaune and Paris. The farmers and workers went, antique dealers and arty-craftsmen moved in. The town looks much better but the atmosphere has changed very radically. Visitors must leave their cars on Esplanade des Remparts – a wise rule.

From the middle ages to the occupation around 1588–9 by the Catholic Leaguers, Flavigny was an important fortified town, which is why the mansions were built. Two gateways are still there – Porte du Bourg, fifteenth century with a statue of the Virgin in a niche, leads into Grande-rue in which is the seventeenth-century mansion Couthier de Souhey with terraced gardens, now occupied by nuns. Porte de Val is flanked by two round towers. Nearby is Maison Lacordaire where, in 1848, Jean-Baptiste Lacordaire, the Dominican preacher, and six companions moved in with as little as one chair each. That, too, is now occupied by nuns.

The thirteenth-century church of St Genest has an interesting statue inside, Angel of the Annunciation, a fine piece of the Burgundian school, found in thirty pieces in the vaults in 1933. It is known locally as the 'Smiling Angel'.

In the crypt of the old abbey church of AD758 is the tomb of St Reine, the Christian girl beheaded for refusing to sleep with the Roman Governor (*see* Alise-Ste-Reine, page 98).

HOTEL
Bon Coin, place des Halles (80.96.21.53): simple inn. Very cheap meals. ROOMS B. MEALS A–C. Shut first half November; 2–30 January.

FLEURIE
[BEAUJOLAIS]

'Easy to say and easy to drink,' is the local feeling about Fleurie wine. It is seductive and charming, and *very* fruity. Most

Frenchmen drink it within eighteen months, locals often keep it three years. And they also drink it at cave temperature of 15°C – not at room temperature. The vineyards are on a long hill topped by a chapel. At the south entrance to the pleasant village is the Cave Co-operative, started in 1927, one of the oldest in Beaujolais, and run for years by a splendid lady, Mademoiselle Marguerite Chabert, known as 'Queen of the Beaujolais'. One of the best wines is called after her, 'Cuvée Président Marguerite', and it is said locally to be elegant, charming and feminine, with a lovely bouquet. For a small sum, you can taste wines there. On special occasions you will be entertained by the local folklorique group, 'La Grappe Fleurie'. Another good place to taste the best wines of Fleurie, chosen by a tasting jury (for a small sum), is the vaulted cellars Caveau de Dégustation des Viticulteurs.

On the first Sunday after All Saints Day (1 November) Fleurie holds an important International Market of Wines of Beaujolais and Burgundy South.

HOTEL

Grands Vins, 1km S by D119E (74.69.81.43): modern hotel in country. No restaurant. ROOMS D–E. Shut 1–9 August; mid-December–mid-January.

RESTAURANT

Auberge du Cep, place Église (74.04.10.77): small village auberge with a deserved Michelin star and prices to match. Book. MEALS F–G. Shut mid-December–10 January, 1–8 August, Monday, Sunday evening, Tuesday lunch.

FLEURIGNY – Château
[YONNE]

Thirteenth-century château surrounded by a moat 15km NE of Sens, with huge round corner towers at the entrance, which leads to a courtyard. The inner walls, patterned in brick and stone and with ground-floor arcades, is Renaissance. The chapel has a good painted coffered ceiling and one room has a series of seventeenth-century painted panels. (Open Saturday and Sunday afternoons mid-April–mid-September; also weekday afternoons except Wednesday in July, August.)

FONTAINE-FRANÇAISE
[CÔTE D'OR]

A very pleasant place in the Vingeanne valley on D960, 36km NE of Dijon. It lies between two lakes. The Rococo château, built for François Billoud de Saint Julien in 1754 on the site of a medieval fortress, is beside one of the lakes. Billoud's wife, Anne-Madeleine, was a lively hostess who entertained the bright spirits of her day. Voltaire, who appreciated her charms, called her a 'philosophical butterfly'. (Open afternoons 1 July–end September except Tuesday, Thursday.)

At Fontaine-Française in 1595, Henri IV had a victory remarkable even for him over the Spaniards and the Catholic League under their commander-in-chief the Duke de Mayenne. With a force of 510 knights, he defeated 15,000 of the enemy. 'This time, I was fighting for my life,' he wrote afterwards. It meant the end of the Catholic League and of a Religious War which had lasted thirty years.

Château Beaumont-sur-Vingeanne (*see* page 117) is 8km S.

FONTENAY ABBEY
[CÔTE D'OR]

This former abbey of the Cistercians is outstandingly interesting because it shows you what a medieval monastery was really like.

It was made into a paper mill after the Revolution, but in 1906 new owners set about restoring it to its original state. A few features, like the church porch, are missing.

The abbey, 5km NE of Montbard, was founded by St Bernard in 1118, one of the first three daughter abbeys of

Cîteaux, and the monks lived under the austere rules of Cistercians. The abbey was expected to be self-sufficient, and it grew very quickly, soon luring three hundred monks. The abbey church was built while St Bernard was still alive, because of the generosity of a Bishop of Norwich who fled here from the wrath of the English Court during the war between King Stephen and Matilda. In Cistercian tradition, the façade disdains ornament. Inside, a night staircase leads to the monks' dormitory so that they could perform their duty of praying from one to two in the morning.

The monks slept in their clothes on the floor on straw mattresses, without heating and covered by one blanket. They attended services for seven hours a day and devoted the rest to work in the gardens or intellectual studies, and copying the Bible or religious manuscripts. Gradually they stopped physical labour because it interfered with their long programme of worship and it was done by lay brothers, who were less educated, and by serfs instead. For the first hundred years of the abbey's existence, the monks lived on two meals a day of bread, made in their own bakery, water and boiled vegetables. No meat or fish was allowed, and even in Clos Vougeot they were not permitted to drink the superb wine they made.

Monks and lay brothers were forbidden to talk except in the chapter house, where they discussed the abbey's business and received daily ôrders. They confessed publicly and were given physical punishment as penance on the spot. There is a big forge worked by a watermill. Only two fires were allowed apart from those in the forge and kitchen, one in the scriptorium, where copying was done and the other in a warming room where the monks could go to warm up when and if they were allowed a few minutes' free time.

The cloisters are superb. But how could they walk round them with their fellow monks without saying a word to each other?

One of the oddities of their meals was that the monks bred trout, which had a gastronomic reputation, and made trout pâté which was always served to kings who visited Burgundy. Yet for those first years the monks were never allowed to taste it. That is true abstinence. The trout was saved for any visitors of importance. The water in their stream and lake was so pure that it was always served on Louis XV's table. After the abbey was sold, the first trout farm in France was started in the old abbey domaines at La Fontaine de l'Orme. It stopped in World War I but was restarted in 1947. The stream flows past the forge and down a waterfall to a pond which holds four thousand fish. The hatchery is downstream towards Marmagne. You can hire a rod at the hatchery and catch your own fish.

The family who bought Fontenay and made it into a paper mill after the Revolution, knocking parts down and building on to it, were the Montgolfiers. Two of the Montgolfier sons, Joseph and Jacques, invented the first balloon to carry human beings in flight, which flew over Paris in 1782. So now you can sometimes see balloons over Fontenay. When the Revolution came, the abbey had long since gone into terminal decline, partly from damage in the Wars of Religion but mostly because kings had appointed commendatory abbots – laymen who just took the abbey's income but very often did not even visit it. This pernicious system, particularly practised under Richelieu, who collected abbeys, almost destroyed the whole monastery system.

FUISSÉ
[BEAUJOLAIS – *see* Pouilly and Fuissé, page 206]

GERMOLLES – Château
[SAÔNE-ET-LOIRE]

Outside a village on D981, 6km N of Givry, is this thirteenth-century fortress which in the fourteenth century Philip the Bold, Duke of Burgundy, made into a house for his wife Margaret of Flanders, an ugly lady whom he had married quickly after she was widowed to gain control of her vast lands. Perhaps he wanted to keep her as far from where he was, in Dijon, as possible. It is recorded that in 1390, in honour of a visit of

Charles VI of France, who was still sane at that time, Margaret topped up her cellar with sixty hogsheads of Givry wine. Then Gabrielle d'Estrées, favourite mistress of Henri IV, stayed there, introduced Henri to Givry wine and the king made it his daily table tipple.

The old Romanesque cellar is vast. The château has an impressive entrance gateway with two round towers and a two-storey chapel. There are staircase-turrets in the main building. (Open July, August except Tuesday.)

GEVREY-CHAMBERTIN
[CÔTE D'OR – *see also* Wine, pages 28–30]

Much more commercialized and tourist-minded than most Côte d'Or wine villages. In 1950 French Railways opened a big marshalling yard here, and there are two important roads, the D122 wine road and the N74 Dijon–Beaune road, passing on its outskirts, thus squeezing most of the town between them, so that it is long and thin.

The old town is grouped round the thirteenth- to fifteenth-century church and the château. The busier part, where the *vignerons* live and have their caves, is called Les Baraques, and N74 runs through it. 'Nono', the greatest creation of the Dijon novelist, poet and historian Gaston Roupnel (1871–1946), lived proudly in Les Baraques, as did Roupnel himself for most of his life.

The village of Gevrey tacked Chambertin on to its name for publicity reasons. There is often a great difference between the wines called Gevrey-Chambertin, excellent as most are, and the nectar called Chambertin, which must come from the old monks' vineyard, Clos de Bèze, or its neighbour, Chambertin itself ('Champ de Bertin'). How *could* Napoleon put water in Chambertin? He was certainly no gastronome or Master of Wine. There are only sixty-nine acres producing Chambertin and 988 acres producing Gevrey-Chambertin.

The tenth-century château, restored by the monks of Cluny

in the thirteenth century, has vaulted cellars inevitably used for maturing wine. (Château open daily except Sundays but by appointment in winter. 80.34.36.13.)

TOURIST INFORMATION place Mairie (May–September, 80.34.38.40).

FESTIVAL Prix du Roi Chambertin, first Friday in September.

HOTELS

Aux Vendanges de Bourgogne, 47 route de Beaune (80.34.30.24): pleasant hotel appreciated by my *The Complete Travellers' France* readers. ROOMS B–D. MEALS A–D. Shut 27 January–10 March; Sunday evening, Monday.

Grands Crus, D122 near church (80.34.34.15): big attractive Burgundian house. Rooms overlooking garden and vineyards. No restaurant. ROOMS D–E. Shut 1 December–25 February.

RESTAURANTS

Rôtisserie du Chambertin (80.34.33.20): made famous by Célestine Menneveau, whose coq au vin and apple tarts were renowned all over France. A new chef copies her recipes successfully. Book. Carte is very pricey. Superb wines. MEALS F–G. Shut first week August; February; Sunday evening, Monday.

Sommellerie (80.34.31.48): a little cheaper than the top restaurants of Gevrey. Good. MEALS D–G. Shut 22–31 December; February; Saturday lunch in winter; Sunday.

GIVRY
[SAÔNE-ET-LOIRE]

One of the few of the small wine towns with some outstanding buildings. Its town hall is in a town gateway of 1771 and its church, a sort of rotunda with domes and half-domes, is regarded by some architects as a masterpiece. It was designed by Emiland Gauthey, who was also the engineer of the Canal du Centre. Germolles Château (page 169) is very near the town.

TOURIST INFORMATION Halle Ronde
(22 June–31 August, 85.44.43.36).

HOTEL

La Halle, place Halle (85.44.32.45): 1-star. ROOMS C. MEALS
A–E. Shut 16–22 September; 12–24 November; Sunday
evening, Monday.

GLEIZÉ
[SAÔNE-ET-LOIRE]

A village west of Villefranche-sur-Saône with the Château de
Vauxrenard, where the Baron de Richemont lived. When Louis
XVI was beheaded at the Revolution in 1793, he left behind a
son aged eight, the Dauphin called Charles. He was kept in
prison after his parents' death and was known as 'le petit prison-
nier du Temple'. His death was reported in 1795 and the
rumour was that he had been poisoned, but all his life, Baron de
Richemont claimed that *he* was Louis XVII. He was not the only
one to make the claim, but was the most plausible. He died in
1853 and is buried in the little village cemetery. (Château open
May–September.)

HAUT-FOLIN
[SAÔNE-ET-LOIRE – *see* Château Chinon, page 138]

IGÉ
[BEAUJOLAIS]

Fourteen kilometres NW of Mâcon, 11km SE of Cluny. Its
imposing thirteenth-century château in woods close to vineyards
is now a Relais et Châteaux hotel. Built by the Counts of Mâcon,
it has two round towers. Its formidable walls are softened by
climbing plants. The countryside around is delightful.

Igé produces a white Mâcon Villages wine which is well above average if not drunk too young, when it can be sulphury like much white Mâcon. The red produced by the Cave Co-operative d'Igé is recommended, too. You need to phone if visiting (85.33.33.65). At le Musée du Vin you can taste on weekends.

HOTEL

Château d'Igé (85.33.33.99): *see* text. ROOMS E–G. MEALS E–G. Hotel shut 15 November–1 March. Restaurant shut 20 December–20 January.

IRANCY
[YONNE]

Leave Auxerre by N6 south, branch left after 4km on to the attractive D956 through St Bris-le-Vineux for 5km, then turn right down a local road to Irancy, a village in the Yonne valley. This is fruit-growing country, especially cherries, and the blossom is superb in late April to early May. Irancy and Coulanges-la-Vineuse produce earthy red wines from Pinot Noir grapes. Irancy is regarded as the best. The local grape César is added, giving the wine rustic fruitiness. It is officially 'Bourgogne Irancy'. St Bris-le-Vineux and Chitry-le-Fort nearby produce Aligoté, white Sauvignon and Bourgogne Blanc.

Irancy was the birthplace of J. G. Soufflot (1713–80), architect of neo-classical buildings, including the Panthéon in Paris.

JOIGNY
[YONNE]

A very attractive and busy little commercial town built on terraces above the river Yonne, 24km NW of Auxerre. Joigny is something of a phoenix. Destroyed by fire in 1530 during the Wars of Religion, it was hit again by the Luftwaffe in 1940 and many of its old houses were destroyed in a terrible gas explosion in 1981. But each time it has been restored, and it is a joy to walk round the narrow, shady streets of the old part of the town among the fine sixteenth-century timbered houses, especially near place St Thibault, where on the corner of rue Montant-au-Palais and rue Gabriel Cortel is a lovely restored house called Rod de Jesse.

Joigny is on the N6, but the A6 motorway runs near to it here so that the traffic is nothing to what it used to be. This was a wine area until the phylloxera disease struck late last century. The only vineyard I know here is the little Côte St Jacques. It was part of a medieval winery. One Lord of Joigny named Leboeuf claimed that the large number of male children conceived in the town was due to the wine! The quaysides are fairly quiet now, though there is still barge traffic on the Yonne. There is a good view of the river and town from just across the six-arched eighteenth-century bridge.

St Thibault church was built from 1490–1529 and is thus a mixture of Gothic and Renaissance. Above its seventeenth-century tower is a very graceful bell-tower. It stands at the top of a hill, truly overlooking the town. Inside is a delightful stone fourteenth-century smiling Virgin. Strange how the Virgin was shown smiling through most of the medieval 'Dark Ages' but became more and more sad and thoughtful about 1400.

The people of Joigny had the happy name of Joviniens. However in 1483 they rebelled against their lord, Count Guy de la Trémoille, attacked and captured the castle and killed the count with mallets used in the vineyards – *mailles* – so they have been called Maillotins ever since. The old town walls have become pleasant boulevards.

The museum, Musée Pasteur Vincent, is devoted to the history of Protestantism in France.

TOURIST INFORMATION quai H. Ragobert
(86.62.11.05).
MARKETS Wednesday, Saturday.
FESTIVALS Fête of St Andre, end July. Melon and
Onion Fair, mid-September.

HOTELS

La Côte St Jacques, 14 faubourg Paris (86.62.09.70): remarkable Relais et Châteaux hotel with 3 Michelin stars. A splendid residence with white stone balustraded balconies by the river, with indoor swimming pool, extremely pricey. *Cheapest* possible meal in 1991 was 300 francs – and that was for weekday lunch only, without wines. Cheapest evening meal was 500 francs, or Menu de Surprise at 750 francs. Michel Lorain and his son do cook uncommonly well. ROOMS G. MEALS G. Shut 2 January– 2 February.

Modern, rue Robert Petit (86.62.16.28): only one Michelin star and a Logis de France, it seems quite cheap after Côte St Jacques. Pool. ROOMS E–F. MEALS E–G. Shut 2–25 February.

Paris-Nice, rond point de la Résistance (86.62.06.72): down-to-earth 1-star, 2-chimney Logis. ROOMS B–C. MEALS B–D. Shut Sunday evening, Monday.

JULIÉNAS
[BEAUJOLAIS – *see also* Wine, page 52]

Juliénas, second of the Beaujolais Cru villages after St Amour coming from the Mâconnais, has some interesting old buildings. The thirteenth-century fortress-château with a round and a square tower, now a big house among the vines, has had its ups and downs through history. In the last century the daughter, then the granddaughter of the owner, the Countess of Ballore, married brothers of the Albon family, and the château became Château d'Albon.

The impressive sixteenth-century Château du Bois de la Salle looks more imposing now. The title 'Salle' meant that it was where the local courts were held. It was maintained for a long time as a fief by the strange Priory of La Salle, founded in 1659. The priory had no monks, just a prior who had to say Mass only eighteen times a year, 'in a low voice', in the Chapel of Notre-Dame-de-Pitié, which was in a Mâcon church, and to give vegetables to the poor on All Souls Day. In return he got the revenues from certain properties, including the château. A family called Charrier more or less cornered the job of prior until the Revolution. Now the Château du Bois de la Salle is the headquarters and wine cave of the Co-opérative des Grands Vins, where you can taste and buy. You pay to taste, and it is best to telephone (74.04.42.91).

The château is worth seeing, but you can taste the same wines in Le Cellier de la Vieille Église, where the Association des Producteurs du Cru Juliénas have set up a tasting cave where you *don't* have to pay. Le Cellier is the old church, deconsecrated (*désaffecté*) and now has coloured frescoes of Bacchus. The three wines you can taste are St Amour (the neighbouring commune, named after the pleasant duties of the Seigneur carried out devotedly by the owners, the Canons of Mâcon Cathedral), Beaujolais Villages and Juliénas itself, the sturdy traditional Beaujolais, not for lovers of lightweight wines. You can see another fine building as you leave the village on D137, the sixteenth- to seventeenth-century Maison de la Dîme. The Dîme was the ecclesiastical tithe (tax) in goods or money which the village priest had to collect from the parishioners. The priest, who was poor, did not get the 'Dîme', it went to the bishop in Mâcon.

HOTEL

Chez La Rose (74.04.41.20): Logis used by *vignerons*. ROOMS B–C. MEALS B–E. Shut end December–early January; Sunday evening, Monday.

KAGYU-LING TIBETAN MONASTERY
[NIÈVRE]

I confess that I have not seen this monastery in the Château du Plaige 18km SE of Luzy (page 180) and 7km N of Toulon-sur-Arroux on D994. I thought that the friend who told me about it was joking until I found it in Michelin. Michelin does *not* make jokes. It is marked on the yellow Michelin map, 69 or 238, 28km SW of Autun. It was founded in 1974 and has a small Tibetan staff of lamas teaching European men and women about

Buddhism and its culture. There is a monument with a conical spire containing two statues of Buddha, and a temple 19.5 metres (64 feet) tall containing a sanctuary with a 7-metre (23-feet) Buddha, a museum and a craft shop. (Tel. 85.79.43.41. Tours in afternoons. Shut Wednesday and third week in March.)

LAROCHEMILLE – Château
[NIÈVRE]

Eighteenth-century château at the south end of the Morvan near the meeting of D192 and D27 on the route from St Honoré-les-Bains to Mont Beuvray. It replaced a feudal fortress and is remarkable for its site dominating the whole Roche valley.

LORMES
[NIÈVRE]

Charming summer resort in lovely countryside at the meeting of Nivernais and Morvan, 26km S of Vézelay by D958 and D42. There are fine views, and delightful roads lead to Lac des Settons and the dams and lakes of Chaumeçon, Pannesière-Chaumard (page 197) and Le Crescent. The area is hilly, crossed by many small rivers and dotted with shallow lakes (*étangs*).

One splendid view is from the top of rue Panorama where there is a modern church, built in Romanesque style, and a cemetery. From the terrace 470 metres high (1542 feet) you can see the thickly wooded hills of the Morvan to the SE and the Nivernais to the SW – its farmlands, villages and little woods.

Two km NW is Mont de la Justice, the same height, with a different but equally superb panorama. It is beside the D42, and a path leads to the viewing table at the top. On fine days you can see Vézelay to the N, and across the Yonne depression W all the way to the hill of Montenoison. South-west you can see to the Bazois and SE as far as the mountain ski resort of Haut-Folin in the Morvan. There is good fishing, canoeing, bathing, walking and horse riding around here.

Perhaps this delightful spot is little known because it does not have enough hotels. It is only 33km from Château Chinon, with the long lake whose beaches were formed by the Pannesière-Chaumard dam on the Yonne in between the two. It still has some old buildings including a mill.

MARKET Thursday.

HOTELS

Perreau, 8 route d'Avallon (86.22.53.21): 2-star, 2-chimney Logis with 14 bedrooms and good-value menus. ROOMS C–D. MEALS B–E. Shut February; Sunday evening, Monday in winter.
At Vauclaix, 8km S, *Poste* (86.22.71.38): on charming roads. Another 2-star, 2-chimney Logis with 10 rooms. ROOMS B–D. MEALS B–E. Shut February; Sunday evening, Monday in winter.

LOUHANS
[SAÔNE-ET-LOIRE]

Almost as much a gourmet's delight as Bourg-en-Bresse (50km S) and very much more attractive. It is in the old plaine de la Bresse – on the banks of the Seille river, 37km SE of Chalon. With Bourg, it is the market centre for Bresse chickens – handsome white birds with blue feet which must roam free on grass and be fed on corn and buckwheat (*see* Food, page 20 for details). When killed the chickens are bathed in milk, and you can identify them by their Appellation Contrôlée tag on the left leg. They cost about three times as much as a lesser bird and have a lot more flavour. Louhans is also a market town for cattle and pigs. Poultry is sold every week at the Monday market.

The charming arcaded Grande Rue is lined with seventeenth- to eighteenth-century houses, and the town has a fourteenth-century church, and an eighteenth-century Hôtel-Dieu with a fine collection of sixteenth-century brown glass flagons and Spanish and Moorish pottery.

There is canoeing on the river.

TOURIST INFORMATION ave du 8 Mai 1945
(85.75.05.02).
MARKET Monday.

FESTIVALS F. Point Gastronomic Exhibition – last
Sunday in November. Chapitre de Confrérie des
Poulardiers de Bresse (Annual dinner of the Bresse
Chicken Producers) end November.

HOTELS

Moulin de Bourgchâteau, rue Guidon (85.75.37.12): large old mill
on the river, built 1778, stopped milling in 1973, became a hotel
in 1986. River flows under the mill in two arches. ROOMS C–D.
MEALS C–F. Shut 23 December–20 January; Sunday evening in
winter; Monday lunch.
Cheval Rouge (85.75.21.42): 2-chimney Logis. ROOMS B–D.
MEALS B–E. Shut 15–25 June; 2–22 January; Sunday evening,
Monday in winter.

LUGNY
[SAÔNE-ET-LOIRE]

On the Mâcon wine trail, it is just E of Bissy-la-Mâconnaise,
20km SW of Tournus by D56, in lovely countryside. Lugny
produces very good white Mâcon and a Mâcon Rouge. It has a
good modern wine co-operative. You can taste wine at the Cave
St Pierre from which there are spectacular views of the vineyards.

The village has a ruined castle and an old church with a
sixteenth-century stone altarpiece of Jesus and the Apostles.

HOTEL

Centre, place Halles (85.33.22.82): comfortable. Country cooking. ROOMS C–D. MEALS A–C. Shut 20 December–20 January;
Sunday evening, Monday in November–end June.

LUZY
[NIÈVRE]

Attractive little medieval town on the river Alène at the south
edge of Morvan. It is 34km SW of Autun by N81 and 22km SE
of St Honoré-les-Bains by D985, a road winding and very beautiful in places.

On the highest point of Luzy at 272 metres (892 feet) still
stands the fourteenth-century tower of the Barons of Luzy, and
in the town hall are seventeenth-century tapestries and interesting doorway paintings. But the main reason people go to stay at
Luzy's three little hotels is to explore the countryside and drive
into the nearby Morvan forest.

HOTEL

Morvan, 73 rue Dr Dollet (86.30.00.66): good country cooking.
ROOMS B–C. MEALS A–D.

MÂCON
[SAÔNE-ET-LOIRE – *see* Major Towns, pages 86–9]

MAGNY-COURS – Motor Racing Circuit
[NIÈVRE]

Twelve km S of Nevers down N7 to Magny-Cours village, then
small road left. It has a school for racing drivers and international races are held here, such as Trophées Federals in July.
The track has facilities for Formula I, and they sometimes hold
the French Grand Prix there. It is possible to get a test drive in a
Renault. Information from Technopole de Magny-Cours (tel.
86.21.20.74). Magny-Cours also has a good golf course (tel.
86.58.18.30).

An African Village Museum is open in the village from 15
April–31 October.

FESTIVALS Motor races, July

HOTEL

Renaissance (86.58.10.40): renowned over France for its cooking, with both classical and modern dishes offered. Comfortable modern rooms. Pricey. ROOMS D–F. MEALS E–G. Shut 24 February–20 March; 4–27 August; Sunday evening, Monday.

MAILLY-LE-CHÂTEAU
[YONNE]

A most pleasant fortified village of five hundred people overlooking the Yonne river and its backwater with the attractive Nivernais canal sweeping in a slow meander alongside. Seen from the shady terrace of the hillside village, it is one of the prettiest river scenes in Burgundy. The fifteenth-century bridge over the river has its own chapel. The terrace view stretches to the distant hills of the Morvan.

The D39 road by the river is attractive, as is the D100 as far as Vincelles, which is 15km north from Mailly on the way to Auxerre. Mailly is 32km NW of Vézelay.

The thirteenth-century St Adrien's church has a belfry ornamented with gargoyles and inside the twelfth-century cemetery chapel are wall paintings showing the life of Christ.

HOTEL

Castel, near church (86.81.43.06): quiet, pleasant, fine cooking; enclosed flower garden, terrace. ROOMS C–D. MEALS B–E. Shut mid-November–mid-March; Wednesday.

MARCIGNY
[SAÔNE-ET-LOIRE]

Fine little town near the Loire and Roanne rivers and close to the SW border of Burgundy, blessedly by-passed by the D982

Digoin–Roanne road. It is only 30km N of the grand temple of gastronomy, the Troisgros restaurant by Roanne station.

Marcigny has old houses, many of which around the church are half-timbered. Here in 1056, St Hugh, the great Abbot of Cluny, and his brother Geoffroy II of Semur started the first Cluny nunnery on their family estates, and made their sister, Ermengarde, the first prioress. A small monastery was started nearby, so that monks were around to supply the *religious* needs of the nuns. That, it seems, is all they supplied, unlike some other priories where degeneracy took over by the fourteenth and fifteenth centuries. In fact, when the nunnery caught alight, it is said that the nuns of Cluny refused to come out or be saved by the monks because it would have meant breaking their vows. Happily and fortuitously there was a bishop around at the time who used his authority by commanding the fire to go out – which it did.

All that remains of the priory is a stout, round windmill tower belonging to the monks. It contains a small local museum with excellent woodwork and some fine old pottery (open afternoons mid-February–late November).

Two km south in the village of St Martin du Lac is Château La Garde which has a most interesting Carriage Museum, showing carriages of the Belles Époques – included are barouches, those elegant four-wheeled coaches with two couples sitting opposite, like those you might see at Ascot and in Royal processions; Berlins, the hooded four-seaters popular in France and England in the eighteenth century, and cabriolets, the light two-wheeled hooded one-horse chaise which gave its name to hooded four-wheeled cars. (Open afternoons Easter–1 November.)

MARKET Monday.

FESTIVAL Famous turkey and goose fair, second Sunday in December.

HOTEL

St Antoine (85.25.11.23): simple Logis. ROOMS A–C. MEALS A–D. Shut March; Friday evening, Saturday lunch except in July, August.

MARSANNAY LA-CÔTE
[CÔTE D'OR]

Though only 8km from Dijon on D122, the wine town of Marsannay is known nationally for its rosé wines (Bourgogne Rosé Marsannay) and locally for its gourmet restaurant, Les Gourmets. Red wines and a little white are also produced.
MARKET Thursday.

RESTAURANT
Les Gourmets, 8 rue du Puits de Têt (80.52.16.32): *see* text. Joel Perreaut's cooking is classic, mixed with his own ideas. Away from Dijon's crowds. MEALS D–G. Shut first 2 weeks August; 7–31 January; Sunday evening, Monday.

MATOUR
[SAÔNE-ET-LOIRE]

Due west of Mâcon by little roads, on the boundaries of Mâconnais and Beaujolais, at the source of the Grosne river, Matour is almost entirely surrounded by mountains, with agricultural land on the lower slopes and woods covering the summits. There are some fine panoramic views from the hills. Montagne de St Cyr, 7km NW by D211 and a local road left, reaches 771 metres (2530 feet). A path leads up the final stretch to a viewing table with views to the Charolles mountains.

Pézanin Arboretum, on the banks of a little lake formed by the Ozolette river, is very attractive and interesting. Take the pretty D987 road NE, then turn left on to the little D95. The arboretum covers 45 acres and has several hundred different species of trees, mostly planted between 1903 and 1923, including exotic varieties from China, Japan, Australia and the Americas.
MARKET (Matour) Thursday.

MERCUREY
[Saône-et-Loire]

Mercurey, 13km NW of Chalon on D978, produces the most
Chalonnais wine and has long been regarded as the 'wine capital'
– in fact, the Côte Chalonnaise wine is often called 'Mercurey
Region' (*see* Wine, pages 43–6). Most of the wine is from the
Pinot Noir grape, which grows well in the region's poor soil,
similar to that of the Côte d'Or.

   The name comes from a Roman temple to Mercury and its
wine charters go back to AD557. The wine is from three communes: Mercurey, Bourgneuf-Val-d'Or and Montaigne. There
are five Premiers Crus and their growers have formed a Confrérie to promote their wines – Confrérie-St-Vincent et des
Disciples de la Chante Flûté de Mercurey. It meets annually to
pick the best wines, which are allowed to carry the 'Chante Flûté'
label. ('Chante Flûté' means a song flowing as softly and sweetly
as a flute.) The Premiers Crus are Clos-du-Roi, Clos-les-Voyens,
Clos-Marcilly, Clos-des-Fourneaux and Clos-des-Montaignes.
Tastings in Caveau du Mercurey (old chapel in vineyards). Open
Saturdays, Sundays, also weekdays in July, August, September.

HOTEL

Hostellerie du Val d'Or on D978 (85.45.13.70): truly Burgundian.
Big country-style rooms. A superb place to eat. True Burgun-
dian dishes and some more original, excellently cooked by Jean-
Claude Cogny. Nice Montagny white wines and best of
Mercurey reds. ROOMS D–E. MEALS D–G. Shut 25 August–
2 September; 15 December–15 January; Tuesday lunch, Monday.

MERRY and MISERY
[Yonne]

Merry-sur-Yonne is a village in a delightful spot on the river. It
is on the beautiful D100 running alongside the river southward
from just below Vincelles. After you have passed the double

hump-backed bridge leading to Mailly-le-Château (page 181), you cross the Nivernais canal and follow the east bank to Merry. Then take the D21 right at Châtel-Censoir to Lucy-sur-Yonne, cross the river and canal and, believe it or not, you come to a village called Misery!

MEURSAULT
[CÔTE D'OR]

I love the village of Meursault, not only for its magnificent white wine but for its atmosphere and charming old buildings. It is such a friendly, unassuming and bright village. Alas, a lot of others like it, too – especially since Château de Meursault was taken over from the Comte de Moucheron by the go-ahead Beaune producers and *négociants* Patriarche. But most visitors are there in midsummer or on the Monday in November after the Beaune sales when the *vignerons* hold their paulée. This party used to be for all the vineyard workers to celebrate the successful *vendange*. It is now one of the three prestigious 'Trois Joyeuses', when the *vignerons* themselves hold a dinner to which each brings two bottles of his best wine, (*see* Wine, pages 38–9).

Despite its tourist attraction, Meursault seems such a genuine village, with its little shops proudly offering their own products like *jambon persillé*, the locals drinking in the inns with the visitors and a travelling shop parking in the square opposite the town hall to sell everything from plastic buckets and washing up bowls and pegs to cheap shirts, braces and safety pins.

Meursault's lovely old houses of the fifteenth and sixteenth centuries are lived in by local people, not sold as weekend hideouts. Many surround the fifteenth-century church with a beautiful Gothic stone spire. Nearby is the strange but pleasant town hall, with a huge square tower, a medieval round tower, and yellow ochre walls topped by steep roofs tiled with greeny and yellow glazed slates in zig-zag design. A true Burgundian building, it was based on a fourteenth-century manor house which was much restored in the eighteenth to nineteenth centuries.

One reason why Meursault has such a delightful old wine village atmosphere is that the N74 misses it by 1½km and the D973 passes it 1½km on the other side. It shares a little road with Puligny-Montrachet. Only 2km from Meursault is Auxey-Duresses on the D973. So three of the best white wines in the world are within 6km of each other.

The château is an elegant, stately home. It was built in the sixteenth century by the Moucheron family on the site of a ruined château from 1337 and it belonged to the Comte de Moucheron until very recently. It still has its dovecote, forge, stables, a fine courtyard, old wine presses in its huge cellars, and in the park are still streams with a fishery and orchards. The cellars are incredible. They stretch under the château itself to the outbuildings, which include an old fermenting house. About 500,000 bottles and 2000 oak casks are stored in the cellars. The Moucherons must have liked their own wines. Some of the cellars were dug out before their time by the monks of Cluny, who had a big estate at Meursault in the twelfth century. The château wines are excellent. (Visits daily, including Sunday, 9.30 a.m.–11.30 a.m.; 2.30 p.m.–5.30 p.m. – highly organized.)

Many of the old houses in the village are from the same time as the château was built, but some are older. In the twelfth century the Duke of Burgundy built a hospital for lepers at the crossroads of what is now N74 and the village street. It was restored in 1931 and its cellars (Caves de l'Hôpital) are now used by Ropiteau Frères, very reputed producers (tastings). Several *vignerons* in the village offer tastings.

HOTELS

Les Arts, 4 place de l'Hôtel-de-Ville (80.21.20.28): old inn where locals drink. Burgundian country meals. Friendly. Good value. ROOMS B–C. MEALS B–E. Shut 8 December–15 January; Tuesday evening, Wednesday lunch.

Le Chevreuil, facing Hôtel-de-Ville (80.21.23.25): La Mère Daugier built up its great reputation for Burgundy cooking long since and she has not been let down. Meals pricey for a village hotel. ROOMS D. MEALS E–F. Shut 23 December–end February.

RESTAURANT

Relais Diligence, at station SE, 2km on D23 (80.21.21.32): country cooking, great choice of menus. MEALS A–E. Shut end November–mid-January; Tuesday evening, Wednesday.

Canal at Montargis

MILLY-LAMARTINE and
MONCEAU CHÂTEAU
[Beaujolais]

A village on a hill above a pretty valley west of Mâcon. The poet Lamartine's name (*see* pages 15–16) was added because his family's old stone house where he lived from the age of seven is here. Here, too, he wrote 'L'Isolement', the first of his *Méditations*. A bust of him stands outside the town hall at the top of the village, from where there is a good view of the vineyards. The twelfth-century church is restored.

Down on the main N79 road to Mâcon 4km away is the golden-brown Château de Monceau, one of Lamartine's favourite homes, where in his middle years he lived as a great vineyard owner. He was no businessman and was swindled by his tenants, and he was also a spendthrift who loved pomp and spent too freely to achieve his political ambitions. It was a sad day when he had to sell Monceau.

MONTBARD
[Côte d'Or]

An old port on the Burgundy canal and a small industrial town, producing steel tubes but known for a man born there – Georges-Louis Leclerc de Buffon (1707–88), the great naturalist who became so famous in his day that the kings and leaders and scientists from Europe and America came to see him or honoured him and sought his friendship. When very young he was passionately interested in science and nature and as a young man travelled around France, Italy, Switzerland and England to study. He inherited a fortune at twenty-five from his mother, who had led a lively life at Court. He was elected as botanist to the Academy of Science at twenty-six, then became Administrator of the Royal Garden (Jardin du Roi in Paris, now Jardin des Plantes). But this great appointment tied him down too much and he disliked Paris so he decided to write a history of nature. The first volumes appeared in 1749. Over twenty-five years he wrote forty-four volumes of his *Histoire Naturelle* (*Natural History*). With Louis Daubenton (1716–1800), another Montbard naturalist, who had followed him at the Royal Garden, he reorganized it and introduced new species and increased the collections in the museum.

As Lord of Montbard, he set up forges which started its industrial tradition and knocked down a keep and most of the rest of the old castle of the Dukes of Burgundy, keeping only two of the ten towers and the walls, inside which he made a garden with different trees, some rare, a wide range of vegetables and flowers. It is now called Buffon Parc and although much altered it is a delightful place to walk, with some paths following the old castle ramparts (shut Monday in winter, Tuesday). You can see Buffon's small pavilion where he worked surrounded by wall paintings of birds, and his laboratory in St Louis Tower. The other remaining tower, Aubespin, is restored, gargoyles and all. It is 40 metres (131 feet) high. By climbing 142 steps you have good views over Montbard, the canal and countryside.

Buffon never liked the castle and after it was pulled down he built himself a fine mansion, which still stands at No. 1 place Buffon. As he got older, he became coarse and very vain. He advised one bright young lawyer that he should read the works of the five great geniuses – 'Newton, Bacon, Leibniz, Montesquieu and me.' He was buried in the vault of a little chapel adjoining the church of St Usse.

In the Beaux Arts Museum is Picasso's portrait of Cézanne among interesting nineteenth- and twentieth-century paintings and sculptures. (Open afternoons April–end October except Tuesday.)

Fontenay Abbey (page 167) is 6km E by D905 and D32 to Marmagne, then by a lane down the valley into the forest.

TOURIST INFORMATION rue Carnot (shut mornings in winter, 80.92.03.75).

MARKETS Tuesday, Friday.

HOTELS

Gare, 10 ave Foch (80.92.02.12): good restaurant 'Gilles Agathy',

excellent wines. ROOMS C–D. MEALS B–E. Shut 20 December–
5 January; restaurant shut Sunday evening, Saturday and Sunday lunch in winter.

At Fain-lès-Montbard, 6km SE on N905, *Château de Malaisy*
(80.89.46.54): lovely seventeenth-century manor, quiet, in park;
pool. ROOMS C–G. MEALS C–G.

MONTRÉAL
[YONNE]

This delightful medieval village rising up a hill above the river
Serein, 12km NE of Avallon, was the 'Mount Royal' of the
dastardly Queen Brunhilda, who died a ghastly death and rated
an opera to tell her story. From 1255 it was the favourite hideaway
of the Capetian Dukes of Burgundy, who threw out the owner.
From Porte d'En-bas, the lowergate with thirteenth-century
arcades, the road passes typically Burgundian fifteenth- to

Wood carving of the brothers Rigolley

sixteenth-century houses, some with towers, to Porte d'En-haut at the hilltop. The gate is bell-tower to the church, founded in 1168, restored last century by Viollet-le-Duc and renowned for its twenty-six carved-oak choir stalls of the sixteenth century. Many interesting scenes are shown, such as the carpenter's shop in Nazareth, and the artists themselves, the famous Rigolley brothers, resting from their carving, seated at a table drinking wine from a pot de Bourgogne. The beautiful English fifteenth-century altarpiece was damaged a little when it was stolen in the Revolution.

From the terrace by the cemetery there are splendid views.

MONT-ST-VINCENT
[Saône-et-Loire]

To mark Midsummer's Eve, a great bonfire is lit at this village 603 metres (1987 feet) up in the Charollais – an old Celtic festival which takes place on the Sunday nearest 24 June. There is a viewing tower up there with a table pointing to the Morvan hills to the NW, the Mâconnais SE, the Charollais highlands to the SW, and north to Creusot and Autun.

The village church, built in the eleventh century, has unusual transverse-barrel vaulting in the nave, interesting to amateurs. The village is in attractive country but is just SE of the old mining town of Montceau-lès-Mines (10km) and Le Creusot, the steel town (28km).

MONTSAUCHE-LÈS-SETTONS
[Nièvre]

Village 650 metres (2133 feet) up at the centre of the Morvan Nature Park, 4km NW of the little resort of Les Settons and Lac des Settons, the big reservoir lake, famous for fishing (*see* page 245). The river Cure runs below Montsauche. The village had to be rebuilt after destruction during fighting in 1944.

HOTELS
see Settons (page 245)

RESTAURANT
Idéal (86.84.51.26): MEALS A–C. Open Easter–end October.

MOREY ST DENIS
[CÔTE D'OR – *see* Wine, pages 29–30]

MORGON
[BEAUJOLAIS – *see* Villié-Morgon, page 268, and Wine, page 53]

MOULINS-ENGILBERT
[NIÈVRE]

Sixteen km SW of Château Chinon, among cattle pastures, it holds cattle markets and is the centre for many hamlets and villages. Old houses, some with turrets, cluster round its Gothic church. Two and a half km SW is the old Benedictine Priory of Commagny with a Romanesque church and fifteenth-century prior's house with tower and belfry.

HOTEL
Bon Laboureur (86.84.20.55): simple Logis, country cooking. ROOMS B–C. MEALS A–D.

RESTAURANT
Cadran (86.84.33.44): good chef, huge choice of regional country dishes; good value. MEALS A–E. Shut Tuesday evening, Wednesday except in summer.

NEVERS
[NIÈVRE – *see* Major Towns, pages 89–93]

NOLAY
[CÔTE-D'OR]

Charming small town 15km NW of Chagny, on the Cosanne, typically Burgundian, with a small covered market, a place to visit for a taste of peaceful old Burgundy. It is known for a talented local family, the Carnots, famous in modern French history.

The Carnot family still own the house in the square named after them, place Carnot, facing a statue called 'Organizer of Victory' which was dedicated to one of them. It all started with Lazare Carnot, born 1753, who became an army engineer and scientist, then joined the Revolution, and became a member of the Legislative Assembly. Given the job of organizing the Revolutionary Armies, he introduced mass conscription, raised fourteen armies, planned the campaigns and munitions for them which resulted in the defeat of the European troops sent to destroy the Revolution. Thus he was called 'Organizer of Victory'. He selected Napoleon for command, but cast the only vote in the Senate against him when he was made Emperor, and when he saw that Napoleon was fighting wars of aggression, Carnot retired. But he rejoined Napoleon during the hundred days between Napoleon's escape from Elba and defeat at Waterloo. When the monarchy returned, he fled to Magdebourg, became a scientist again and died there. In 1889, his body was brought back to France and buried in the Panthéon. He wrote late in his life of the Revolution: 'We thought that it was possible to obtain an unbounded liberty without disorder, a perfect system of equality without factions. We were cruelly undeceived by our experience.' And of Napoleon: 'Few men have exercised a more pernicious influence on the fate of their country as Napoleon, despite his prodigious ability, keen judgement, inflexible character and brave heart.'

His elder son Sadi, who died at thirty-six, was called 'one of science's most original and profound thinkers' and is still known for researches into thermodynamics. His younger brother became Minister of Education but on trying to bring in free and compulsory education for all and to extend secondary education to girls, he was forced to resign. He also resigned his parliamentary seat in protest against Napoleon III making himself Emperor. *His* son, Sadi, became President of the French Republic in 1887 but was assassinated by an anarchist in 1894.

The restored fifteenth-century church of Nolay has a strange stone belfry by Jacquemart – two mechanical figures striking the hours. There are sixteenth- and seventeenth-century houses, some with towers, in the older streets.

Five km NE by D973 is Château La Rochepot (*see* page 213). A walk of 5km N through Tournée valley takes you past Cormot cliffs, well known to climbers. The steepest is called Dame de Paris. Then you reach the village of Vauchignon from where the left fork goes up Cosanne river valley under high rock walls. A steep path on the left through woods leads to a cave where the Cosanne flows most attractively in a waterfall. Another meadow path leads to Cirque du Bout du Monde (World's End), a beauty spot in a natural amphitheatre where a waterfall of fine spray falls 28 metres.

TOURIST INFORMATION Maison des Halles (July, August, 80.21.80.37) or rue St Pierre (80.21.70.96). MARKET Monday.

HOTEL

Chevreuil, place Hôtel-de-Ville (80.21.71.89): comfortable Logis, good cooking. ROOMS C. MEALS A–D. Shut December; Wednesday out of season.

NOYERS
[YONNE]

Pronounced 'Noyaire', Noyers is a delightful tiny town in the wine country between Tonnerre and Avallon. It is well worth

staying in or diverting from the D944, N6, or A6 to see it. The
D86 south of it is pretty. Noyers is built in a bend of the river
Serein. Around it are ramparts and sixteen round towers, and in
its streets and squares are many old half-timbered and gable-
ended houses, as if its defences had kept out time itself. 'Picturesque' in the best sense. Gaston Roupnel, the novelist, described
it as 'background for a historical pageant'. Or a film, perhaps.

In the ramparts are two gates, Porte Peint and Porte Sainte-
Verrotte, which has a statue of the Virgin in a niche in the arch.
Each year on 15 August (Feast of the Assumption) local *vignerons*

Noyers

used to put a bunch of grapes in the Virgin's hand. The grapes, *verrots*, were still green – hence the name. There is another story behind the rue Franche. It was called Franche (free) because the residents were exempt from manorial taxes. The local story is that during a depression the townspeople appealed for tax relief and the Countess of Noyers pleaded their cause with her husband. The Count said that he would exempt the houses as far down the street as she could throw a bowl, so long as she performed naked. Like Lady Godiva, she stripped – but there is no suggestion that the men of Noyers were as coy as the men of Coventry.

Wooden Renaissance houses and others with arcades line the little place de l'Hôtel-de-Ville, with its seventeenth-century town hall and there are more round Marché-au-Blé and other little squares, old cobbled streets and narrow passages. You will notice that many houses have front doors reached by flights of stairs. The little Serein may look quiet enough but has flooded the town in winters past.

Le Petit Train de l'Yonne runs between Noyers and Avallon on Sundays (1 May–30 September) from 3 p.m. until 5.30 p.m. every quarter of an hour, taking you on an old line, partly through the Serein valley.

HOTEL

Pail, at A6 Exit Nitry (86.33.64.33): no restaurant. ROOMS C–D.

NUITS-ST-GEORGES
[CÔTE D'OR]

Not a pretty town but attractive for its friendliness, its alive atmosphere and its superb wine. A place to sit outside a café or eat a hearty meal of simple Burgundian country dishes. It has a huge austere Romanesque thirteenth-century church, St Symphorien, a modern church Notre Dame with stained glass by J. J. Borghetto, and a seventeenth-century belfry of the former town hall. As a wine commercial centre, it is second to Beaune. A good place to eat at *moderate prices*.

The Dufouleur family have been *vignerons* in Nuits since the sixteenth century and have marketed their own wines since 1848. Xavier Dufouleur still produces traditional wine reaching its best in ten to twenty years. (His tasting cave is at 17 rue Thurot, open 8.30 a.m.–12 noon, 2 p.m.–6 p.m.) Henri Remoriquet's family were vineyard workers who bought a few parcels of vines in 1892. He now produces not only wines respected in the trade for taste and flavour but has also a vineyard in the Hautes Côtes de Nuits area, the hills south of Nuits where vineyards had collapsed until a recent revival. Wines must pass a test to use the name. His tasting cave is at 25 rue Charmoise (Monday–Friday 8 a.m.–7 p.m.).

TOURIST INFORMATION rue Sonays (80.61.22.47).

MARKETS Tuesday, Friday.

FESTIVALS Hospice Wine Sales, two Sundays before Easter.

HOTELS

Côte d'Or, 37 rue Thurot (80.61.06.10): immoderate prices. I knew it as a Logis de France. Now it has a Michelin star and more modern cooking. Six rooms. ROOMS D–F. MEALS D–G. Shut February; Thursday lunch, Wednesday.

Cultivateurs, 12 rue Gén. de Gaulle (80.61.10.41): simple rooms. Good-value cheap meals of Burgundy dishes, well cooked. I eat here. So do locals. ROOMS B–C. MEALS A–C. Shut 5 December–15 January; Sunday.

Hostellerie Gentilhommière, 1.5km on D25 route Meuilley (80.61.12.06): big sixteenth-century hunting lodge in a park, bedrooms in annexe. Cooking improved, now very good. Regional. ROOMS E. MEALS D–F. Shut end December–end February. Restaurant shut Tuesday lunch, Monday.

PANNESIÈRE-CHAUMARD – Barrage
[NIÈVRE]

This huge reservoir 8km N of Château Chinon, 7½km long, makes a beautiful lake among wooded hills of the Morvan. It was made by damming the Yonne river. The surrounding roads are all attractive and you can drive right over the top of the great dam, which is 340 metres long and 50 metres high, with many arches in the centre and twelve supporting buttresses from the gorge. It controls the flow of water in the Seine basin and downstream is a hydro-electric plant. A second control dam 220 metres long near D944 allows water from the electric turbines to be returned to the Yonne, finally supplying the Nivernais canal.

PARAY-LE-MONIAL
[SAÔNE-ET-LOIRE]

On the river Bourbince and Canal du Centre, midway between Mâcon and Moulins (68km each way), Paray is almost a 'Holy City', so many religious communities have been established there. For it was the place where the worship of the Sacred Heart started around 1673 when a nun in the Convent of the Visitation claimed to receive visits from Christ in a little chapel. With the help of her confessor she revealed Christ's message: 'Here is this heart which so loved mankind.' She was beatified in 1873 when a huge pilgrimage was organized in Paray, with 30,000 people attending a ceremony to dedicate France to the Sacred Heart. At the same time the local church of Our Lady, built by St Hugh of Cluny in 1109, was made a basilica, and a national subscription was started to build the Sacré Coeur (Sacred Heart) in Montmartre in Paris. It was all done to counter divine displeasure, as shown by France's defeat in the Franco-Prussian War – or perhaps to take the people's mind off this humiliation.

Since 1873, a pilgrimage to Paray has taken place yearly in May on the Friday after Corpus Christi Sunday. In 1920 Sister Marguerite-Marie was made a saint. She had been an unusual girl – from the age of four the very sight of a male person offended her, and she suffered from a number of psycho-somatic illnesses which came and went. Her fellow nuns believed that her visitations were delusions. The little chapel where she claimed to receive them and where her body is preserved in a

Basilica of the Sacred Heart

silver and gilt shrine is called Chapel of the Visitation by some, Sanctuary of the Apparitions by others. Souvenirs of the saint and a reconstruction of her cell are in the Chamber of Relics in an old house (open April–late October). The pilgrimage services take place in the big park called Parc des Chapelains. Here there is a diorama (early April–late October).

The pale golden stone Basilica is lovely. It stands on the banks of the river Bourbince and you can see it well from the nearest bridge. It is said to be a small version of what the great abbey at Cluny looked like until it was almost totally destroyed in the Revolution. At the west end are two very tall square towers with spires and an even higher octagonal tower over the transept. From inside the great height of the nave is almost truly breathtaking. It soars to 22 metres (72 feet).

Even the museum in Paray (Musée Hiéron) has a religious theme, but is blessedly devoid of plaster saints, its masterpiece being a tympanum which came from above the door of the old priory of Anzy-le-Duc.

The one great secular building is the Renaissance town hall, with a fine, rich façade decorated with medallion heads of

French kings. It was the home of a rich draper, built in 1525. Opposite is the massive, domed Tour St Nicolas, bell-tower of a sixteenth-century church now gone.

Paray has other strings to its bow. Its factories produce building materials and it is the economic centre of this area. Its Musée de Faïence has two thousand pieces of pottery from 1836 to the present day.

Paray has a Brotherhood of the Free Cacous. Cacous is a milk pudding containing stoned local cherries. The nickname is given to the people of Paray, and they all claim an imaginary ancestor Jean-Marie Cacou, a much jollier fellow than their saint.

TOURIST INFORMATION ave Jean-Paul II (85.81.10.92).

FESTIVALS Sacred Heart Pilgrimage – May/June, Friday after Corpus Christi Sunday. Fête de Magnificat, celebrating the Arts 8–12 July (artists, dancers, musicians, actors, singers and sculptors take part). Sessions of Renewal, July–August. Fête de Ste Marguerite-Marie mid-October.

HOTELS

Vendanges de Bourgogne, 5 rue Denis-Papin (85.81.13.43): classic, simple hotel; Burgundian meals (coq au Beaujolais) are good value. ROOMS B–D. MEALS A–E. Shut Sunday evening in winter.

Trois Pigeons, 2 rue Dargaud (85.81.03.77): near Basilica. Bedrooms vary, so look first. Range of menus. ROOMS A–D. MEALS B–F. Open 1 March–1 December.

Prieuré du Coeur de Jésus, 8 ave Jean-Paul II (85.88.83.17): new, between river bank and parc des Chapelains. Simple modern comfort. ROOMS D. MEALS A–E. Shut 1 December–1 March.

RESTAURANT

Poste, at Poisson 8km S by D34 (85.81.10.72): in tiny village; best restaurant around here. MEALS B–F. Shut February; Monday evening, Tuesday.

PERNAND-VERGELESSE
[CÔTE D'OR]

This attractive wine village NW of Aloxe (Wine, page 35) has built a theatrical tradition in recent times. Jacques Copeau, director of the Vieux Colombier Theatre in Paris, producer at La Comédie Française, co-founder in 1908 of Nouvelle Revue, and a man who had a profound influence on French dramatic art, decided in 1925, when he was forty-six, that the French theatre needed to spread way beyond Paris and clear away its cobwebs. So he and his close associates moved to this village in Burgundy and those of his troupe who could not find a place to lodge moved into Aloxe-Corton. They were an international group, some rather strange: there was a Dutchman, a white Russian called Popov, two Americans who climbed the outside staircase of their Burgundian house astride a donkey, and assorted French stage staff, actors and actresses. The big house where Copeau lived is still owned by his family and contains mementoes.

New houses fit into the old village, which is one of the most attractive in Burgundy. Built on the side of a hill, with old houses, alleyways, lanes, and two old *lavoirs* fed by La Mère Fontaine – where the women did their washing before the washing machine was invented and passed around news before the radio took over – the whole village is surrounded by vineyards and woods, as if in a world of its own. Yet it is only 7km north of Beaune. Pictures of it are used often for books and posters, and many artists paint it.

PIERRECLOS
[BEAUJOLAIS]

On the trail of the poet Lamartine, 2km W of Bussières and just SW of Milly-Lamartine (page 188). It was the home of the girl called Laurence in his love story *Jocelyn*, based on the true romance of his friend Father Dumont, Curate of Bussières, and

Mademoiselle de Milly, daughter of the owner of Pierreclos. Unfortunately it is not open to the public. It looks splendid in its romantic setting and is very old but became a house in the seventeenth century when additions were made within its fortifications.

Lamartine used to visit Pierreclos and was very fond of the Comte de Pierreclos and his whole family. In fact, he was so fond of the Count's relations who lived at Château Cormatin, Antoine de Pierreclos and his notoriously bedworthy and willing wife Nina, that he had a son by Nina, which her husband acknowledged as being Lamartine's. The poet was very fond of him and greatly distressed when he died at the age of twenty-eight. It was Nina's sister-in-law, Marguerite de Pierreclos, Mademoiselle de Milly, who fell in love with the curate Father Dumont and had a baby by him, which was brought up in Lyon. She later married a banker.

PIERRE-DE-BRESSE
[SAÔNE-ET-LOIRE]

Only part of Bresse is in Burgundy and that part tends to be neglected by travellers. East of the Saône to the Jura, it is mostly maize country, grown on a big plain broken by woods and little lakes. It is part of the Bresse chicken country, too. Louhans to the south is the centre.

Pierre-de-Bresse, a pleasant little town south of the Doubs river, 34km N of Louhans and 45km SE of Beaune, is on the plain, with lakes, rivers and streams all around it. It grew around a seventeenth-century château of limestone bricks in a deer park. The château towers have slated dome roofs topped by bell-towers, and its centre has semi-circular arches supporting a balcony. A bridge crossing the moat leads to a courtyard. Exhibitions are held in part of it (open afternoons Easter–1 November). Terrans Château, 3km W by D73, built in 1765, is unexciting and not open to the public.

MARKET Monday.

HOTEL
Poste, place du Château (85.76.24.47): simple village inn. Rooms B–C. Meals B–D. Shut January. Restaurant shut Monday evening, Tuesday.

PIERRE PERTHUIS
[Yonne]

Delicious spot, 6km S of Vézelay with a hamlet around the ruins of a twelfth-century feudal castle looking down on a narrow gorge through which the river Cure hurries over rocks. The gorge is crossed by a modern single-arched bridge of 33 metres (108 feet) span, from which you can see the Roche Percée, a rock forming a natural arch, and along the gorge to Vézelay in the distance. Further along is an eighteenth-century hump-backed bridge.

The fortress was dismantled after the Wars of Religion. Vauban, the great military engineer who was born at St Léger-Vauban to the east, was Lord of the Manor of Pierre Perthuis and nearby Bazoches and may have built the old stone bridge.

PIERRE-QUI-VIRE – Abbey
[Yonne]

I should like to visit this wild spot in the Morvan on Christmas Eve. Then, they say, the huge rock of granite standing on another, the Rocking Stone (Pierre Qui Vire), rotates unaided. It is so remote that I do not think many people go there to find out, for although you are invited to join the monks in their chapel services, theirs is a Closed Order, cut off from the world. Strange if the rock does choose Christmas Eve for its gyrations. Like Stonehenge it is a Druidic monument. You can rock it by hand if you push hard enough.

The abbey is 10km E of Quarré-les-Tombes (page 211) by the zig-zagging D55 to St Léger-Vauban, then a right turn. It is in the depths of the St Léger forest, on the banks of the river

Cousin (called Trinquelin here) below granite rocks – one of the loneliest spots in the Morvan. The abbey was not founded until 1850 and building went on until 1953. There are around one hundred monks there and men and women visitors do go for a temporary retreat from the overpowering world outside, called 'a time of reflection'. Father Muard founded it. Born at Sens in 1809, he became a foreign missionary, then started this abbey with the aid of the Chastellux (de Beauvoir) family. You cannot look around but at the entrance is an exhibition and an audio-visual presentation of the life and work of the monks. As well as attending four services a day and five on Sundays, they *do* work. They research in art and architecture, and print and publish the delightful Zodiac books on those subjects. They also make and sell a lovely cream cheese, made from cows' milk, either eaten fresh or matured on straw, when it is strong in taste and smell. A version with herbs is called Boulette de la Pierre-Qui-Vire or Boules des Moines (Balls of the Monks).

The exhibition is shut in January (when the Morvan weather can be rugged, anyway). Mass is at 9.15 a.m. weekdays, 10 a.m. on Sundays.

POMMARD
[Côte d'Or – *see* Wine, page 39]

PONTIGNY
[Yonne]

The abbey of Pontigny, on the river Serein 11km NE of Auxerre, has seen some remarkable times. Founded in 1114 by twelve monks and an abbot from the great austere abbey of Cîteaux, it became in the middle ages a bolt-hole for English bishops and archbishops fleeing the wrath of English kings during the fight for power between the Crown and the Catholic Church. Thomas à Becket, Archbishop of Canterbury, came there in 1164 for two years when wandering France to escape the wrath of Henry II, only to be murdered on his return to England through a misunderstanding between the king and his knights. Stephen Langton was appointed Archbishop of Canterbury by Pope Innocent III, an old friend of his from Paris University, in 1207 but King John of England refused to accept him and he lived at Pontigny until 1213, when he was allowed to take up the position. He supported the English barons against the king and was the first witness on the Magna Carta document. Then Edmund Rich of Abingdon, appointed by the Pope to preach the Sixth Crusade in England, became Archbishop of Canterbury in 1234 but joined the opposition to King Henry III, even threatening him with excommunication from the Church. He gave up the struggle in 1240 and retired to Pontigny. Made a saint (St Edmé) soon after his death, he is still venerated throughout the Auxerre region. Miracles have been attributed to his relics.

The monks were thrown out of the abbey during the Revolution and much of the stone was used for building nearby villages. Most of the church was saved. The Archbishop of Sens bought it in 1840 and gave it to the Missionary Fathers of Champagne (founded by Father Muard of Pierre-Qui-Vire) to rebuild. The fathers were expelled under the anti-clerical laws of 1905 and the philosopher Paul Desjardins bought the abbey ruins and church at auction. He used it for 'secular retreats', bringing together great scholars to discuss art and literature. Until the outbreak of World War II, these meetings, called 'Decades', were held at frequent intervals. Such men as André Gide, T. S. Eliot, François Mauriac, Thomas Mann and Edmund Gosse took part. They stopped when Desjardins died in 1940.

The abbey church is truly beautiful, a delightful low Gothic building almost as big as Notre Dame in Paris. Inside is austere, with little decoration, as laid down by St Bernard for the Cistercian Order. There was a wooden shrine to St Edmund at the end of the choir but it was replaced by a more elaborate shrine in the eighteenth century and is now in a side chapel.

In the village is a fine thirteenth-century bridge. It was said that on it three bishops (Sens, Auxerre and Langres), three counts (of Auxerre, Champagne and Tonnerre) and an abbot (of Pontigny itself) could dine together, while each remained on his own land. But it was the Count of Champagne who proved the best protector, for in 1150 he gave the monks the money to expand the abbey.

POUGES-LES-EAUX
[Nièvre]

On the N7 NW of Nevers near the Loire river, it is in a very pleasant position in a shady valley below Mont Givre. Pouges was a health spa until quite recently, and it still has parks with beautiful old trees. The park on Mont Givre, aptly called Belle-vue, has a fine wide view from its terrace over the Loire valley and countryside. Good walks and various entertainments and sports. A retreat from Nevers but near enough to explore the big town.

TOURIST INFORMATION ave Paris (June–September, 86.58.71.15).

HOTEL

Paradou, 6 ave Paris (86.68.55.50): away from N7, in its own quiet park. Pleasant dishes. ROOMS C. MEALS B–F. Shut mid-January–mid-February; Wednesday.

POUILLY and FUISSÉ
[Saône-et-Loire]

Not everyone realizes that these are separate Mâconnais villages. We just think of the great dry white wine made from Chardon-nay, Pouilly-Fuissé (*see* Wine, page 48). In fact, the wine is also produced in Solutré, Vergisson and Chaintré. Pouilly likes to think that its wines are just a *little* better than the others. Four million bottles of Pouilly-Fuissé are produced yearly, usually too few, hence the high prices. Pouilly also gives its name to two other wines: Pouilly-Loché, same style wine from the Loché commune, not quite so good as Pouilly-Fuissé but cheaper,

The rock at Solutré

though not much of it is produced and most of it is drunk on the spot or by French who give regular orders; and Pouilly-Vinzelles from Vinzelles commune, better known than Loché and slightly pricier.

Fuissé is the most attractive of the villages – typical of a successful *vigneron* village. Solutré is the most interesting. Here, rising out of the vineyards, is the sinister great Solutré rock, under which men lived in the Upper Palaeolithic age (15000–12000BC). No skeletons of these people have been found here, only remains of earlier and later people. But among their tools are eyed needles, showing that they were making clothes. They used flaked stones for most purposes. In 1866 excavations unearthed a huge heath (Cros du Charnier) containing the bones of about 100,000 horses, enough to have fed generations. A gentle slope leads up to the clifftop. It is believed that terrified wild horses were driven up there by noise, sticks and fires until they ran and plunged over the cliff to their death. A nightmare scene indeed. But not so bad, perhaps, as deliberately keeping calves in the dark in a crate too small to move with no bedding, just to make their flesh whiter and softer for the table, which, apart from Britain, is still done legally all over Western Europe.

A Route des Vins is marked round the villages.

HOTELS

Solutré – *Relais de Solutré* (85.35.80.81): attractive inn; restaurant around wood-burning stove. Rooms in annexe. Views over Pouilly, Roche de Solutré and Beaujolais hills. ROOMS B–D. MEALS B–E. Shut January.

Fuissé – *Vigne Blanche* (85.35.60.50): 2-star village inn. ROOMS B–D. MEALS B–E. Shut February.

RESTAURANT

Fuissé – *Pouilly-Fuissé* (85.35.60.68): MEALS A–E. Shut mid-January–mid-February; first week August.

POUILLY-EN-AUXOIS
[CÔTE D'OR]

Not a very exciting town except for inland waterways sailors. Here the Burgundy canal goes through a 3300-metre (2-mile) long tunnel. A towing chain anchored at the bottom of the canal draws boats and barges through it. It is, too, the meeting place of motorways – the A38 to Dijon joins the A6 to Beaune.

Halfway up a hill, by a cemetery with an old stone open

pulpit, is a fourteenth-century church which used to draw pilgrims to revere an ancient statue called Notre-Dame-Trouvée (Our Lady Discovered) because of the 'miraculous' way it was found.

POUILLY-SUR-LOIRE
[NIÈVRE]

On the Loire 13km N of La Charité-sur-Loire, this Pouilly produces the delicious Pouilly-Fumé 'smoky' dry white wine from the Sauvignon grape, which tastes like a Loire wine, is called a Loire wine, but is made in Burgundy. Across the river just north is Sancerre, actually in Loire, and producing a very similar wine – but don't say that to the people of either little town as each thinks its own wine to be superior. Now that the N7 main road by-passes it, Pouilly can get on with its serious business of making Fumé and the lesser but quaffable dry white called Pouilly-sur-Loire, made from the Chasselas grape. You can taste them at Caves de Pouilly-sur-Loire, a co-operative, opposite the Relais Fleuri at the south entrance of the village (Monday–Saturday 8 a.m.–12 noon, 2 p.m.–6 p.m.) or at the two Blondelet domaines 250 metres past Relais Fleuri (phone if possible, 86.39.13.83, English spoken – 8 a.m.–12.15 p.m., 1.30 p.m.–7.30 p.m.). They produce one of the best Fumé wines. My favourite is produced by Guy Saget at Caves St Vincent in the village centre (open 8 a.m.–12 p.m., 2 p.m.–6 p.m.).

TOURIST INFORMATION Mairie (July, August 86.39.12.55).

MARKET Friday.

FESTIVALS Wine Fair, mid-August.

HOTELS

Relais Fleuri, 42 ave Tuilerie (86.39.12.99): delightful old village inn. Jean-Claude Astruc's good-value regional meals are part of the local scene. He is also a Pouilly wine expert. Flower garden with river views. ROOMS C. MEALS C–E. Shut 15 January–15 February; Wednesday evening, Thursday in winter.

Bouteille d'Or, route Paris (86.39.13.84): classic small-town hotel with reliable food. ROOMS C. MEALS B–F. Shut 10 January–25 February; Sunday evening, Monday except summer.

POURRAIN
[YONNE]

Village 10km E of Toucy on D965 to Auxerre has a surprisingly interesting World War II museum, with American, British and German exhibits including vehicles, arms and medals, an aircraft cockpit, parachutes and German Army and Air Force uniforms. (Open daily.)

PRÉCY-SOUS-THIL
[CÔTE D'OR]

This beauty spot in the Serein valley at the foot of Thil mountain, 16km N of Saulieu on D980, was once the centre of an iron-ore industry with eighty ironworks in the area. Long before, it was an important fortified village of the Barons of Thil who built the castle between the ninth and twelfth centuries. The keep, built in the fourteenth century, was called 'l'espionne de l'Auxois' ('the spy of Auxois') by its builder, John II of Thil, Constable of Burgundy. You can still see for about 50km (31 miles) around it. An avenue of limes leads to its outer walls and the old collegiate church which John also built in 1340.

PULIGNY-MONTRACHET,
CHASSAGNE-MONTRACHET
[CÔTE D'OR – *see also* Wine, pages 41–2]

The two villages are divided by the N6 and apart from their wine are quite different. Puligny has charm. Its château in its own park is not open to the public but it has the super Montrachet hotel in the middle of the village. Its land is said to be the most expensive agricultural land in Europe. An acre was estimated to be worth £2 million in 1985, and the French Government paid a fortune to completely re-route the A6 motorway to avoid the vineyards. The four Grands Crus vineyards are Le Montrachet (known in 1482), Chevalier-Montrachet, Bâtard-Montrachet and Bienvenues-Bâtard-Montrachet. Chassagne-Montrachet is a sprawling village with a troubled past. When Louis XI was taking over Burgundy, using Swiss mercenaries to do the job for him, Mary, the only surviving child of Charles the Rash, the last Duke of Burgundy, asked the Prince of Orange, Charles de Chalon, to help her. He was in Chassagne-Montrachet when a big Swiss force advanced and he was forced to flee. When the Swiss found that he had escaped, they burned down the village and killed most of the people.

HOTEL

Le Montrachet, Puligny-Montrachet (80.21.30.06): Burgundian dishes at their best. Rooms in old country style. Not cheap but really good. ROOMS E–F. MEALS D–G. Shut end November–10 January. Restaurant shut Wednesday.

QUARRÉ-LES-TOMBES
[YONNE]

The sombre-sounding name refers to the 112 limestone coffins or covers (sarcophagi) found near the church and the remains of around a thousand more. They are from the sixth to eighth centuries, Merovingian period, but no one knows why or how they got there. Theories range from the unlikely, such as that pilgrims came to die under the protection of some long-forgotten saint, to the highly improbable theory that after Christians had been slaughtered by invading Norsemen or Saracens, the stone coffins fell from Heaven to give them a decent Christian burial. The locals may have been undertakers, of course. St George is now the patron of the church, hardly a long-forgotten saint. Quarré-les-Tombes is in a wild, attractive part of the Morvan 5km W of St Léger-Vauban (*see* page 229) and in season is used by visitors as a centre for exploring the land of lakes and forests. In winter this wild part is not for tourism. The valleys of the Cure and Cousin rivers are nearby.

Five kilometres S through the hamlet of Busson is Les Isles Ménéfrier an old village near a beautiful spot where the Cure rushes in a torrent through rocks.

HOTEL

Nord et Poste, 25 place Église (86.32.24.55): farspread reputation for Morvandelles and Burgundian cooking. ROOMS C–D. MEALS B–E.

RESTAURANT

Auberge de l'Atre, at les Lavauts, SE 5km by D10 (86.32.20.79): rather remote; another restaurant offering true local and Burgundian dishes with local trout, sandre, beef, even local mushrooms and herbs. MEALS (book) E–F. Shut end January–6 March; Tuesday evening, Wednesday in winter.

RATILLY – Château
[YONNE]

Ratilly is a truly charming thirteenth-century castle hidden away among dense woods in the Puisaye, a little known area of forests, lakes, pools, scrub and meadows to the SW of Auxerre around Toucy, Bléneau, St Sauveur and St Fargeau (*see* pages 221 and 233). Colette, the writer (*see* Writers, page 15), came from the Puisaye. It is 16km SE of St Fargeau by the attractive little D185, hidden in a secret world of its own behind trees. From the gateway, a straight drive lined by old chestnut trees and walls crosses a bridge over the deep moat to an entrance with two huge round towers with conical caps. Between them is a high pavilion. The castle is in ochre stone and covered with creepers. Standing away from the main part are two more round towers, their cones of different heights. The castle became a hideout in the seventeenth century for the Jansenists, the Catholics who had very different beliefs regarding original sin and grace from the Jesuits, who persecuted them. They became deeply involved in politics, too. Louis XIV expelled them from Paris and they hid in Ratilly, from where they printed secretly their forbidden literature.

The château has found new life as a pottery and stoneware school, with holiday courses in summer, an exhibition of Puisaye stoneware and a hall for temporary art exhibitions.

Two kilometres E is the village of Treigny, which has a beautiful fifteenth- to sixteenth-century Flamboyant Gothic church called the 'Cathedral of the Puisaye' because of its size.

REULLE-VERGY
[CÔTE D'OR]

A hamlet W of Clos Vougeot and Chambolle-Musigny, with an interesting exhibition in a barn showing traditions, daily life and arts of the Hautes Côtes de Nuits wines and vineyards, including day-to-day life in the vineyards this century and last, and history of the region. (Open Sundays all the year, all afternoons from early July–mid-September.) The hamlet has about ninety inhabitants, a town hall built on top of a *lavoir* (clothes-washing house), and a twelfth-century church.

LA ROCHEPOT – Château
[CÔTE D'OR]

A village 5km E of Nolay with a fine castle in an impressive and attractive setting where a powerful man called Philippe Pot was born in 1428.

His father, Regnier Pot, was one of 10,000 knights who followed the Duke of Nevers (later John the Fearless, Duke of Burgundy) on a disastrous crusade to Jerusalem against the Saracens in 1396. They went in a spirit of adventure and chivalry, as if going to a joust, and were utterly defeated at Nicopolos. Regnier was one of the lucky ones to be taken prisoner with the Duke and held to ransom.

The crusaders came back with some tall stories about their adventures and the story told about Regnier is as tall as most. Regnier's bravery had so won the admiration of Sultan Bayazid that he proposed to get Regnier on his side by marrying him to the Sultan's sister. Regnier was already married and anyway did not fancy becoming a Moslem, so he refused. You don't refuse a Sultan who offers you such an honour when you are his prisoner. He was sentenced to fight in the arena the next day, and that night the Virgin Mary appeared to him and gave him some good advice: 'Strike low,' she said simply. He was at least given a scimitar when he was led into the arena, where he faced a half-starved lion. He struck low, and cut off the poor lion's front legs. The Sultan set Regnier free.

On his return Regnier became chamberlain to the Duke of Burgundy, ambassador to Hungary and a Knight of the Golden Fleece. He bought the castle, then called Roche-Nolay, and spent a fortune improving it.

His grandson Philippe Pot was heaped with even more honours. Of course it helped to be a godson of Duke Philippe the Good, who made him Knight of the Golden Fleece, chamberlain, Steward of the Duke's Household, governor of Lille (a very important city in the Duke's Flemish lands) and ambassador to England. But when the last Duke of Burgundy, Charles the Rash, was killed in battle by Louis XI's Swiss mercenaries, he abandoned poor Mary, Charles's only child, and joined Louis XI, who grabbed Burgundy and made him Seneschal of Burgundy and guardian of Louis's son, the Dauphin. At Dijon the Burgundians wiped his name from the rolls of the Golden Fleece, so Louis gave him the Order of St Michael.

He was the diplomat *par excellence* and he used gentle humour as his weapon, pacifying Charles the Rash by jokes when he threw a fit of temper. At the banquet of the Vow of the Pheasant in Dijon when Duke Philippe the Good announced a crusade and the nobles tried to outbid each other in making extravagant vows (no doubt assisted by good Burgundy wine), Philippe Pot pledged not to eat sitting down on Tuesdays and to fight the Saracen with his right arm bare. Philippe the Good seemed to take this second vow quite seriously, for he solemnly rejected it. Luckily for all of them the crusade never took place.

Later in his life, when the Dauphin was thirteen and had become King of France (though his sister, the strong Anne of Beaujeu, was really ruling France), Pot made a speech which in Louis XIV's day might have cost him his life. The State belongs to the people, he said, and the kings were there by the people's suffrage. They were there not to enrich themselves but to forget their own interests and enrich the people. If they did the opposite, they were tyrants. In fact, he was suggesting a Constitutional Monarchy, unbelievable in those days. He himself had become very rich indeed. He owned the great château of Châteauneuf as well as Rochepot and when he died in 1494 he was buried in Cîteaux Abbey in a magnificent tomb by the sculptor who designed the tomb of John the Fearless, now in the Ducal Palace in Dijon, Le Moiturier. Pot's tomb is now in the Louvre.

Rochepot Château, sitting on a hilltop surrounded by trees, rich in pointed towers, its roof Burgundian glazed tiles in traditional zig-zag pattern, is one of the symbols of Burgundy. It was a wreck after the Revolution, when the stone from one side and the keep were taken for the buildings. But in 1893 it was bought by Madame Carnot, wife of Sadi Carnot, President of France and a member of the great Carnot family of Nolay. He was assassinated the year after. She and her family made a superb job of restoring Rochepot. You can cross the drawbridge to see the courtyard, then the great guard room with a vast fireplace, the kitchens, the sumptuously furnished dining room, a tower, and a room with a museum of gifts given to the president on his world travels.

ROMANÈCHE-THORINS
[Saône-et-Loire]

Large by Beaujolais wine village standards, Romanèche shares with Chénas the production of Moulin-à-Vent wine (*see* Wine, pages 52–3). The area actually straddles the border between Saône-et-Loire and Beaujolais, which is in Rhône *département*.

Its most famous villager was the *vigneron* Benoist Roclet. In the 1820s Beaujolais was attacked by a parasite called pyrale, which destroyed whole vineyards. Roclet noticed that vines planted close to the outlet of his kitchen sink were not attacked. He tried scalding vine-stock during the parasites' hibernation and had instant success. Not even his friends took him seriously for twelve years, until they finally realized he was right. The method was used throughout the world until 1945, when pesticides took over. In his house in the village is a little exhibition of implements used for this scalding operation, including boilers and even coffee percolators. The fête of new wine in Romanèche is called after him.

There is a new king of Beaujolais in Romanèche-Thorins now – Georges Duboeuf, grower, wine-maker, '*éleveur, négociant*, sometimes called the Pope of Beaujolais (*see also* Wine, page 51). Some say that he has the best nose and palate in Burgundy. He travels each year through the Beaujolais and Mâconnais tasting wines (eight thousand in a year, I am told), taking back about three thousand for exhaustive laboratory analysis. From these he finally takes only those fine wines which are (to use his own words) 'balanced, fruity, stylish and have individuality'. He supplies leading restaurants around the world. It was he who made Beaujolais Nouveau a considered wine, not just any old cheap Beaujolais to be rushed to Paris as a stunt. He did it by analysis to find which wines were suited to be drunk young. He has a fine turn of phrase, too. How is this for a description of a vintage? 'The quintessence of Beaujolais, brilliant ruby with violet hue, strong floral note in which raspberries, blackcurrants and bananas dominate, wines that are well-balanced, elegant, artistocratic, subtle and finish with the delightful taste of fresh grapes.'

Alas, so many professional buyers from the whole world descend on Georges's at La Chapelle de Guinchay at Romanèche that he can no longer give tastings to passing travellers. But if you are serious about Beaujolais and would like to take a case or more home – paying duty, perhaps, but still saving money and getting the best – telephone 85.35.51.13 or call during office hours to make an appointment.

Otherwise you can find excellent Moulin-à-Vents to taste at Caveau des Viticulteurs on the N6 (85.35.51.03, shut Wednesdays). It also has a restaurant.

Originally Beaujolais Nouveau was not a fashion. There was good reason for this. Beaujolais was a wine sold from barrels in the cafés and bistros of Paris, and after a year in that atmosphere it grew somewhat nasty and vinegary. So the new wine was rushed there as a replacement and when it came the cafés would put out a notice 'Le Beaujolais Nouveau est arrivé'.

Guillon Craft Museum in Romanèche has wood-craft exhibits from last century by Pierre-François Guillon, who had a workshop here, and his pupils.

Near Romanèche is a good zoo for breeding rarer birds and animals. Parc Zoologique Touroparc is eastward. At Maison Blanche crossroads on N6 take D466E towards St Romain-les-Iles. In 25 acres animals and birds wander at liberty (except the Big Cats!). There is an adventure playground, aerial monorail and picnic areas with snack bar.

HOTEL

Maritonnes, near station, route de Fleurie (85.35.51.70): travellers leave the nearby A6 motorway to eat the excellent local dishes here. Comfortable rooms. Attractive garden. Pool. ROOMS D–F. MEALS E–G. Shut 15 December–end January; Sunday low season; Tuesday lunch, Monday.

RULLY
[SAÔNE-ET-LOIRE]

Rully wines (*see* page 44), and the village that produces them, have come out of hiding in the last fifteen years. The search for 'country' wines to replace the great Burgundy white wines, which were shooting up in price, and for similar reds, led the buyers to this pleasant village, hidden between the D981 and

D974 in the Chalonnais 5km S of Chagny. They discovered that
the Chardonnay white wine, elegant, with a little spice, made a
good substitute for Chablis, and the light ruby-coloured Pinot
Noir red with a fruity bouquet and palate could be drunk after
two years, which fitted the current fashion for lighter, younger
reds. Previously, nearly all the white wine had been made into
sparkling Burgundy and Crémant de Bourgogne, a superior
sparkling wine. The grapes used were Chardonnay and Aligoté.
It started way back in 1822 when a wine merchant from Chalon
nearby, looking for a cheaper substitute for champagne,
recruited a cellarman from Champagne, Francis Brazile Hubert.
Until recently, more than three-quarters of Rully wine production was sparkling. The village of Mercurey, a deadly rival
and much more influential, got a regulation passed that Rully
could not use its own name on wines, so even the red was made
into sparkling Burgundy, popular mostly in the United States
during Prohibition there. Now still wine is the main product, it is
getting better and better, and there are no fewer than nineteen
Premiers Crus, all good to excellent. But new-found popularity
has pushed up the price of white wines so much that they can
cost more than AOC Chablis, though not so much as Chablis
Premiers Crus.

Popularity of its wines has brought many more visitors to the
village. Ten years ago I arrived there to taste wine and found
Rully so deserted that you would have believed everyone had
suddenly emigrated – the deserted village. Not a person nor car
did I see as I parked by the hilltop church which dominates the
village, and walked around for about twenty minutes. Then a
dog, noisily defending the courtyard of Domaine du Prieuré,
brought Armand Monassier's cellarman from the cellars. Everyone, it seemed, was in the cellars or the vineyards. Times have
indeed changed. The old Commerce hotel, until recently a very
simple inn where you could take a glass of the white or red with
locals and a good solid meal of Burgundian country dishes, now
has some expensive dishes à la carte as well as its cheap menu
and a notice outside saying that drinks are not served to people
not taking meals. I suppose the locals do as I did last time –
drink in a friend's cellar, surrounded by fine old bottles which
experts would say had been kept too long. The experts are

wrong. From 1973 to 1985 the wines were all just right for drinking. I know – I tasted them in Armand Monassier's cellar.

You can visit on weekends (15 April–30 October) the thirteenth- to fourteenth-century fortress château where they make and keep wine.

HOTEL

Commerce, place Sainte-Marie (85.87.20.09): *see* text. 16 rooms (4 with private facilities) ROOMS B–C. MEALS A–F. Shut Sunday evening, Monday.

Burgundy rooftops

ST AMAND-EN-PUISAYE
[Nièvre]

Centre of the Puisaye pottery industry. Puisaye pottery is made from local white or red clay, as it has been since the middle ages. New craftsmen are trained in the town. It is close to Ratilly Château (page 212) and St Fargeau (page 221). There are guided tours of the pottery-making shops (ask at Tourist Office).
Tourist Information square de la Poste
(86.39.65.70).
Market Monday.

ST AMOUR-BELLEVUE
[Beaujolais – see Wine, page 52 for story of its name and its wine]

ST AUBIN-SUR-LOIRE – Château
[Saône-et-Loire]

Simple but well-proportioned eighteenth-century château 6km S of Bourbon-Lancy. The main staircase is decorated with superb tapestries and the bedrooms have delightful panelling and furnishings. Still a private home so open only afternoons mid-July to late August and shut on Tuesday.

ST BRIS-LE-VINEUX
[Yonne]

Vignerons village SE of Auxerre producing Sauvignon de St Bris with the VDQS denomination (Vin Délimité de Qualité Supérieure – one below AOC) and a good Aligoté. The Sauvignon is good as an aperitif or for making Kir. Other grapes such as Gamay, Pinot Noir and Chardonnay are grown, so that Bourgogne Rouge and Blanc are made, Bourgogne Grande-Ordinaire, Passe-Tout-Grains and sparkling Bourgogne Crémant.

The village has fourteenth- to fifteenth-century houses and a thirteenth-century Gothic church with Renaissance stained glass windows and a great fresco of the Tree of Jesse from 1500.

ST BRISSON
[NIÈVRE]

Village in the heart of the Morvan, SE of Quarré-les-Tombes (page 211). St Brisson has now the administrative centre for the Morvan Regional Park (Maison du Parc), from which you can get detailed maps and news of any events (86.78.70.16). It is a centre for walking and fishing with lakes of St Agnan and Settons and the river Cure quite near and the Forêt au Duc with a stone commemorating the first parachute dropping of arms and munitions from England to the famous Morvan Resistance men. You will notice many memorials to Resistance fighters in the Morvan, and in St Brisson is a Musée de la Résistance (open late June–15 September). There is also a botanical garden outside Maison du Parc, with plants typical of the area.

ST FARGEAU
[YONNE]

This most interesting little village of under two thousand people is the main town of the Puisaye, the silent land of forests, marshes and lakes west of Auxerre, for centuries a secret region, hardly known even to the rest of Burgundy. Its enormous primeval oaks were used to build great cathedrals – their trunks were the only ones long enough for the beams. As the forests were cleared, cattle were grazed, and today it is one-third pastureland, with superb woods and lakes around the meadows,

which are enclosed by hedges. Most of the trees are oaks but
there are dozens of other varieties. Farms and homesteads are
still scarce. The clay has been dug for pottery since the middle
ages. There are forestry and sawmills, a few cement works and,
at St Fargeau, smelting works to treat minerals taken from the
soil.

Colette, the romantic novelist, came from Puisaye (*see*
Writers, page 15), and her mother, Sido, told her of wolves still
haunting those forests late last century, and of one hungry wolf
following her carriage for five hours.

St Fargeau is reminded of its history by the old château
which still stands guard over it. Very impressive, with massive
towers over the main gateway and solid ones at the corners, it
would look forbidding but for the warm rose-coloured brick
with which it was built, and the water-filled moat and greenery
surrounding it. It is mostly fifteenth-century, but in the seventeenth century La Grande Mademoiselle, Anne-Marie-Louise
d'Orléans (*see below*), added magnificent touches.

Jacques Coeur built the château in the fifteenth century on
the site of a medieval fortress. He was the great merchant and
financier who put up the money for Joan of Arc's campaigns
and Charles VII's wars to drive out the English. Jacques became
one of the richest and most powerful men in France and
inevitably made enemies. A group of them, led by Antoine de
Chabannes, accused him of embezzlement. Charles VII, an
ungrateful, cunning man who had not raised a hand to save
Joan of Arc, turned against Coeur. Always broke, Charles was
after Coeur's fortune. Coeur fled to Italy and died in the Greek
Isles leading a fleet to try to drive out the Turks. Chabannes was
given Coeur's château at St Fargeau.

La Grande Mademoiselle, Anne-Marie-Louise d'Orléans,
was Duchess of Montpensier, daughter of Gaston d'Orléans and
first cousin of Louis XIV – a lady born before her time. During
the Fronde uprising of the parliament and aristocrats against
Cardinal Mazarin, the king's powerful chancellor, she commanded a Fronde Army and fired cannon at the Royal troops at the
Bastille. When the Fronde collapsed, instead of marrying Louis
XIV, as she had always hoped, she was exiled for five years to St
Fargeau. She arrived at the château and found that it had no

windows or doors and its courtyard was knee-high in grass. 'I was so frightened and unhappy that I began to cry,' she said. But not for long. La Grande Mademoiselle called in François Le Vau to make the place habitable. She updated the six round towers with domed roofs and great tall lanterns, had seventy new fire-places put in to warm up the place, modernized all the rooms, and put a fine semi-circular staircase in the courtyard opposite the main entrance. It leads to a domed vestibule. The whole must have looked more ostentatious than now, for in 1752 a fire damaged two wings and they were restored in simpler style.

Mademoiselle held great parties with theatre and music. Her guests were among the most important people in France – Vicomte de Turenne, the commander-in-chief of the French Army, the Prince of Condé, her father Gaston, Duc d'Orléans and Madame de Sévigné, as well as the amusing Roger de Bussy-Rabutin, also exiled to Burgundy (*see* Bussy-Rabutin, page 125). She was allowed to return to Paris in 1657 but was exiled to St Fargeau again in 1662 for refusing to marry the King of Portugal – sensible of her for he turned out to be impotent and mad.

In 1681, against the King Louis XIV's wishes, she married a very dubious character called Lauzun, who sold the castle in 1714. It was bought by an important legal family called Le Peletier. One of them was President of the National Assembly in 1790 and voted for the execution of the king. He was assassin-ated by Louis' former bodyguard, and became the first official Martyr of the Revolution, buried as a national hero in the Panthéon. When French Royals returned to power last century, regicides lost their popularity in Paris and his body was removed to the chapel in a round tower in St Fargeau Château.

If the château looks formidable from the front, it has another side which opens on to an English-style park of lawns and great trees, its towers reflected in a large lake fed by the little river Bourdin. The park covers 292 acres and includes a horse museum. The main street of St Fargeau passes beneath a pretty tower of pink brick and stone which was a fortified gateway of the fifteenth century. The church (eleventh to fifteenth century) has a gorgeous rose window.

The château now belongs to relations of the writer Jean

d'Ormesson, who made it a setting for his novel *Au Plaisir de Dieu*, which was televized there. An historic 'spectacle' is shown Wednesday and Saturday in July and August, with six hundred actors, fifty horses, dancers, musicians, troubadours (book at the château 86.74.05.67). Château is open daily from early April to 10 November. The farm of the château, showing farm life at the beginning of the twentieth century, is 500 metres from the château. (Open daily – local produce for sale.) Three kilometres SE is the beautiful Bourdon reservoir lake covering 494 acres.

At Boutissaint Château, 9km SE from St Fargeau on D185 is St Hubert Wildlife Park of deer, fallow deer, wild boar, European bison and moufflons, mostly free ranging (open daily from sunrise to sundown). On one day in mid-July and one in mid-August is held a Fête de la Chasse et de la Nature, with huntsmen blowing hunting horns and various shows.

TOURIST INFORMATION place du Château (shut
Saturday, Sunday in winter, 86.74.15.72).
FESTIVALS *see* text.

HOTEL

Relais du Château, promenade Grillon (86.74.01.75): made from two old houses. Big dining room with rôtisserie. ROOMS C. MEALS B–F.

ST FLORENTIN
[YONNE]

Though it is a small industrial town, St Florentin has a lot to recommend it. It stands on a terraced hill overlooking the meeting of the Armance and Armançon rivers with the Burgundy canal, and it has become a centre for leisure boat hire on this attractive and interesting canal, as well as a delight for anglers. Its attractive church, started in 1500, stands on a hill surrounded by charming old streets. It has some beautiful Renaissance stained glass windows in remarkably brilliant colours, showing scenes from the saints and the Bible. Two forests are nearby, Forêt de Pontigny and Forêt d'Othe, which is just over the border in Champagne. Furthermore, St Florentin is only 22km N of Chablis and produces two outstanding cheeses – Soumaintrain (a wonderful brine-washed cheese made mostly by farmers in the Armançon valley, kept six weeks in humid cellars, but becoming scarce) and St Florentin itself (also brine-washed, a lovely spicy, strong cheese rather like Munster from Alsace, once a farm cheese, now produced mostly in dairies or factories).

From the terrace of Promenade du Prieuré are fine views over the old town and the Armançon valley.

Boat hire companies using St Florentin are Rive de France, 172 boulevard Berthier, 75017 Paris (tel. 46.22.10.86) and in Britain VFB, Normandy House, High Street, Cheltenham, Gloucestershire GL50 3HW (tel. 0242 526338).

TOURIST INFORMATION 10 rue de la Terrasse (86.35.11.86): shut Tuesday except high summer.

MARKETS Monday, Saturday (vegetables).

HOTELS

Grande Chaumière, 3 rue Capucins, (86.35.15.12): very good classic-regional cooking. Rooms now comfortable. ROOMS D–F. MEALS C–G. Shut first week of September; mid-December–mid-January; Wednesday low season.

Tilleuls, 3 rue Decourtive (86.35.09.09): nice little peaceful hotel. ROOMS C–D. MEALS C–E. Shut early November–early December; Sunday evening, Monday.

At Venizy, 3km N by D30 and D129, *Moulin des Pommerats* (86.35.08.04): charming old mill by a small trout river with attractive garden. Fishing. Pleasant rooms vary in size. Paul Reumaux d'Equainville, the owner, fought with RAF in World War II. Fresh ingredients excellently cooked. ROOMS D–F. MEALS D–F. Shut Sunday evening, Monday low season.

ST HONORÉ-LES-BAINS
[NIÈVRE]

The Romans originally discovered the helpful properties of the sulphurous radioactive waters of this little town on the SW edge

of the Morvan. Unlike most spas, which have faded, St Honoré
has become increasingly popular, probably because it is a very
pleasant centre for exploring the Morvan forest and Regional
Park, including the wilder areas in the Haut Morvan. Its waters
are used to treat asthma and bronchitis. (Établissement Thermal, tel. 86.30.73.27.) It has a casino and sports facilities.

An interesting and scenic drive is through the gorges of the
Cauche to Autun. Just south of St Honoré is a shallow lake,
Étang du Seu. At Vandenesse, 6km W, you can see a huge
fifteenth-century castle with several towers from the road.

TOURIST INFORMATION place F. Bazot (86.30.71.70):
1 May–end September.

MARKETS Monday, Tuesday, Thursday, Friday (May–
end September).

FESTIVALS Flower Fête, August; Regional Food Fare,
August.

HOTELS

Henry Robert, 47 ave Général d'Espeuilles (86.30.72.33): interest-
ing old house in nice gardens. Comfortable; elegant furnishings.
ROOMS C. MEALS C–E. Shut 30 September–1 May.
Auberge du Pré-Fleuri, 22 ave Jean-Mermoz (86.30.74.96): 2-star
local hotel, open out of season, unlike most in the spa. ROOMS D.
MEALS B–E. Shut February holidays.

ST HUBERT WILDLIFE PARK
[YONNE – *see* St Fargeau, page 221]

ST JEAN D'ARDIÈRES
[BEAUJOLAIS]

On N6 NW of Belleville-sur-Saône (page oo) is La Maison de
Beaujolais, a little paradise for Beaujolais drinkers, where you
can taste all the Grands Crus with local cheeses or eat at a
restaurant (tel. 74.66.16.46, shut Wednesday afternoon and

Thursday). La Cave de Bel Air gives tastings except Sunday. Château de Pizay, 2km from N6, has a fourteenth-century donjon, huge cellars and a beautiful French-style formal garden.

ST JEAN-DE-LOSNE
[CÔTE D'OR]

This old fortified town is indeed at the Meeting of the Waters, a crossroads of inland waterways. The Saône skirts it, the Ouche and Vouge rivers join the Saône within 3km, the great Burgundy canal ends in the town on its journey from Seine to Saône and the Rhône–Rhine canal begins 3km NE, where there is also a dam forming a long narrow lake. There is a small craft port, used by pleasure craft, at the mouth of the Burgundy canal. Not surprisingly, the town lures fishermen. Beside this stretch of the Saône is a land famed for pochouse, the freshwater equivalent of bouillabaisse, a soup-stew of thick slices of perch, tench, carp and eels, which are cooked in a sauce made from fish stock, fat bacon, garlic, chopped onions, herbs and white Burgundy wine, then strained. A glass of *marc*, the wine spirit, is poured in and set alight. The fish is cooked in the sauce for about twenty minutes, taken out and kept hot, then the juice reduced and thickened with cream. It is served on croûtons of bread fried in butter and rubbed with garlic.

The Saône was the seventeenth-century frontier between Burgundy, which was French, and Franche Comté, which belonged to the Habsburg Austro-Spanish Empire. In 1636 Louis XIII and Cardinal Richelieu joined in the war, later called the Thirty Years War, between the German Protestant States, seeking their freedom, their allies the Protestant Swedes and the Habsburg Empire. The Habsburg forces, under their commander-in-chief General Mathias Gallas, crossed the Saône and laid waste the countryside. But a few hundred men of St Jean-de-Losne held out against 60,000 of the enemy who besieged them – a success still remembered proudly. The defenders were helped by a propitious flood of the river. In the

Revolution, when religious names for towns were altered, it was temporarily renamed Belle-Défense.

Last century, St Jean was a very important port, centre of traffic from the North Sea to the Rhine, Maine and Danube. Little barge traffic is seen now on this part of the Burgundy canal but St Jean is a base for Blue Line pleasure boats (La Gare d'Eau, 21170 St Jean-de-Losne, tel. 80.29.12.86). As a result of its previous importance, St Jean is still one of the most crowded little towns in Burgundy, though it has only two thousand inhabitants.

TOURIST INFORMATION ave Gare d'Eau (May–September, 80.29.05.48) or Mairie (off-season 80.29.05.44).
MARKET Saturday.

HOTEL

Auberge de la Marine, at Losne (80.29.05.11): 2-star, 2-chimney comfortable Logis. ROOMS B–D. MEALS A–D. Shut 20 December–22 January. Restaurant shut Monday.

ST JULIEN-DE-JONZY
[SAÔNE-ET-LOIRE]

Village 12km N of Charlieu, which is over the Rhône border, and 8km SE of Marcigny, it has lovely views across Brionnais countryside to the distant hills of Beaujolais. It is known for its twelfth-century Romanesque church with wonderful craftsmanship, especially the tympanum and lintel over the door, carved from one piece of sandstone. Alas, the heads of all the disciples at the Last Supper were mutilated with a chisel in the Revolution.

ST JULIEN-EN-MONTMELAS
[Saône-et-Loire]

Village in the Beaujolais hills NW of Villefranche which produces wine, of course, but is suprisingly better known for producing one of France's greatest medical men, the physiologist
Claude Bernard (1813–78). In the house which he bought in St
Julien is a museum showing his many medical discoveries, from
connections between liver and the nervous system to blood temperatures and oxygen content. His book *Leçons de Physiologie
Expérimentale* is still a standard work. He was the son of a poor
vigneron in St Julien and was taught a little Latin by the village
priest. He became a chemist's assistant in Lyon, but wanted to be
a writer, and went to Paris. Failing to make a living, he studied
medicine, and succeeded brilliantly. A chair of Physiology was
created for him at the Sorbonne. His work was the basis of much
modern knowledge. (Museum shut mid-February–mid-March
and Monday.)

Cross the garden of his house, go through the vines, and you
reach the humbler house where he was born.

ST LÉGER-VAUBAN
[Yonne]

This village, 5km NE of Quarré-les-Tombes in the Morvan, was
called St Léger-de-Foucheret when Sébastien Le Prestre was
born there in 1633 (*see* page 14). He became the greatest military
engineer in French history, and was created Marquis de
Vauban, so his home village took his name. Dozens of French
towns and villages owed their security to his brilliant fortifications. He surrounded the French kingdom with a cordon of
fortresses and invented weapons from the socket bayonet to new
types of gun batteries. He is not buried at St Léger. Napoleon
had his heart placed in Les Invalides, and his body is in the
church of Bazoches, 12km SW of Avallon, where he had a
château. In St Léger is La Maison de Vauban, a museum opened

in 1980, with an audio-vision (twenty minutes) of his life and work. (Open mid-June–mid-September.)

The village church is most unusual. It was built in the fifteenth century, altered last century, and decorated quite recently by the sculptor-architect Marc Hénard, who lived at St Léger for a while. He carved the panels of the doorway, and in 1973 designed attractive blue and pink ceramic tiles around the altar. A doorway at the abbey of Pierre-Qui-Vire, 4km S, (page 203) is his work. Ten kilometres S is Lac de St Agnan, an attractive reservoir with wooded banks.

ST MARTIN DU LAC
[SAÔNE-ET-LOIRE – see Marcigny, page 181]

ST PARIZE-LE-CHÂTEL
[NIÈVRE]

At one end of the Magny-Cours racing circuit (page 180), St Parize has been known since Gallo-Roman times for its gazeous waters, which are still sought after. The crypt of its twelfth-century church has capitals with strange carvings, some of animals, acrobats and fantastic figures, others of pagan motifs.

ST PÈRE-SOUS-VÉZELAY
[YONNE]

Village 3km SE of Vézelay (page 260) on the river Cure has a lovely thirteenth- to fifteenth-century Gothic church rather overshadowed by the famous basilica at Vézelay, but worth seeing outside and inside. In a twelfth-century Presbytery house is an interesting archaeological museum of finds from Les Fontaines Salées (2km near D958). There Gallo-Roman baths have been found, fed by saline springs. They are built on a Gallic temple from the second century BC in an area which was dedicated to the God of the Springs.

The springs have been used since the Iron Age. They were very popular with the Romans and in the middle ages. They were filled in during the seventeenth century by gatherers of the pernicious salt tax. Unearthed, they are used for treating arthritis. A Celtic church and a field of burial urns from 900BC have also been unearthed.

St Père is known these days for its Relais et Châteaux Hotel L'Espérance (*see below*).

HOTEL

L'Espérance (86.33.20.45): *see* text. Lovely country garden, superb meals (3-star Michelin); luxury bedrooms and very high prices indeed. Cheapest menu (1991) was 300 francs served weekday lunch only; cheapest evening menu was 550 francs. ROOMS G. MEALS G. Shut early January–early February; Wednesday lunch, Tuesday.

ST PIERRE-LE-MOUTIER
[NIÈVRE]

This market town by the N7, 23km S of Nevers, was the scene of Joan of Arc's last victory. After she had persuaded the Dauphin to be crowned Charles VII at Reims, she wanted to try to retake Paris, but the king and his council stopped her – probably wisely, although the French now insist that it was through jealousy of her success and popularity. After doing nothing for months, in 1429 she was sent to rid the Nevers barony of the freelance commander Perrinet-Gressard, who was fighting for the Duke of Burgundy and the English. She took little St Pierre, but failed to take La Charité-sur-Loire (page 134), and had to give up. She was captured next year at Compiègne by the Burgundians.

The church at St Pierre was part of a Benedictine priory founded at the time of Queen Brunhilda in the seventh century. St Pierre has fine Renaissance houses.

TOURIST INFORMATION Mairie (86.37.42.09).

MARKETS Thursday, Friday.

HOTEL

La Vigne, route de Decize, D978A (86.37.41.66): Relais Gastronomique in same family since 1930. Very interesting dishes; good value. Bedrooms in pavilion in the park. ROOMS D. MEALS B–F. Shut mid-January–mid-February. Restaurant also shut Wednesday.

ST POINT
[SAÔNE-ET-LOIRE]

The château in this little village was given to Lamartine, the poet, as a wedding present in 1820 by his father, a landowner and minor aristocrat. The village is on the river Valouze, W of Mâcon beyond Bussières and Pierreclos. Lamartine was fond of his old manor house and lived in it often, receiving many visitors, including Liszt, Victor Hugo, and the songwriter Béranger. He and his English artist wife could not resist adding to it in the fashionable pseudo-Gothic style. It is open to visitors and you can see Lamartine's bed, writing desk in his study, and his salon housing his portrait by his wife and a seventeenth-century tapestry. In the garden, a stone bench where he wrote many of the *Méditations* and an oak under which he wrote much of *Jocelyn* are both still there. (Open early March–mid-November. Shut all Wednesday and Sunday morning.)

In the village church, built in Cluny style, are two pictures by his wife. The couple are buried in the family chapel with his daughter, his mother and niece. In the chapel is a bust of Lamartine in white stone with a white stone tomb.

Nearby on the same road, D22, is an artificial lake used as a leisure and watersports centre.

ST SAUVEUR-EN-PUISAYE
[YONNE]

Colette, the writer, was born in this big village SW of Auxerre in 1873 (*see* page 15). She went to the local school and lived there until she was in her late teens with her mother Sido, to whom she was devoted, and her father, an invalided army officer bewildered by civilian life. Their home is a grey stone 'bourgeois' house with three small gardens, which she described so lovingly in *La Maison de Claudine*. It was in rue des Vignes in her day – now it is in rue Colette, and there is a red marble plaque inscribed *Colette est née ici* (Colette was born here). But that is all. She described the house as 'solemn, rather forbidding', but the back, it seems, was quite different: 'The house smiled only on its garden side.' It was not just the flowers and trees which made it smile, but the children's toys and books and the voice of her mother calling them. Alas, her father was bankrupted by bad management of his estate and cunning tenants who did not pay the rent, and she had the sad experience of seeing the family move out and their possessions auctioned on the steps.

You cannot see inside the house although John Ardagh did recently and described it in his delightful book *Writers' France*. It belongs to a retired doctor who also brought up his family there. Colette's room was filled with a model railway.

Colette called St Sauveur 'Montigny' in her books. The steep streets down which the showers ran in little 'torrents' are now paved. The château where, in her time, impoverished aristocrats lived, still stands on the hilltop. Local cheeses St Florentin and the scarcer Soumaintrain are still sold at the Wednesday market, with chickens and vegetables. But Colette would not recognize much of her beloved village now.

ST SEINE L'ABBAYE
[Côte d'Or]

Village on the N71, 27km NW of Dijon, 10km SE of the source of the Seine. Seine (or Seigne), son of a Count of Mesmont, founded an abbey here in the sixth century. The early thirteenth-century abbey church which remains is beautiful. The front dates from the fifteenth century, restored at that time after a fire. The porch is set between two buttressed towers.

As the N71 climbs on its way north from the village, you pass on the right (eastward) the source of the Ignon river, whose waters find their way to the Saône and so eventually to the Mediterranean, then almost immediately the source of the Seine is 2km to your left (westward), and these waters flow to Paris and on to the Channel at Le Havre.

ST THIBAULT
[Côte d'Or]

A hamlet 19km SE of Semur-en-Auxois, with an abbey church whose priceless treasures of Burgundian sculpture would have been lost if the local peasants had not stood their ground and received Communion in rain and all weathers to save them.

The priory was small when it acquired the relics of St Thibault (Theobald of Provins) in the thirteenth century. News spread of miracles that were attributed to the saint, the pilgrims poured in and wealth with them, the village alongside took the saint's name, and finally Duke Robert II of Burgundy put up much of the money for an abbey rebuilding programme. The monks had built a magnificently sculptured new entrance door-way, a chapel for the saint's bones and a superb new chancel for themselves. Before they could build the rest of their new monastery, the Black Death and the Hundred Years War brought chaos.

A fire and other tragedies resulted in the collapse of the nave in the eighteenth century. The architect called in to restore insisted that he would have to pull everything down, but the villagers were not having it. They insisted that a builder was found who would leave the chancel, the doorway and the chapel. They heard Mass in the churchyard for years.

The doorway is brilliant but four of the five figures on it are still a mystery. The saint is there but the others are still in doubt. They have been identified as Duke Robert, his son Duke Hugues V, his wife Agnes, daughter of St Louis, and their friend the Bishop of Autun, Hugues d'Arcy. Other people believe that they are Solomon, David, Aaron, and the Queen of Sheba! Among many treasures in the church is a charming fourteenth-century statue of Mary watching Jesus playing with a bird.

HOTEL
Auberge Chez Guite, 15 rue Carnot (80. 35.01.46): simple Logis de France. Home cooking. Rooms all with facilities. ROOMS B–C. MEALS A–E.

SANTENAY
[CÔTE D'OR]

Last of the important wine-producing communes of the Côte d'Or, at the south end of the Côte de Beaune, it has something the others don't have – spa water! Inevitably, its spa has a casino. The spa water which is used to treat rheumatism and digestive and liver problems, is in Santenay-le-Bas. The other two districts producing the wine are Santenay-le-Haut and St Jean. They are spread along the river Dheune amid big vineyards. Wines are red, can be tannic when young. Of the twelve Premiers Crus, Les Gravières has the most finesse. Generally, the wines are robust. You will find very many caves offering tastings and direct sales.

You can taste in the old château built by Duke Philip the Bold (open 11 a.m.–3 p.m. but phone 80.20.61.87), or Caves Prieuré-Brunet, rue Narosse, in fifteenth-century cellars with old tools used by winegrowers (open 9 a.m.–12 p.m.; 2 p.m.– 7 p.m. – for Sunday visits phone 80.20.60.56).

RESTAURANT

RESTAURANT

Terroir, place Jet d'Eau (80.20.63.47): Burgundian dishes; grill.
MEALS B–E. Shut Thursday except in July, August.

SAULIEU
[CÔTE D'OR]

Saulieu has only about three thousand inhabitants but it is in a
very pleasant setting, is interesting and has several strings to its
bow. At the boundaries of the Auxois and the Morvan on the
N6, SE of Avallon, among forests, it has a timber industry which
sends more than one million Christmas trees (*sapins de Noël*) each
year not only to cities of France but to many all round Europe
and Africa. Large tree nurseries also send hundreds of thousands of saplings all over France and beyond. Furniture is made
there, too. Its own forest of 1900 acres, which reaches the north
and west edges of the town, is owned by the State and is provided with walks and trails, picnic sites, adventure playgrounds,
bicycle tracks and trout fishing in its small lakes.

Long before Christmas trees became fashionable in France,
Saulieu was famed as a gastronomic centre. The old Paris–Lyon
road made it an important stopping place in the middle ages. Its
cuisine was praised by Rabelais. Then in 1651 the Burgundian
states restored the old road and Saulieu became a great posting
stage for horses, then an eating or overnight stop for motorists
on the N6. This lasted until very recently, when the A6 motorway took away much of its trade. But Saulieu is still holding its
own. For those with money, Bernard Loiseau's Côte d'Or restaurant is still one of the best in France. He is a magnificent
cook, even if some critics may criticize his attitude. You will pay
300 francs (1991) for his cheapest lunch menu, about 600 francs
at night. This was the restaurant made world famous by Alexandre Dumaine between the world wars. Bernard Loiseau is near
to doing the same. For those with less money and Burgundian
tastes and appetites, the old Relais de Poste where the coaches
once changed horses still gives a smiling welcome, and truly
good meals.

For many people Saulieu's fame rests on its church of St Andoche, begun in 1112, and for the curious relic of history that makes the curé of this little town 'Bishop of the Morvan'. The church was started by Stephen of Bagé, Bishop of Autun and Abbot of Saulieu, who also rebuilt Autun Cathedral, so the Bishop of Morvan's title, as well as the unofficial title of 'cathedral' for the church were bequeathed by him. Andoche was martyred here by the Romans. The church was partly destroyed by the English in the Hundred Years War and by the Huguenots in the Wars of Religion, and simplified in rebuilding, but the sculptures of the Romanesque capitals are lovely and very imaginative. I cannot help wondering about the unknown local artists who created such beauty in churches like this. The foliage alone is magnificent. The Biblical scenes are fascinating. Even the donkeys truly live. And any peasant of the middle ages or much later must have gone in fear of the Devil after seeing this Arch-Fiend.

A later work is a beautiful Virgin and Child given to the church by Madame de Sévigné – perhaps a penance for having got drunk in Saulieu, which she admitted in her writing. It is said that the angel has the face of Sévigné herself.

At the north entrance to the town, in a little square off the N6, is a statue of a bull by a local man, François Pompon (1855–1933), a brilliant animal sculptor. More of his works are in the little Musée Pompon in a seventeenth-century presbytery beside St Andoche basilica. In the museum, too, are rooms showing a last-century Morvan cottage, and a nineteenth-century sabot-maker's workshop, flax-weaving room, blacksmith's forge and pottery. (Museum open May–October except Tuesday and Sunday; also in February and spring school holidays.)

Pompon's tomb is in the charming fifteenth-century church of St Saturnin at the south end of the town. Above it is one of his own sculptures of a condor.

Pompon worked for years as assistant to Rodin, and used to study animals and their movements in Jardin des Plantes zoo in Paris. Success came late in life.

TOURIST INFORMATION rue d'Argentine (80.64.00.21).

MARKET Saturday.

FESTIVAL Charolais Cattle Show, Saturday, Sunday
following 15 August.

Côte d'Or, 2 rue d'Argentine (80.64.07.66): all gastronomes
agree that it is a 'gastronomic experience'. Bernard Loiseau has
admitted that his is a 'cuisine inimitable' (unparalleled cooking).
See text. Charming walled garden, luxury bedrooms. *Very*
expensive. ROOMS E–G. MEALS G+.
Poste, rue Grillot (80.64.05.67): *see* text. Classic and Burgundian
dishes. Pleasant rooms C–E. MEALS C–E.
Relais, 8 rue d'Argentine (80.64.13.16): only 5 rooms. Hearty
Burgundian dishes are good value. ROOMS C. MEALS B–E. Shut
first week December; 16–23 January; Wednesday evening,
Thursday except summer.

SAVIGNY LÈS BEAUNE
[CÔTE D'OR]

I am very fond of this *vigneron* village NW of Beaune, W of
Aloxe-Corton. It is not only for wine-lovers, but for people like
me who love aeroplanes, cars and old motor-cycles.

The perfumed wines, very similar to Beaune, loosen the
tongue into making fine phrases, as I have reported in the
chapter on Wine. Even the private houses have inscriptions
carved into the stone lintels over their doors.

There are 950 acres of vineyards. The A6 motorway was
driven through them but only after the precious topsoil was
removed and spread around. The stream that also runs through
the vineyards is called the river Rhoin and is important to the
winegrowers, for they say that wine from one side is lighter than
from the other. Wines from the north side, grown on clay, are
fuller. Those from the south, grown in gravel, are lighter and
grapes ripen a week earlier. There are no Grands Crus, but
twelve Premiers Crus, and I have found them very good value.
It is a wine that satisfies both me and my bank manager.

There are some spectacular vineyard views from the village,

which has a lovely church dating back to the twelfth century, with a fifteenth-century fresco.

The fourteenth-century château in the centre of the village, built by a Maréchal of Burgundy, has four medieval pepper-pot towers, a U-shaped courtyard and an attractive staircase. It was altered in the seventeenth century. The Duchess of Maine, wife of the favourite son of Louis XIV and of Madame de Montespan, was exiled from Paris to the château by the Duke of Orléans, Regent of France, after Louis's death.

You have to walk to the top of the stairs to find, hidden away, a remarkable collection of motor-cycles from 1903 to 1960. There are magnificent bikes with names almost unknown to young people – Rudge, Velocette, Vincent, NSU, as well as great names like Norton, AJS, Honda, BSA, BMW and Peugeot. I did not know that Blériot's aircraft company made motor-bikes, too. In the stable end of the château are fifteen racing cars, all Abarth, the Italian car with a Fiat engine, all driven in races by the owner of the château, Michel Pont, who won the world sportscar championship two or three times in the sixties.

In the château park alongside vines, are more than twenty fighter aircraft, in use from the end of World War II until quite recently – French, US, British and Soviet, including Mirage, Mystère, Sabre, Soviet TF, Gloster, Météor, Vampire and Hunter.

Of course, the large château cellars are used to store and mature wine. You can taste and buy. (Museum open daily. Shut for lunch 12 p.m.–2 p.m.)

The delightful eighteenth-century Manoir Nicolay in rue Goby (which I covet) has a formal French-style garden and important wine cellars.

HOTEL

Ouvrée, route Bouilland (80.21.51.52): superb-value meals. Burgundian dishes. Owner is a wine producer. ROOMS C. MEALS B–E. Shut 1 February–10 March.

SEIGNELAY
[Yonne]

Once Seignelay was very important, a barony raised by Louis XIV's ambitious minister Colbert to the status of Marquisate after he bought the château. It is now a pleasant, very small town, little known to the outside world, although it is only 14km N of Auxerre and 18km SW of St Florentin, with the river Yonne looping a few km to the west and the Serein 2km N. It spreads pleasantly down a hillside overlooking the Serein.

Colbert bought the barony in 1657. His great task was to make Louis XIV and France solvent when the king had wasted France's money waging a disastrous war on the English and on expensive living and building. That meant that Colbert had to break the power of the aristocrats, who did not deign to pay taxes. Yet Colbert himself longed for a title. Rich members of the French middle-class got titles by buying a château that had a title attached. In the same way kings gave titles to their mistresses – Madame de Pompadour, born Jeanne Poisson, hardly bothered even to visit Château de Pompadour after Louis XV bought it for her to give her the title of Marquise.

But Colbert was interested in his château as well as in being a Marquis. He had it completely restored by the Royal architect. It was destroyed in the Revolution which Louis XIV's spending sprees had made inevitable. The park remains, with an eighteenth-century entrance and a tower. Colbert's name is given to the pleasant seventeenth-century main square approached by an attractive lime-shaded avenue. Colbert's Court of Justice is now the town hall. He would surely have approved of the governor's house next door becoming an income tax office. Opposite is a fine seventeenth-century covered market, with an unusual roof supported by thirty-two columns.

The Romanesque church, mostly rebuilt in the fifteenth century, has an interesting Renaissance doorway, a Louis XIII churchwarden's pew, Louis XVI chandeliers rescued from the château, a seventeenth-century painted statue of the Virgin and two reliquaries carrying Colbert's coat of arms.

SEINE'S – River Source
[CÔTE D'OR]

The beloved Seine bubbles up from a cave containing the statue of a nymph, in a little valley of fir trees on D103, a mile W of the N7 and 10km NW of St Seine l'Abbaye (page 234).

Last century the city of Paris bought the site and the nymph that was erected is a copy of one sculptured by Jouffroy in 1865. Just downstream have been dug up the remains of a Gallo-Roman temple and bronzes which include the goddess Sequana and a faun, and wooden statues and votive offerings, including flat sticks carved into human outline. These are in Dijon's Archaeological Museum.

Sequana was the daughter of Bacchus, god of wine, so it is fitting that the river named after her (Seine) should be born in Burgundy. She was one of the loveliest nymphs befriended by Ceres, goddess of corn, and inevitably that old lecher Neptune propositioned her. Refusing, she asked her father and Ceres to turn her to water to escape. The Yonne was a nymph, too.

Another story sets the scene later when St Seine, son of the Comte de Mesmont, had founded the nearby abbey. When he was old, his donkey thoughtfully bent its knees to let the old monk dismount and so dug a small hole in the ground. The river sprung from the hole. I am afraid, however, that the river was flowing long before the sixth century AD. I shall settle for Bacchus' daughter and drink to her in her father's wine each time I go to Paris.

SEMUR-EN-AUXOIS
[CÔTE D'OR]

A most attractive peaceful old town of cobbled streets, ramparts and four solid, round defence towers, on a high rock of pink granite, almost surrounded by a loop of the river Armançon. It is 19km S of Montbard and the D980 skirts it. From the north approaching Pont Joly, the single-span river bridge, it looks

Semur-en-Auxois

splendid, especially when floodlit in the evenings. From the bridge itself are fine views up and down the river, with old houses and trees beside the water. Little houses are packed on the hillside under the castle keep beside which the stone spire of Notre Dame church looks slender and frail.

The town must have been incredibly well defended in ancient times. It was said to have been founded by Hercules. In the fourteenth century its ramparts had eighteen defence towers, and extra walls divided the town into three. The château (dismantled in 1602) was on the western end and you can walk under lime trees round the edge of its ramparts and look into the river below. To reach the promenade you pass a hospital which was the handsome seventeenth- to eighteenth-century home of the Governors of Semur. The one who sold it, the Marquis de Châtelet, was the husband of the beautiful Emilie de Breteuil, a brilliant mathematician and scientist who seduced Voltaire and became his mistress, only to dump him for a dashing army captain. She also translated Newton into French.

The huge keep which almost covered the spur of rock had a sheer drop to the river valley to the north and south and was flanked by four towers. You reach Notre Dame church through a narrow medieval street leading to a square of old houses. The church was founded in the eleventh century by Duke Robert I as recompense for killing his father-in-law. It was rebuilt in the thirteenth century and much damaged and restored later. It is attractive, with two square towers and a huge porch at one end and an octagonal tower with the slim stone spire over the transept. Inside, the nave is extraordinarily narrow, so it seems even higher than it is, which is why the church is one of several called a miniature cathedral. A row of side chapels is along one side.

The museum in a former Dominican convent contains old manuscripts and paintings and sculpture, including three landscapes by one of the greatest landscape painters, Corot (1796–1875).

Semur claims to run the oldest race in France. In the middle ages it was a foot race for men with a prize of a pair of hose (medieval tights) – of which the men had need, for they ran in the nude. In 1630 the wife of the governor (*not* Emilie!) objected and it became a horse race with a prize of a gold ring inscribed with the town's coat of arms and a pair of gloves. The course is of 2275 metres between Pont Villenotte and the top of rue Liberté (Course des Chausses).

Three kilometres S by D103B is Lac de Pont, a 6km reservoir lake made from the river Armançon from Pont-et-Massène to Montigny-sur-Armançon. It has a watersport centre and is very popular on weekends in summer.

TOURIST INFORMATION 2 place Gaveau (80.97.05.96).

MARKETS Tuesday, Thursday, Saturday.

FESTIVALS Course des Chausses et Fête de la Bagne (*see* text), Sunday nearest to 31 May. Cultural Festival, July. Theatre Festival, August.

HOTELS

Côte d'Or, 3 place Gaveau (80.97.03.13): pleasant atmosphere. Simple traditional cooking. Good value. ROOMS B–D. MEALS B–E. Shut mid-November–5 January; Sunday evening January–April; Thursday lunch May–November; Wednesday.

Lac, 3km at Lac de Pont, Pont-et-Massène (80.97.11.11): very pleasant. Fishing, bathing. Burgundian meals. ROOMS B–D. MEALS B–E. Shut mid-December–1 February; Sunday evening, Monday except July, August.

SEMUR-EN-BRIONNAIS
[SAÔNE-ET-LOIRE]

An old village S of Paray-le-Monial (page 198), E of Marcigny, perched on a hill covered in fruit trees and vines, it has a castle with a heavy ninth-century rectangular keep which dominates it. Here St Hugues (St Hugh, the great abbot of Cluny) was born. The two round towers were used as a prison in the eighteenth century. There are superb views over the vineyards to the hills beyond. A later abbot of Cluny, Renaud, Hugh's great-nephew, was also son of the Seigneur of Semur-en-Brionnais. (Castle open early April–late October except Tuesday.) There is a Son-et-Lumière on Thursday evenings July, August.

Semur has a Romanesque church with a doorframe carved with the story of St Hilaire (St Hilary of Poitiers) condemned to exile by the Council of Bishops. It shows an angel trying to lift him back to his rightful place while the Devil runs away with the Council President's soul. The eighteenth-century courtroom, now the town hall, is also attractive.

SÈNE-MONT
[CÔTE D'OR]

Called also Montagne des Trois Croix because of three crosses on the top, it is 10km W of Chagny along steep narrow roads with sharp bends, and just NW of Santenay. From the summit you have superb views N over Santenay vineyards, and Chassagne Montrachet, past La Rochepot, E over the Saône valley to the Juras and sometimes to the Alps, and to the W over the Morvan.

SENS
[YONNE – *see* Major Towns, pages 93–7]

LES SETTONS
[NIÈVRE]

Lac des Settons, a reservoir covering 887 acres of the river Cure valley, SW of Saulieu, is in one of the wildest and most isolated areas of the Morvan. It is at a height of 573 metres (1880 feet) but is popular with active holidaymakers in spring, summer and autumn. The reservoir dam was built in 1861 to release water to float logs down the river. Later a dike was added and the lake became a reservoir to regulate the flow of the Yonne into which the Cure runs.

There are pleasant walks and drives round the lake, and two nautical bases with accommodation. Les Brantlasses (86.84.51.98) is open Easter–October and has facilities for sailing, sail-board, kayak canoeing and water-skiing, as well as horse-riding and tennis. Base Baye (86.84.51.98) also has all these except water-skiing and tennis. You have to stay at least five days, but there are other places where you can hire sailing boats or sail-boards.

Les Settons is a pleasant little resort at the north end of the lake (*see also* Montsauche, page 191).

HOTELS
Morvandelle (86.84.50.62): 2-star, 2-chimney Logis. ROOMS C–D. MEALS B–E. Open Easter–1 November.
Grillons (86.84.51.43): another 2-star, 2-chimney Logis. ROOMS C–D. MEALS B–E. Shut 15 November–15 March.

SOLUTRÉ

[Saône-et-Loire – *see* Pouilly, page 206]

SULLY – Château
[Saône-et-Loire]

One of the most beautiful châteaux in France. It was called the 'Fontainebleau of Burgundy' by Madame de Sévigné. Certainly it has the same blend of elegant formality with fairy-tale dreaminess as Fontainebleau. Perhaps it is so little known because it is in the rather uninspiring countryside 14km NE of Autun where few of us have occasion to go and at present (1991) only the grounds and servants' quarters are open, although there is talk of opening the whole estate at certain times (open Palm Sunday–30 October).

It was built around 1567 at much the same time as the better-known Ancy-le-France and Tanlay, for Maréchal de Saulx-Tavannes, and, as at Tanlay, the medieval towers of an old fortress, four square towers, have been incorporated and water adds greatly to its beauty. The moat, fed by the river Drée, widens into a pretty lake. From the eighteenth-century façade, a great flight of steps goes down to a semi-circular terrace, with beautiful balustrade, from which more steps descend to the edge of the water. The moat is crossed by a five-arched bridge. Its vast park, too, adds greatly to the scene.

Sévigné called the Renaissance courtyard 'the most beautiful in France'. Alas, you cannot see it. I am still hoping to do that.

Marshall MacMahon, who became President of France in 1873, was born here in 1808.

TAIZÉ
[Saône-et-Loire]

In 1940 a Catholic priest, Father Schutz, formed, just 10km from the former great old abbey of Cluny, an ecumenical religious community of men of several Christian denominations from twenty different countries. All finally took Holy Orders and Schutz became a monk, Brother Roger. It is a lively community with a bungalow village and tents, to which young people are invited to stay to reflect and think. Anyone can drop in. There are craft workshops and stands. Easter brings the most visitors.

The flat-roofed concrete church of the Reconciliation was opened in 1962. There is a simple Romanesque village church, too.

TALANT
[CÔTE D'OR]

Until Philip the Bold and the Valois Dukes of Burgundy made Dijon a true capital, Dukes preferred to live at their castle 359 metres up on the hill at Talant, 5km NW, probably because it was in a good defensive position. Although Talant is a town of 11,000 people, it is virtually a suburb of Dijon, looking towards Lac Kir. There are still splendid views from its hilltop. The thirteenth-century church has interesting old statues.

TALMAY – Château
[CÔTE D'OR]

Six kilometres N of Pontailler-sur-Saône. Even demolition could be a costly, difficult business when medieval fortresses were giving way to homes and bits of the old building were left. At Talmay, when rebuilding took place in 1762, the architect left a strong square tower of the thirteenth-century castle, using it as a sort of annexe to the charming classical house. The house itself is decorated with a sculpture of the goddess Cybele, mother of the gods, with the sun and moon on either side. A French-style garden surrounds it. (Open July, August afternoons.)

Marie-Thérèse Figeur, born at Talmay in 1774, joined the

army at nineteen and became a dragoon, fighting in many battles including Jena and Austerlitz. She was called Sans-Gêne. Retiring in 1814, she admitted that she was a woman, and wrote her memoirs.

Louis Thénard, the chemist (1777–1857), lived at the château and had a laboratory in the tower. He discovered sodium and potassium peroxides, and 'Thénard's blue', which is used to colour pottery and which made him a fortune. He became a baron.

TANLAY – Château
[YONNE]

The château of Tanlay, begun in 1550 9km E of Tonnerre, is unusual and beautiful. Its beauty is enhanced by its great moat of running water and lovely park. A rather rambling house, it is an elegant monument to French Renaissance architecture which in the mid-sixteenth century broke away from the more ornate Italian style from which it sprung.

You approach Tanlay through its wooded park and down a long double avenue of elms. You come first to the Petit Château (a monumental gatehouse), then you cross a solid bridge over the wide moat, which leads to the Court of Honour.

Tanlay had been bought in 1535 by Louise de Montmorency, mother of the Coligny brothers who played such an important part in the Wars of Religion on the Protestant side. Gaspard de Coligny was an Admiral of France and a national hero from fighting against Spain. Odet was a bishop who turned Protestant, married, but remained a bishop and cardinal for many years and his wife was known as 'Madame La Cardinale'. Their mother gave Tanlay to her fourth son François d'Andelot, who added to it and had begun the Petit Château gatehouse, a château in itself, when he died in 1569. It was finished by his son-in-law. But the main château was not finished. That was done by Michel Particelli, a tax-collector who bought the estate in 1642 with ill-gotten gains from squeezing the people so hard that he had to be removed temporarily from his job to avoid a revolt. He hired the classical architect Le Muet to finish Tanlay. It was completed in six years with a workforce so big that two surgeons were employed full time to tend the sick and injured. Even a tax-collector could not afford such an outlay and Particelli died owing 200,000 écus, to the intense fury of his son and heir.

The château, which is beautiful, has round domed towers, steep roofs and arcades round its court of Honour. In the park, Le Muet built a 530-metre-long canal, called Grand Canal, with an ornamental water-tower which feeds the 22-metre (nearly 70-feet) wide moat with spring water.

Inside, the apartments are sumptuously furnished and decorated, especially the long gallery and a tower room where there is a strong allegorical painting based on the rivalry between Catholics and Protestants at the Court of Catherine de' Medici, wife of Henri II, with figures in various states of undress, including Catherine appearing naked as Juno with her peacock, Henri II's mistress Diane de Poitiers looking more becoming as Venus and the Catholic leader François de Guise as Mars, his followers forging weapons of war. Gaspard and François de Coligny are Neptune and Hercules. In life, François de Guise was assassinated by a Protestant, and Gaspard de Coligny was murdered in his sick bed on St Bartholomew's night when hundreds of other Protestants were killed. He has been described as 'the noblest Frenchman of his time'. He became a Protestant mainly to defeat the scheming of Spain, for whom Guise's son was a spy and collaborator. Odet de Coligny fled to England, only to be poisoned by one of his servants. Only François d'Andelot de Coligny died a natural death. It was in the tower room that the Protestant leaders met during the Wars of Religion. (Guided tours 1 April–1 November except Tuesday.)

TERNANT
[NIÈVRE]

Thirteen kilometres SW of Luzy, the little village's tiny church has two fifteenth-century Flemish triptychs of carved wood, painted and gilded, one of the Passion of Christ, the other of the Virgin.

TERNIN – Valley
[NIÈVRE, SAÔNE-ET-LOIRE]

From Saulieu to Autun, winding through small green hills with wooded summits. Take D26 from Saulieu. Two villages on the 45km route are Chissey-en-Morvan and Lucenay-L'Évêque.

TIL-CHÂTEL
[CÔTE D'OR]

Where the river Ignon joins the Tille river, a tributary of the Saône, a village on N74 NE of Dijon with some beautiful medieval and Renaissance houses. The Lords of Til-Châtel were very important in the days of the Dukes of Burgundy. What little is left of their château is on a hill where the very fine twelfth-century Romanesque village church stands. Although slightly restored in the fifteenth century, it is almost a perfect example of Romanesque art.

TONNERRE
[YONNE]

Busy but very pleasant town terraced up the steep banks of the Armançon river and Canal de Bourgogne among vineyards and greenery. It still has a medieval atmosphere in its narrow streets and old quarter below the eleventh-century St Pierre church. A fire destroyed much in the sixteenth century, but the thirteenth-century Ancien Hôpital survived. It has a tall roof covering a huge area and an impressive ward 80 metres long and 18 metres wide with a remarkable oak roof. The sick were in beds in alcoves along the walls placed so that they could see an altar, as in the Hospice de Beaune built 150 years later. The hospital was founded by Margaret of Burgundy, sister-in-law of Louis IX (St Louis). Her tomb here is a nineteenth-century restoration. Most interesting is a sculpted 'Entombment' with life-size figures, presented in 1454 by a rich local merchant. Another monument is the tomb of the Duke of Louvois (1628–1716), one of Louis XIV's war ministers, who had acquired the Château of Ancy-le-Franc and the county of Tonnerre in 1684. The tomb was originally in the Capuchin Convent in Paris. It was commissioned from the sculptors Martin Desjardins and François Girardon (leading French sculptor of Louis XIV's reign) by Louvois' wife who had herself placed at her dead husband's feet pointing out in a book his 'victories' – destroying the old cities of Worms and Heidelberg as a warning to France's enemies. The only part of the tomb missing is the green marble sarcophagus on which Louvois' effigy had laid. Napoleon took it as a bath tub!

Tonnerre's most notorious townsperson was Charles Eon de Beaumont, Chevalier d'Eon, born in 1728 in Hôtel d'Uzies, now a bank. Even his parents could not make up their mind if 'he' was a girl or boy. When he was three, they put him in girls' clothes and called him Charlotte. But he had a military education as a man, and was said to be a courageous soldier. He was well suited to intelligence work, and the French sent him (as a woman) to St Petersburg where he (or she!) gained the confidence of the Tsarina Elizabeth and became her personal reader.

He was then sent in 1762 to the French Embassy in London as a French secret agent, but eleven years later Paris began to suspect that he was a double agent, working for the British, and recalled him. Compromising documents were found and Louis XVI imposed a condition that he must always in future wear women's clothes. Whilst in London he had become the subject of heavy betting about his sex at the Hell-Fire Club which met at Medmenham Castle, a lechers' association to which belonged Lord Sandwich (the gambler who invented sandwiches to eat at the card table so that he would not have to stop playing to eat supper) and John Wilkes (the politician and editor who won a great battle for freedom of press comment). The gambling members persuaded d'Eon to attend the club to be examined by a jury of 'Ladies of Quality' to decide his sex. The jury's verdict was indecisive.

He returned to England from France in 1785 as a man and gave fencing exhibitions. He was re-examined by the 'Ladies of Quality' who pronounced him to be a woman. He spent the rest of his life dressed as one. He died in 1810. A post-mortem reported that he was without any doubt a man! What were those 'Ladies of Quality' trying to hide?

TOURIST INFORMATION place Marguerite-de-Bourgogne (April–October, 86.55.14.48).
MARKETS Wednesday, Saturday.

HOTELS

Abbaye St-Michel, rue St-Michel (86.55.05.99): tenth-century Benedictine abbey in a park made into luxurious Relais et Châteaux hotel. Brilliant chef. Very expensive. ROOMS G. MEALS F–G. Shut 1 January–early February.
Centre, 65 rue Hôpital (86.55.10.56): pleasant small-town hotel. ROOMS B–C. MEALS A–F. Shut 2–15 January.

RESTAURANT

St Père, 2 ave Pompidou (86.55.12.84): classic and interesting dishes. Good value. MEALS A–E. Shut 15–30 March; 9–30 September; Sunday evening, Monday; also Tuesday, Wednesday and Thursday evenings in winter.

TOUCY
[YONNE]

Small town 24km W of Auxerre on the banks of the river Ouanne. The fortress-like church has two twelfth-century towers which were originally part of the fortifications of the local baron's château. Pierre Larousse (1817–75) was born there – a teacher, he wanted to 'teach the world about everything'. He produced the renowned Larousse French language dictionary, works on grammar and started a *Grand Dictionnaire du XIXe Siècle* 'giving answers to all questions'. It was finished after his death and for a long time was not surpassed anywhere in the world. 'Larousse' books are still published, including the great *Larousse Gastronomique*.

TOURNUS
[SAÔNE-ET-LOIRE]

Tournus is just outside the Mâconnais, between Mâcon and Chalon and was a staging post between them in Roman times. It is still a good stopping place for motorists on N6 or A6. Apart from its great abbey of St Philibert, it has old cobbled streets with medieval and Renaissance houses, several good restaurants and rather more than its share of antique shops.

St Philiberts is one of the most remarkable, dignified and imposing of Romanesque buildings, described as 'a piece of music in stone'. It seems appropriate that part of it was chosen as the International Centre for Romanesque Studies. It was the church of a tenth-century abbey, and only after a lot of bickering and ill-will did St Philibert take over from St Valerian, its original patron.

You reach it from the busy traffic of N6 by taking rue Albert Thibaudet, which passes between two towers of the medieval Porte des Champs into the quieter old abbey square. The front looks rather like a castle, with loophole slits in bare walls and two towers linked by a fortified parapet. There was good reason. The monks had already had their fill of looting invaders. The parapet was a little bit of extra defence added by a restorer this century.

The whole of the inside of the abbey from the narthex (the vestibule) with its thick pillars and vaulted roofs and the nave with lighter but still sturdy pillars, to the cool arcades of the cloisters, the thirteenth-century chapter house and the fifteenth-century abbot's lodgings has an unadorned beauty. Even if you are tired of dragging yourself around churches and cathedrals, try to see this one in its beautiful simplicity.

The missionary, Valerian, who came to convert Tournus

was beheaded here in AD179. He became a Christian cult figure and around his tomb grew up a monastery dedicated to him.

In the ninth century the monks of the Île de Noirmoutier (now in Normandy) were fleeing with the remains of their patron St Philibert from the invading Norsemen. They moved gradually right across the country as the Norsemen penetrated further and further up the rivers, looting, raping, burning, killing. The raiders found monasteries particularly rewarding for looting treasures. The Noirmoutier monks wandered for seventy years until Charles the Bold of Burgundy offered to extend Tournus Abbey to accommodate them. So Tournus had two saints, St Valerian and St Philibert. But they (or their monks) did not get along very well. And the Noirmoutier monks had *not* escaped from invaders. The Hungarian Magyars were sweeping westward and in AD937 they pillaged and burned Tournus. Rebuilding began, but the row between supporters of the two saints flared into open conflict and the Philibert monks moved to St Pourçain in the Auvergne, where they had stayed on their travels. A former abbot, Abbot Stephen, got them back together but under the agreement Philibert was top saint, with his bones in the church, while Valerian was down in the crypt, though they were both included in pilgrimages. As the church was rebuilt, craftsmen from Lombardy in Italy had an effect on the new abbey.

Though near Cluny, it was one of the few abbeys within range which remained independent under the rule of St Benedict, and gradually built up considerable civil power beyond its religious duties. It was badly damaged by Calvinists in 1562, declined and was secularized in 1627, the monks being replaced by canons who did not live in. The refectory became a tennis court, called Le Ballon. The buildings survived the Revolution. The abbey was shut down in 1785 and became a national monument in 1841. When the bridge over the Saône was bombed in 1940 and 1944, the stained glass was damaged but rebuilt by Brigitte Simon of the family of wonderful craftsmen and artists who did such a superb job restoring old glass in Reims Cathedral. The church restoration was done between 1946 and 1951 by Questel.

The main museum in Tournus in an eighteenth-century

convent is named after the local painter Jean-Baptiste Greuze (1725–1805) who deserves a better reputation than he has. A portraitist and genre painter of everyday scenes, he rose to international popularity, but was driven out of fashion by the neo-classicism of David, who used episodes from ancient history to extol civil virtues and had the advantage of being virtual dictator of arts in the Revolution and then Napoleon's official painter until Waterloo. Greuze turned to painting sentimental pictures of little girls. There are several of his paintings in the museum, but there are also works of David and Poussin and of artists more critical of life such as Hogarth. Interesting are the paintings of a lesser-known artist Felix Ziem (1821–1911), born at Beaune, a sort of latter-day Turner, with a strong touch of Impressionism, who painted superb sunsets and was brilliant, like Monet, at showing the effect of light on stone. (Museum closed Tuesday and November–March.)

The other museum, Perrin-de-Puycousin, grew from collections of a local lawyer of that name and is in a seventeenth-century house given for the purpose by a famous literary critic, Albert Thibaudet, who died in 1936. It shows very interesting scenes from daily life of the past, with wax models in Burgundian clothes, and includes a Burgundian cellar. (Shut Tuesdays, Sunday mornings and November–March.)

The countryside from Tournus SW and then turn SE through the Mâconnais vineyards to Mâcon is delightful (*see* Mâcon, pages 86–9).

TOURIST INFORMATION 2 place Carnot (March–October, 85.51.13.10).

MARKET Saturday.

FESTIVAL Salon of Antiques, end May–early June.

HOTELS

Rempart, 2 ave Gambetta (85.51.10.56): delicious cooking with Burgundian and Bresse bias. Very comfortable rooms. Expensive but very good. ROOMS E–G. MEALS D–G.

Greuze, 1–5 rue Albert-Thibaudet (Hotel – 85.40.77.77; Restaurant – 85.51.13.52): one of Burgundy's famous restaurants now has a luxury hotel alongside made from an old mansion. Jean Ducloux's gourmand restaurant is true to the great traditions of French cuisine. He is seventy years young – may he live for ever! Rooms in the hotel are prettily furnished, have super bathrooms, open fires and they serve great breakfasts. All expensive – but worth every franc. ROOMS G. MEALS F–G. Restaurant shut 1–10 December.

Sauvage, place Champ de Mars (85.51.14.45): one of several pleasant hotels with good-value meals. Cooking classic regional and good. ROOMS D–E. MEALS B–F. Shut mid-December–mid-January.

VALLERY
[YONNE]

In the NW corner of Burgundy, on the borders of Seine-et-Marne, and 19km NW of Sens, this little village has the remains of two Condé châteaux and a vault of the great Condé family. Even a 350-year-old oak in the park is known as the Great Condé.

Of the medieval château, only part of the ramparts is left. The Renaissance château is rather formidable for this artistic period. It was, in fact, never finished. It is Henri II de Bourbon, third Prince of Condé, you can see in stone reclining on one arm in the church, by the tomb, with Prudence, Temperance, Fortitude and Justice in marble beside him. He died in 1646. He was the grandson of the Protestant leader and army commander in the Wars of Religion, the first Prince of Condé, and the father of the Great Condé, commander-in-chief of Louis XIV's forces and winner of battle after battle against the Spanish and Bavarians. He fell foul of the Queen and Cardinal Mazarin, the king's minister, and was put in prison. When Mazarin was forced out, he was released, but led the Fronde forces of discontented aristocrats against the Royal troops led by Turenne and was finally beaten. He refused to accept Turenne's terms for surrender and fled to Spain, where he fought for the Spaniards against the French. Although he was extremely arrogant, he was so formidable and had such support that Louis took him back and, when Turenne died, made him commander-in-chief again. As his health deteriorated he retired to his splendid château at Chantilly where he kept company with men such as Molière, Racine, Nicolas Boileau, the much-respected literary critic, and La Bruyère who was tutor to both the Royal family and the Condé family, and whose character portraits of men and women of his time brought him great friends and furious enemies.

VARZY
[NIÈVRE]

Once a favourite hideout of the bishops of Auxerre, this little town has very nice shaded boulevards replacing its old ramparts. It is on the N151, 16km SW of Clamecy, 36km NE of La Charité, and is still a pleasant hideout with a thirteenth- to fourteenth-century church, St Pierre, containing treasures from a former abbey, and a museum with a mix of exhibits, some very interesting – furniture, good ceramics (Nevers, Rouen, Delft, Clamecy), tapestries, paintings, sculptures, weapons.

MARKETS Thursday. Big Poultry Market second Thursday of December.

HOTEL
Hotel Poste, fauberg Marcy (86.29.41.89): no restaurant. ROOMS B–C. Shut 27 December–6 January; Sunday evening except in summer.

RESTAURANT
Auberge de la Poste, rue Angle (86.29.41.72): delicate classical cooking. Wide price range. MEALS B–F. Shut February; Monday in winter; Sunday evening.

VAUX-EN-BEAUJOLAIS
[Saône-et-Loire]

Clochemerle to you, if you have read Gabriel Chevallier's delicious novel about the problems caused by a new public convenience in a wine village – and if you have not, please do, if only to learn a lot about Beaujolais of not so long ago. Other places claimed to be Clochemerle – for example La Clayette, where Chevallier lived, rightly said to have provided some of the characters, but on 26 October 1956 Gabriel Chevallier was asked to open Vaux's wine-tasting caveau. He signed his name first in the visitors' book, said that he used to go there on holidays, and

The pissotière *of Clochemerle*

gave Vaux the right to be Clochemerle. There is an upper town and a lower town, which fits with the story, and there used to be a pump room, which appears in the sequel *Clochemerle-les-Bains*. Of course, they have built a fine pissotière, and the auberge has become Auberge de Clochemerle (74.65.91.11), still serving local dishes and, of course, local wine in a delightful setting.

Vaux is 12km W of the N6 at St Georges de Reneins. The tasting and buying caveau is open 10 a.m.–12 noon, 2.30 p.m.–7 p.m.

VERDUN-SUR-LE-DOUBS
[SAÔNE-ET-LOIRE]

Little town in a delightful position 22km SE of Beaune, close to N73. The quiet river Saône meets the turbulent river Doubs. Good fishing. Excellent pochouse – freshwater fish bouillabaisse. You can taste it at good local restaurants in season. You can take boat trips on the Saône in luxury forty-passenger boats (Croisières de Bourgogne, Bragny-sur-Saône, 71350 Verdun-sur-le-Doubs, tel. 85.91.58.17).

TOURIST INFORMATION Mairie (85.91.52.52 or in season at Capitainerie, 85.91.87.52).
MARKET Thursday.

HOTELS

Hostellerie Bourguignonne, ave Président Borgeot (85.91.51.45): renowned through generations of the Lauriot family for excellent and true Burgundian cooking, including real pochouse from fish caught on the Saône. Generous helpings. Rooms cosy and comfortable. ROOMS C–E. MEALS C–G. Shut early February–mid-March; 1–7 October; Tuesday evening except July, August.

Trois Maures, place Liberté (85.91.91.17): big auberge beside the river Doubs serving very good local dishes – *fritures* (fried little fishes) of the Doubs, pochouse of Verdun, Bresse chicken. Good value. Rooms simple. ROOMS B–C. MEALS B–E. Shut early December–mid-January; Sunday evening, Monday.

Moulin d'Hauterive at Chaublanc, 10km by D184 and D183 (85.91.55.56): charming mill by the river Dheune started by the monks of Cîteaux Abbey in the twelfth century as an oil mill, converted to a corn mill later. At work until 1962 it became an hotel-restaurant in 1977. Renowned lady chef Christianne Moille. Fairly pricey. ROOMS F–G. MEALS E–G. Shut 22 December–1 February; Sunday evening, Monday except July, August.

VÉZELAY
[YONNE]

In a gorgeous setting on a climbing ridge, overlooking beautiful, wild Morvan scenery, this tiny town of six hundred people is one of the treasures of France. If you are travelling the N6 south of Auxerre, do turn on to D951 NW of Avallon to see it. The D951, which follows the Cure river, is very attractive.

You do not have to be an amateur of old churches to enjoy Vézelay's historic basilica, Ste Madeleine (Mary Magdalene) which stands above its old houses and ramparts.

Leave your car at Champ de Foire and walk up the sloping narrow and winding old streets to the church past old houses with sculptured doorways, staircase turrets, mullioned windows and wells with fine wrought-iron well-heads. The walk may tire you – but no more than it did hundreds of thousands of pilgrims back to the middle ages when they were on their way to the tomb of St James at Compostella and may well have already walked more than one thousand miles. The original abbey was founded in the middle of the ninth century at St Père nearby (page 230) by Girart de Roussillon, Count of Burgundy, a soldier so heroic that the stories of his exploits were told in ballads and by troubadours, including the famous Chanson de Geste. But the Norsemen destroyed the abbey, so the count rebuilt it on top of a hill to make defence easier.

Then, in the tenth century, one of the monks claimed to have brought the relics of Mary Magdelene from Provence. It was a highly improbable claim, but typical of the time and it was not only the simple people who believed it. Pilgrims poured into Vézelay and a basilica was built to accommodate them. A thousand pilgrims were killed in a fire in 1120, but the church was rebuilt and in 1146 St Bernard arrived to recruit for the Second Crusade against the Moslems in Jerusalem. He preached the crusade to Louis VII of France, Eleanor of Aquitaine who was still Louis' wife, his family and many powerful barons who, with

La Madeleine at Vézelay

Louis, were so impressed that most of them volunteered to go. Louis took Eleanor with him, later accused her of going to bed with other crusaders and divorced her on her return. Whereupon she married the future King of England Henry Plantagenet (Henry II). When the Third Crusade set out in 1190, those great rivals King Philippe-Auguste of France and King Richard the Lionheart of England, Eleanor's favourite son, joined forces at Vézelay, to fight the Saracens together, brothers in arms. When Philippe-Auguste left the fight before Richard, he swore an oath that he would not lay a finger on Richard's lands before Richard returned. But, of course, he did, finding Richard's younger brother John a much weaker opponent and a collaborator. Richard was held in prison in Austria for ransom on his way home, and Philippe had done quite well in the take-over business by the time Richard got back to put a stop to it.

St Francis of Assisi was at Vézelay when he decided to build his first monastery of Minorite monks in France and chose a spot near the place where St Bernard preached and where Ste Croix chapel had been built.

St Louis (King Louis IX) went to Vézelay on pilgrimage several times before going on two crusades. The abbey was now extremely rich, but at the end of the thirteenth century other relics claimed to be the true remains of Mary Magdalene were 'discovered' at St Maximin in Provence, and when Pope Boniface VIII announced that those, and not the ones at Vézelay, were the true relics, pilgrimages began to fall off, and the once-lucrative fairs and festivals lost their importance.

By 1538 secularized canons replaced the monks, under a commandatory abbot (absentee who just took a lot of the abbey's income). In the Revolution the monastery buildings were virtually demolished. The basilica was closed. When the poet and novelist Prosper Mérimée saw it in 1834 he found the beautiful basilica falling apart. Hens were running in and out of it. He was dismayed, but luckily he was then Inspector of Historic Monuments at the Interior Ministry and his report made the ministry take action. They decided to restore it but could not find an architect to take it on until in 1840 young Viollet-le-Duc, aged twenty-seven, offered to restore it. The work took nineteen years. Then he restored Notre Dame in Paris.

The basilica is known now as La Madeleine (Mary Mag-dalene). It used to have two towers and two bell-towers. The Protestants destroyed half of them. They might have destroyed them all if Théodore de Bèze, Calvin's successor, had not been born in Vézelay! The thirteenth-century St Anthony's tower is 30 metres (98 feet) high. Lovely gardens cover the site where the abbey buildings stood. From the tree-shaded terrace behind the church where the abbots' palace stood in the eighteenth century, you have a lovely view of the Cure river and Morvan.

Viollet-le-Duc was criticized, as usual, for using too much of his imagination in restoring, but there was little he could do in some sections if the basilica were to be complete. He had to remake what was left of the tympanum on the centre doorway, for instance, and it is said that he took the wrecked original as 'his inspiration'.

He did not have to touch the beautiful tympanum over the wonderful central doorway of the narthex, the entrance ves-tibule. Some of the capitals had to be recarved but most are original and all are absolutely superb. They are well worth studying in detail. The nave is superb, too, with alternating white and greenish-grey stone in its transverse arches. When I first looked down the nave, all 62 metres (203 feet) of it, I was transfixed.

The arches, resting on pillars, are 21 metres (68 feet) high and look higher. It is simple, graceful and peaceful. The light breaks through to the transept and choir at the far end as if it is illuminated by electricity.

A staircase of two hundred steps takes you to the top of the tower, from which there are even better views than from the terrace.

From place Champ de Foire at the lower end of the town you can follow Promenade des Fossés, which is laid out on the medieval ramparts round the town.

Many artists, writers and architects have chosen to live in Vézelay, including the poet, musician, novelist and biographer Romain Rolland (1866–1944) who sought to find in the lives of great men (Beethoven, Tolstoy, Michelangelo, Gandhi, Rama-krishna) evidence of the greatness and brotherhood of man and who ended his life trying to awaken Europe to the evils of

Fascism and Nazism. He spent the last years of his life at No. 20 Grande-Rue. The architect Le Corbusier lived in Vézelay, too, but the daily sight of the basilica did not discourage him from covering acres of the earth with heavy masses of re-inforced concrete.

St Père's fine church and the excavations of Gallo-Roman remains at Fontaines-Salées are about 3km from Vézelay.

TOURIST INFORMATION rue St Pierre (April–November, 86.33.23.69).

FESTIVALS Feast of Ste Madeleine and pilgrimages 22 July.

HOTELS

Le Pontot (86.33.24.40): fifteenth-century house; lovely views, quiet garden. No restaurant. Pricey. ROOMS G. Shut early November–end March.

Poste et Lion d'Or, place Champ de Foire (86.33.21.23): old posting inn; good bourgeois classic-style cooking. ROOMS C–G. MEALS C–F. Shut early November–end March. Restaurant shut Tuesday lunch, Monday.

Relais du Morvan (86.33.25.33): simple Logis with good auberge cooking. ROOMS B–E. MEALS B–F. Shut Tuesday evening, Wednesday.

VILLEFRANCHE
[SAÔNE-ET-LOIRE]

Villefranche, the capital of Beaujolais, has remained an important commercial and industrial town despite the pressure of having the great city of Lyon only 31km away. Villefranche has resisted becoming a mere suburb of Lyon and is a pleasant and independent town which is still very much part of Beaujolais. And it keeps a lot of its old buildings and traditional street markets. Many of the old buildings, including the thirteenth-century Notre-Dame-des-Marais church, are in rue Nationale (called 'Nat' locally).

Villefranche started as a toll-post set up by the Barons of Beaujolais from Beaujeu in the thirteenth century. Under Baron Guichard's great charter of 1260, the town which grew up around the post was given extraordinary privileges. Apart from the more usual provisions, such as freedom from taxes levied by the Baron of Beaujolais, even for the brothel-keeper, there were some considerably less usual. People taken in adultery or reasonably suspected of adultery by their state of undress had to run naked through the town or pay a fine to the baron. The men were allowed to beat their wives provided the results were not fatal!

In front of the church is the old market square paved in stone slabs called 'calades' in the old language, *langue romane*, a transitional tongue between Latin and French. As a result, going to Villefranche was called 'going to the calade' and Villefranche people were called 'Caladois'.

Working clothes were made in the town last century and it still produces sports wear, underwear and gloves. Metal and mechanical industries are well established and now plastics are important. The river port still operates on the Saône.

Though conscription has ended in France, the Festival of Conscripts is still held through the streets of Villefranche on the last Sunday in January and for several days after. It used to be a send-off feast for twenty-year-olds conscripted for the forces; now it is a celebration of 'coming of age'. If the year ends with a 2 (1992, for instance) everyone born in a year ending with a 2 joins in – whether it was 1922, 1932, 1942, etc. They wear top hats and the colour of their hat ribbon signifies their age. (In 1989, I should have worn violet!)

Villefranche has attractive gardens and is a leading sporting centre, including sailing and canoeing.

Wine information from Union Inter-Professionel des Vins de Beaujolais, 210 boul. Vermorel (74.65.45.55).

Across the Saône from Villefranche is the plateau of Dombes. Just off the road from Villefranche to Bresse is Ars-sur-Formans, to which pilgrimages are made because of a nineteenth-century parish curé called St Jean-Baptiste Viannay, despised and ridiculed by his parishioners but with a gift for conversion of people, so that after his death he was made patron saint of parish priests.

TOURIST INFORMATION 290 route Thizy (74.68.05.18).

MARKET new covered market daily.

FESTIVAL Fête of Conscripts (*see* text) last Sunday in January.

HOTELS

Château de Chervinges, 3km by D38 Roanne route (74.65.29.76): pleasant eighteenth-century manor. Park, pool. Disco in season. Pricey rooms. ROOMS G. MEALS E–G. Shut January, February; Sunday evening, Monday.

Plaisance, 96 ave Libération (74.65.33.52): well-run hotel. Restaurant separate (*see* Fontaine Bleue). ROOMS D. Shut 24 December–1 January.

RESTAURANTS

Bressane, at Beauregard, 3km NE by D44 (74.60.93.92): auberge beside Saône river with flowery shaded terrace. Fine traditional cooking. MEALS C–F. Shut Tuesday evening, Wednesday.

Fontaine Bleue, 18 rue J. Moulin (74.68.10.37): good classic cooking. MEALS B–F. Shut 21 December–mid-January; Sunday lunch in July, August; Saturday lunch rest of year.

VILLENEUVE L'ARCHÉVÊQUE
[YONNE]

Little town 24km E of Sens in the river Vanne valley, founded in the twelfth century by an archbishop of Sens, hence its name. There in 1239 Louis IX (St Louis) and Blanche of Castille (his pious mother) received what was claimed to be the 'crown of thorns' worn by Christ, from Baldwin II, Emperor of Constantinople. He was selling it to pay off a debt. Louis built in Paris one of the most beautiful churches in France, La Chapelle Royale, to house it. It is now in Notre Dame Cathedral.

The twelfth- to sixteenth-century church in Villeneuve is also called Notre Dame. It has a lovely thirteenth-century doorway.

MARKET Saturday.

VILLENEUVE-SUR-YONNE
[YONNE]

This town 13km S of Sens on the Yonne river has a grid-style street layout like the dullest modern planning, but it was laid out this way for defence reasons by Louis VII in 1163, when it was called Villefranche-le-Roy. He built it to serve a Royal castle and as a fortress-town to protect the southern flank of his kingdom. The ramparts are now gardens, but two thirteenth-century fortified gateways are still there – Porte de Sens (or de Champagne) and Porte de Joigny (or de Bourgogne), altered in the sixteenth century. Of the original Royal castle, Tour Louis-le-Gros, a massive round keep, has survived. So has the handsome church, built from the thirteenth to sixteenth centuries.

The town gained much notoriety just after World War II for its ex-mayor, Dr Petiot, who was one of France's most prolific mass murderers. A medical practitioner who had a big reputation for curing both people and horses, he was mayor from 1927 to 1933 and popular with many townspeople as the man who had given the town main drainage, new schools, a day nursery, tennis courts and a bowling alley. Others, however, claimed he had embezzled public funds. They also accused him of taking away a cemetery cross on Christmas Eve and throwing it into the river. As it weighed half a ton, he must have been mighty strong.

In 1946, when he was in Paris, he was charged with twenty-seven murders. He admitted nineteen of these killings but said that he had only killed people who were informers for the Gestapo. I cannot help feeling still that he might have been a one-man freelance Resistance movement, seeing himself as a sort of legendary hero. The judges did not see it that way. He was executed.

TOURIST INFORMATION 4bis rue Carnot (86.87.36.28).

HOTEL

Dauphin, 12 rue Carnot (86.87.18.55): 500-year-old inn with modern comforts. Good cooking and choice of menus. ROOMS C–E. MEALS B–F. Shut 1–14 October; February holidays; Sunday evening, Monday low season.

VILLIÉ-MORGON
[BEAUJOLAIS]

Morgon may have been replaced by Chiroubles among Parisian fashionable eaters and drinkers as their most popular Beaujolais, but Morgon remains Beaujolais' biggest seller, rich and substantial after two to three years, really rich and delightful after five to six years.

Villié-Morgon, the village, is not only a good place to taste the wine but for an excursion into the Beaujolais countryside. Le Caveau in a Louis XVII château has an attractive tasting room in the middle of a pretty public park where there is a small zoo and a display of wine-making tools. Tasting (small charge) daily 9 a.m.–12 noon, 2 p.m.–7 p.m. It has a restaurant opposite (Relais des Caveaux, 74.04.21.77).

HOTEL
Villon (74.69.16.16): good local inn. ROOMS C–E. MEALS C–D. Shut 2 January–5 February. Restaurant shut Sunday evening, Monday lunch.

VOLNAY
[CÔTE D'OR – *see* Wine, page 40]

VOSNE-ROMANÉE
[CÔTE D'OR – *see* Wine, pages 32–3]

VOUGEOT
[CÔTE D'OR *see* Wine, pages 31–2]

M A P S

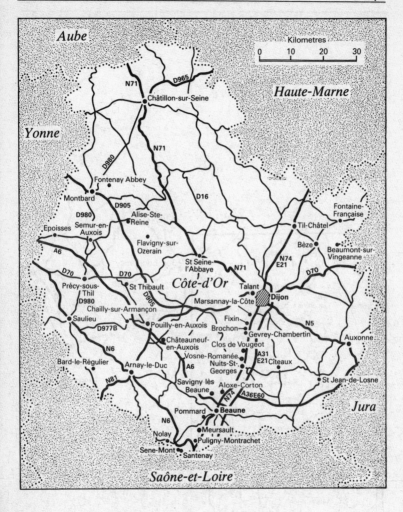

Aube

Haute-Marne

Yonne

Kilometres
0   10   20   30

N71   D965
Châtillon-sur-Seine

N71

D980

Fontenay Abbey   D16

Montbard
D905
D980   Alise-Ste-   Til-Châtel
Epoisses   Semur-en-   Reine
Auxois   Bèze   Fontaine-
A6   Flavigny-sur-   Française
Ozerain
St Seine-   N71   N74   Beaumont-sur-
D70   l'Abbaye   E21   Vingeanne
D70   Côte-d'Or   D70
Précy-sous-   St Thibault   Talant   Dijon
Thil   Marsannay-la-Côte   N5
D980   Chailly-sur-Armançon   Fixin
Saulieu   Pouilly-en-Auxois   Brochon
D977B   Gevrey-Chambertin   Auxonne
Châteauneuf-   Clos de Vougeot
N6   en-Auxois   A31
Bard-le-Régulier   Arnay-le-Duc   Vosne-Romanée   E21   Citeaux
A6   Nuits-St-
Savigny lès   Georges   St Jean-de-Losne
N81   Beaune   Aloxe-Corton
Pommard   Beaune   N74   A36 E60   Jura
N6
Nolay   Meursault
Puligny-Montrachet
Sene-Mont   Santenay

Saône-et-Loire

2   Côte-d'Or

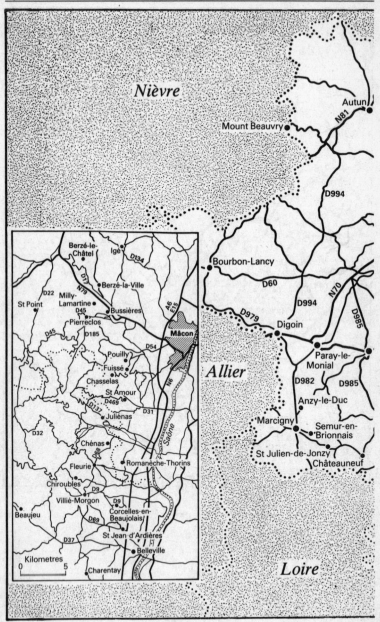

Nièvre

Autun

Mount Beauvry

N81

D994

Berzé-le-
Châtel   Igé   D134

Bourbon-Lancy

Berzé-la-Ville   D60

D17   N79   D994   N70

Milly-
Lamartine   D979   Digoin   D985

St Point   D45   Bussières

Pierreclos   A6 E15   Paray-le-
Monial

D45   D185   Mâcon   D982   D985

Pouilly   D54   Anzy-le-Duc

Fuissé   *Allier*   Marcigny   Semur-en-
Brionnais

Chasselas   St Julien-de-Jonzy

St Amour   Châteauneuf

D469   D31

D13   Juliénas   N6

D32   Chénas   Saône

Fleurie   Romanèche-Thorins

Chiroubles   D9

Villié-Morgon   D9

Beaujeu   Corcelles-en-
Beaujolais

D69   St Jean d'Ardières

D37   Belleville

Kilometres

0   5

Charentay

Loire

3   *Saône-et-Loire*

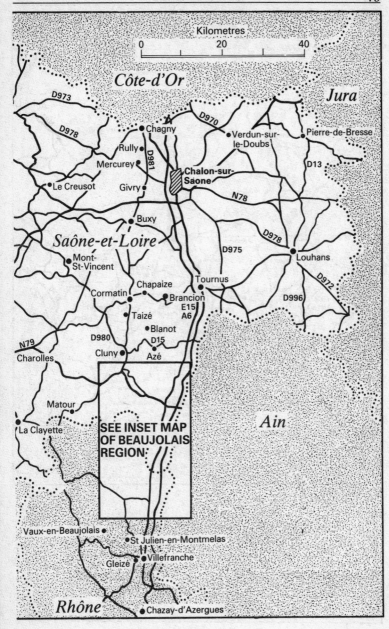

Kilometres
0   20   40

Côte-d'Or

Jura

D973

D978

Chagny

D970

Verdun-sur-le-Doubs

Pierre-de-Bresse

Rully

Mercurey

D981

Chalon-sur-Saône

D13

Le Creusot

Givry

N78

Buxy

Saône-et-Loire

D975

D978

Louhans

Mont-St-Vincent

D972

Chapaize

Tournus

D996

Cormatin

Brancion

E15
A6

Taizé

N79

Blanot

D980

D15

Charolles

Cluny

Azé

Ain

Matour

La Clayette

SEE INSET MAP OF BEAUJOLAIS REGION

Vaux-en-Beaujolais

St Julien-en-Montmelas

Villefranche

Gleizé

Rhône

Chazay-d'Azergues

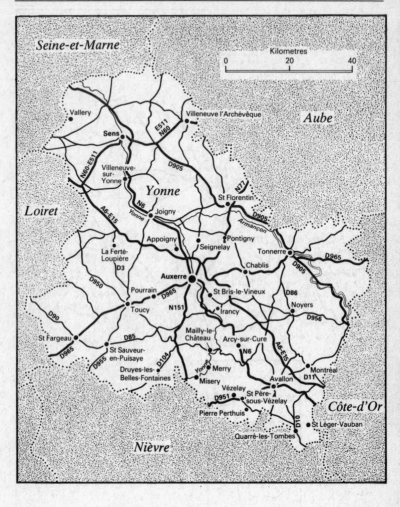

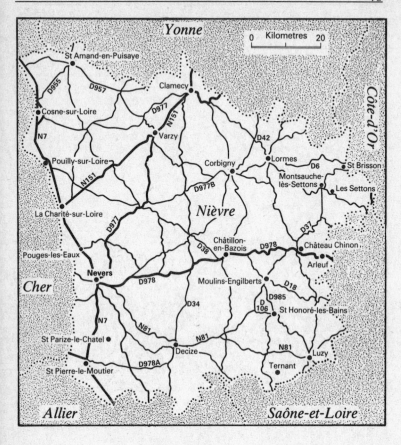

5 *Nièvre*

I N D E X

All Pan books are available at your local bookshop or newsagent, or can be ordered direct from the publisher. Indicate the number of copies required and fill in the form below.

Send to: **CS Department, Pan Books Ltd., P.O. Box 40, Basingstoke, Hants. RG21 2YT.**

or phone: 0256 469551 (Ansaphone), quoting title, author and Credit Card number.

Please enclose a remittance* to the value of the cover price plus: 60p for the first book plus 30p per copy for each additional book ordered to a maximum charge of £2.40 to cover postage and packing.

*Payment may be made in sterling by UK personal cheque, postal order, sterling draft or international money order, made payable to Pan Books Ltd.

Alternatively by Barclaycard/Access:

Card No.

Signature:

Applicable only in the UK and Republic of Ireland.

While every effort is made to keep prices low, it is sometimes necessary to increase prices at short notice. Pan Books reserve the right to show on covers and charge new retail prices which may differ from those advertised in the text or elsewhere.

NAME AND ADDRESS IN BLOCK LETTERS PLEASE:

....

Name————————————————————————————

Address————————————————————————————

3/87